THE GERMAN STUDENT CORPS IN THE THIRD REICH

Mensur with Glockenschläger

THE GERMAN STUDENT CORPS IN THE THIRD REICH

R. G. S. Weber

Palgrave Macmillan

ISBN 978-1-349-18075-2   ISBN 978-1-349-18073-8 (eBook)
DOI 10.1007/978-1-349-18073-8

© R.G.S. Weber 1986
Softcover reprint of the hardcover 1st edition 1986

All rights reserved. For information, write:
St. Martin's Press, Inc., 175 Fifth Avenue, New York, NY 10010
Printed in Hong Kong
Published in the United Kingdom by The Macmillan Press Ltd.
First published in the United States of America in 1986.

ISBN 978-0-312-32623-4

Library of Congress Cataloging-in-Publication Data
Weber, R.G.S.
The German student corps in the Third Reich.
Originally presented as the author's thesis (Ph. D.—
University of London, 1983)
Bibliography: p.
Includes index.
1. College students—Germany—Societies, etc.—History
—20th century. 2. College students—Germany—Political
activity—History—20th century. 3. Germany—Politics and
government—1933—1945. I. Title.
LA729.W4147   1985   378'.1983'0943   85–18254
ISBN 978-0-312-32623-4

To my parents, Kate and Bryce

Contents

Preface	ix
List of Abbreviations	xi

1 GERMAN STUDENT FRATERNITIES — 1
The *Landsmannschaften* — 3
The student orders — 5
The *Kränzchen* — 10
The rise of the *Burschenschaften* — 14
The *Allgemeine Senioren-Convent* — 17
The *Kösener Senioren-Conventen Verband* — 18
Kartell and *Kreis* — 23

2 STUDENTS, LAW AND CODES — 26
The *Corpsstudent* and honour — 31
The *Mensur* — 33
The Erlangen and Erfurt Agreements — 39
Jewish students and the *Kösener Verband* — 48
The *NSDStB* and the student fraternities — 55

3 THE CORPS VERSUS THE *NSDStB* — 64
An affair of honour — 64
The Erfurt *Waffenstudententag*, 1931 — 76
The *Deutsche Studentenschaft* Conference, Graz, 1931 — 78
The lines are drawn — 80
The *Waffenstudententag* in Goslar, 9–10 January 1932 — 82
The *Deutsche Studentschaft* Conference, Königsberg, July 1932 — 86
The Bad Kösen Congress, 1932 — 88
Isolationism — 90
The Extraordinary Bad Kösen Congress of 1933 — 92
1933 and the *Gleichschaltung* — 93
The Extraordinary *Waffenstudententag*, Goslar, 20 May 1933 — 95
The Bad Kösen Congress of May 1933 — 97

4 BLUNCK AS *FÜHRER* OF THE *KSCV*	102
Blunck and the *KSCV* versus Schwab's *DB*	112
A time of decision	116
Attacks against the fraternities	119
The Feickert Plan	120
The *Völkische Waffenring (VWR)*	123
The *Gemeinschaft Studentischer Verbände (GStV)*	125
Lammers' withdrawal	130
The Nuremberg Blood Laws and the Lutze Decree	138
5 THE *VERBOTZEIT*, 1936–45	142
The *Kameradschaften*	142
The corps revived	158
6 EPILOGUE	163
7 SUMMARY AND CONCLUSIONS	167
Glossary	170
Biographical Notes	172
Appendix tables	173
Notes and References	177
Bibliography	196
Index	203

Preface

I have tried to show in this book the extent to which certain of the German student fraternities resisted the imposition of Nazi doctrine and structures upon their community. In general, German university fraternities with their tradition of duelling codes and complex etiquette, appear at first glance to have been the type of para-military organisations which might well have assisted the *NSDAP* during its rise to power. While this was true in a number of instances, the corps, which were one specific denomination of fraternity comprising approximately 8 per cent of the student fraternity population,[1] refused to comply with a number of Nazi directives. Attitudes varied from corps to corps and from member to member, so that a few active and enthusiastic Nazis did exist among the corps; a point which has clouded the picture and given rise to inferences of corps complicity with National Socialism[2] – a notion which I hope this work will dispel.

Previous works to appear on the topic of German student fraternities since the First World War generally have employed a very broad approach in order to encompass the more than 45 federations of student fraternities to appear by 1929; varying anywhere from 200 to 1000 members.[3] I have deliberately not attempted to write another general history of the fraternities, but rather have tried to present a much closer account of the interaction between Nazi organisations and the corps in order to study more closely the tactics and sequence of events of their interplay.

In order to achieve this I first have traced the development of European student communities, particularly those in Germany, to illustrate the origin of many of the traditions and the genealogy of the multiplicity of fraternities which existed by the turn of this century. The first two chapters of this work contain a great deal of not generally known, nor readily available, background material in order to set the stage and to relieve confusion which might otherwise arise due to the rather complex interweaving of terminology, participants and events which appear later in the work.

Brief mention should perhaps be made at this point regarding the end material of the work. A short glossary has been included for some of the fraternity terminology not usually found in contemporary dictionaries. Also a listing of the major fraternity federations, their membership totals and a number of brief biographical outlines have been added to provide background detail. In the text itself, a number of loan-words such as corps, which have no English plural form, appear quite frequently and an effort has been made to keep the context clear in such cases.

This book is based upon a PhD thesis which I wrote under the supervision of Professor F. L. Carsten while I was a research student at the School of Slavonic and East European Studies, in London, and which was accepted by the University of London in 1983. I wish to express my thanks to Professor Carsten for his guidance and patience in helping me bring the original work to fruition and to the Director of SSEES, Dr Michael Branch, for his advice and assistance in the publication of this work.

My research was assisted and encouraged by many people in many ways, particularly by the German Historical Institute and the Wiener Library in London, the German Federal Archives at Coblenz, the Institut für Zeitgeschichte in Munich and the Archiv der ehem. Reichsstudentenführung und NSDStB in Würzburg. However, special mention must be given to the gentlemen of the Institut für Hochschulkunde, the Archiv des Kösener SC-Verbandes in Würzburg and the Verein für Corpsstudentische Geschichtsforschung, who together with the 40 some corps alumni whom I interviewed for this work, all were most helpful in assisting me to fit the pieces of the puzzle together. I would like to express my appreciation both to the Institut für Hochschulkunde and to Ulrich Becker for permission to reproduce the illustrations and my gratitude to Dr Keith Thomas and Dr Elizabeth Ruge for their kind assistance in the later stages of its completion.

I also wish to record my debt to the many other friends, who read and advised me at various stages in the preparation of the manuscript, with particular and special thanks to my dear friend Werner Barthold, for his constant endorsement and friendship which served as an inspiration throughout this work and to Dr Robert Pynsent whose expertise and critical comments helped to clarify many of the issues presented here.

R. G. S. WEBER

List of Abbreviations

ADW	Allgemeine Deutsche Waffenring
CM	Corpsstudentische Monatsblätter
DB	Deutsche Burschenschaft
DCZ	Deutsche Corpzeitung
DOB	Deutsche Offizierbund
DSt	Deutsche Studentenschaft
DW	Deutsche Wehrschaft
GStV	Gemeinschaft Studentische Verbände
HKSCV	Hohe Kösener Senioren-Convents-Verband – variation of KSCV
Inst HK	Institut für Hochschulkunde
Inst RStF	Archiv der ehem. Reichsstudentenführung
Inst ZIG	Institut für Zeitgeschichte
Kobl	Bundesarchiv, Koblenz
Kös Arch	Kösener Archiv
KSCV	Kösener Senioren-Convents-Verband
NDO	Nationalverband Deutscher Offiziere
NSC	Naumburger Senioren-Convent
NSDStB	Nationalsozialistische Deutsche Studentenbund
RSC	Rudolstädter Senioren-Convent
USCHLA	Untersuchungs- und Schlichtungs-Ausschüsse
VAC	Verband Alter Corpsstudenten
WL	Wiener Library
WSC	Weinheimer Senioren-Convent
WVAC	Weinheimer Verband Alter Corpsstudenten

1 German Student Fraternities

When the first central European university was opened at Prague in 1348, the system adopted for the governing and administration of its students was that which had been employed by the older universities of Paris and Padua. This system was based on divisions of the student population, known as nations, which corresponded to the geographical location of each particular student's home.

> The schools of Paris, like those of Bologna, were attended by a multitude of foreign students and young masters from all parts of Europe who, lacking citizenship, banded together for mutual protection and help according to their home countries or provinces.[1]

Bologna recorded as many as fourteen nations in 1265, but the University of Prague following closely the model of Paris, was founded with only four:[2] Bohemia, Saxony, Bavaria and Poland. Similarly, the University of Leipzig which was established as the result of an exodus of scholars from Prague in 1409, also was established on a system of nations which represented and protected scholastic interests. The nations, however, slowly lost their importance at the German universities and the faculties of study gradually developed as the forum representing academic interests.[3] With regard to the founding of the University of Rostock in 1419 Hasting Rashdall writes:

> The national subdivisions of Paris and Bologna were clearly out of place in a merely provincial university; and by this time German universities were becoming essentially provincial. . . . Leipzig was almost the last German university in which this part of the Parisian system was reproduced. There is no trace of nations at Rostock, or any of the subsequently founded universities of Germany except Louvain.[4]

The trend of regional rulers to develop their own universities, both for their associated prestige and for the education of their subjects at home rather than abroad, facilitated the growth of provincial universities within Germany. Furthermore, the adoption of Roman Civil Law within most of Europe helped to remove at least some of the necessity for compatriots to band together for legal solidarity while studying away from home. However, the natural inclination of students to share living accommodations and leisure time with their compatriots would appear by no means to have been affected by the decline of the university nations. In actual fact the practice of students living in academic dormitories, usually organised on the basis of the scholars' provinces of origin, became the rule rather than the exception. Many types of communal dormitories or *Bursen*[5] existed, but most were associated with cloisters, schools or monasteries and had a regional bent in the persons which they housed. This was very clear at the University of Vienna where the regionalism was reflected in such names as *bursa polonica*, *bursa silesorum*, *bursa salisburgensis* and *bursa bavarica*; all of which afforded housing to *conterranei* or countrymen.[6] Similar affiliations can also be seen at Oxford University where Jesus College maintained ties with Wales and Exeter College with the West Country.[7] These *Bursen* were relatively small and generally housed only eight to twelve students, whose studies and activities were strictly supervised by a *regens bursae* or senior scholar; much like a modern Oxford or Cambridge don.[8]

By the fifteenth century the universities, much like the craft guilds, had evolved the practice of initiating their new members, thereby keeping membership exclusively for their 'craft' and discouraging interlopers. Without immatriculation a student was not allowed to be quartered in a *Burse* nor was a lecturer allowed to hold instruction with him present.[9] But immatriculation, which in theory meant only the paying of a fee and enrolment for a new student, in actual practice, also demanded the extraction of the *depositio beanii*. For the eliciting of this *Deposition* the *bean*,[10] as new students were known, was handed over to senior scholars who put him through the rigours of academic initiation.[11] Although the saws, axes, files and planes used during the extraction of the *Deposition* to smooth and shape the rough *bean* into material suitable for scholastic pursuits were constructed of wood, the rule prohibiting the letting of the *bean*'s blood was not always strictly observed. Nor did it in any way guarantee against his subjection to mental and physical pain, which were inflicted at levels that today would be considered torture. During the ordeal, the *bean* was castigated and admonished with statements such as, 'You are hereby freed of all abnormalities of your body and mind.'[12] The ceremony usually was concluded by the *bean* having his mouth filled with salt and wine poured over his head, symbolically absolving him of his *beanismus*.

It should perhaps be mentioned that a few universities and *Bursen* did not practise such ardent initiation rites, but some form of *Deposition* was carried on at certain universities until well into the eighteenth century.[13]

THE *LANDSMANNSCHAFTEN*

By the late Middle Ages the practice of students living in *Bursen* had become so institutionalised that permission was required before scholars could take up quarters elsewhere.[14] Following the Reformation, the importance of the *Bursen* declined very quickly, due, for the most part, to their previous associations with religious foundations such as cloisters and abbeys. Vienna, however, retained *Bursen* until as late as 1785. In the late sixteenth century the *Bursen* were replaced, especially at Protestant universities, by organisations called national colleges or *Landsmannschaften* or in some cases *societates*. These *Landsmannschaften* distinguished themselves from the previous university nations in that they were not official university institutions, but rather private unions of compatriot students at the same university.[15]

Not only the mode of student housing changed following the Reformation.

> With the movement of the later medieval universities toward greater involvement in aristocratic society, the former conceptual divorce between the scholar and the knight was rendered an inappropriate theoretical projection and was replaced by that of the closer identification of the two orders in society.[16]

This trend continued and the post-Reformation scholar changed his self-image from that of his clerical scholastic predecessors to one of a knight errant, sallying out in search of truth. In order to facilitate this quest the traditional clerical robes previously worn at universities were discarded in favour of the costume worn by the contemporary soldier of fortune, the *Landsknecht*.[17] This idea of the knight-scholar was reinforced further by an increased enrolment at the universities by the sons of aristocratic families. This new class of students wished to acquire better juristic qualifications for imperial or princely service following the reception of Roman Law.[18] The adoption of Spanish court dress, Italianesque codes of chivalric behaviour and the carrying of side arms were post-Reformation phenomena.[19] The carrying of swords had previously been denied to scholars in general, as well as the giving and accepting of challenges to armed combat. This was due to the general beliefs that scholars lacked the necessary physical strength to wield arms and that their true weapons were those of wisdom and learning.[20]

The *Landsmannschaften* of the post-Reformation univertisities structured themselves around an executive, appointed from their own ranks, which was led by a *Senior* or president. The University of Rostock apparently had a council composed of the *Senioren* from the various *Landsmannschaften* as early as 1647. These councils of seniors attempted to ease relationships between the various territorial rivalries and personal interests of their members. This is not surprising for regionalism abounded at the universities by the seventeenth century, and patriotic displays of the homeland colours among students, extended even to personal decorations on sword hilts and the wearing of sashes. The spirit of patriotism required of *Landsmannschaft* members that mutual assistance be given to compatriots, such as care of one another when ill, physical protection to the point of duelling on each other's behalf and the assurance of a proper burial should death occur while away from home.[21]

These post-Reformation dauntless Knights of Knowledge continued much as their predecessors had with the practice of initiating new students, changing only the form. By the early eighteenth century an exceedingly harsh fagging system had evolved at most of the German universities which was known as *Pennalismus*. The *Landsmannschaften* had merely substituted the rigours of the *Deposition* for a *Pennaljahr* or year of service, at the end of which the student was given 'absolution' and thereby ended his sentence of subservience to senior students.[22] During this ordeal the *bean* was assigned a mentor in the form of an older student, known as his *praeceptor morum*. The responsibilities of this more experienced scholar were to comfort and council the *bean* through the throes of his initial academic year.[23] Unfortunately in many cases, it proved advantageous only for the senior student whose instructions to his ward were merely a first hand demonstration in the exploitation of trust. Frequently both the *bean*'s property and person were pressed into hard use during his term of fagging, and despite a later opportunity as a senior student to avenge himself on others who were junior in status, the memories of such abuse at the hands of his own countrymen were not often, nor easily forgotten. This resentment festered within the *Lands-*

mannschaften and proved fertile ground for the subsequent growth of dissenting cliques known as Student Orders. These secretive organisations represented a more exclusive extension of the student-knight idea, but proved much more than a mere theoretical acceptance of the quest, for the orders which formed arcane factions within the *Landsmannschaften* attempted to influence and to direct the actions of the larger organisation.[24]

By the mid-eighteenth century, changes in student convention and development which had existed since the Middle Ages were more in form rather than in substance. Students still lived in communal housing and were organised along rather parochial geographic guidelines. *Bursen* and nations evolved into *Landsmannschaften* and the *depositio beanii* was superseded by a *Pennaljahr*; only the adoption of pseudo-chivalric behaviour and attitudes proved new. This allowed the *Landsmannschaften* to adopt codes of honour, but of a very nebulous and *ad hoc* nature. It was into this breach that the student orders moved and were very successful in directing student affairs – albeit through a rather arcane rule of terror.

THE STUDENT ORDERS

Interestingly few modern historians make any mention of the student orders at the German universities. However, Charles McClelland does note the influence of the *Ritterakademien* on the syllabus of studies at the new University of Halle, which soon after its founding became the model for most subsequent university reforms within Germany.

> Halle was initially based upon a previously existing *Ritterakademie*, upon which was grafted a Pietistically oriented theological faculty and a comparatively progressive law faculty . . . One of the leading educational modernisers of early eighteenth-century Germany, Christian Thomasius, sought to combine the educational desiderata of a gentleman (including riding, fencing, foreign languages, and the new sciences) with the state's formal requirements for civil service education.[25]

Regular training of scholars in the cavalier skills of swordsmanship and riding was easily adopted by the *Landsmannschaften* as a means by which their members could settle personal differences. But more importantly it served as a further reinforcement for the image of the scholar as a knight on quest, fighting the world of ignorance and the Philistines for the attainment of truth.[26] The idea of overcoming a hostile environment during such a trial of courage was very simply transposed to the rather less than amiable living conditions within the *Landsmannschaften* as briefly mentioned above. The student orders saw themselves not only metaphorically as knights, but in reality as the members of a chivalric order of brother knights, struggling against the larger and impersonal *Landsmannschaften*.

Not surprisingly, heated conflicts developed between the *Landsmannschaften* and the various orders, and the quarrels in turn spilt over into the student community as a whole, creating an intractable situation which eventually brought about the downfall of both groups. In writing on the stuggle between the *Landsmannschaften* and orders, Meyer-Camberg observes that all activities were centred around the gaining of influence, leadership and power within the student community.[27]

The fact that the student orders were organised into lodges seems to have led to a great deal of speculation by writers, particularly following the First World War, that the student orders were seen as a form of conspiratorial student Freemasonry. It was also speculated that these lodges had recruited members to take part in an international Masonic conspiracy, which working through the Grand Orient Lodge in Paris, had fomented the French Revolution. True, there were in fact student Freemasons in Europe during the latter half of the eighteenth century, but they appear to have been members of regular Masonic lodges such as the 'Zu den drei Rosen' in Jena or the 'Friedrich' Lodge in Göttingen.[28] Other elementary similarities existed between the orders and Freemasonry which might have caused confusion in identifying the two unrelated societies, but their doctrinal differences were almost polar. The *Landsmannschaften* were compatriotic in membership, the tenure of which extended only to the duration of a student's term of studies. The orders, on the other hand, bound their members by an oath of brotherhood for life, regardless of their patriality which was also a basic Masonic tenet and thereby helped to confuse the issue even further. Furthermore, the *Landsmannschaften* tended to restrict their activities to the particular university community in which they existed, while the student orders built a web of affiliated lodges, thereby linking members of the same order at a number of universities. This also has tended to be misleading for researchers attempting to decipher the activities of the student orders. But investigators seem to have been even further confused by sources, both from within and outside Freeemasonry, which alleged a long connection between Masonry and mystically associated crusading orders such as the Knights Templar or the Knights of Malta.[29] The Chevalier Andrew Ramsey, who was closely associated with the Jacobite Court of St Germain, is cited as having been instrumental in establishing such mystical, chivalric Masonic group on the Continent in the mid-1730s.[30] Furthermore, Frederick the Great of Prussia gave monumental support to Freemasonry through his own active membership and by his granting permission for the founding of the Prussian Grand Lodge of the Three Globes in Berlin, during the Silesian Wars.[31] It is therefore very easy to see how faulty conclusions might be drawn. However, the Masonic orders referred to would presumably have been set up as a hierarchy of Masonic degrees with associated rituals, rather than as competing and rival factions, which was definitely the case between the student orders.[32]

Each of the student orders wherever possible, established its own network of individual lodges at a number of universities, thereby creating a situation of competition between the various orders. The most notorious of the many student orders were Constantia, Amicitia, Unitas and Harmonia; the latter was also known as the 'Orden der schwarzen Bruder'.[33]

Franz Christian Laukard, who was himself a member of the Mosellaner or Amicitia Order at the University of Jena, described it as young people who associated with each other *mutua officia*; taking walks to nearby villages, drinking together in pubs and who cared for each other by lending money and supporting each other in following the 'straight and narrow'.[34]

When viewed in comparison with the brutality often and liberally meted out by the *Landsmannschaften* to their members, it is no small wonder that the precepts of life-long fraternity and loyalty were so well received by members of the student orders.[35] These 'student orders', the majority of which were secretative organisations, envisaged themselves as an embodiment of the student-knight idea; yet their activities in this context proved much more than a mere theoretical acceptance of the quest: for the orders, which formed arcane factions within the *Landsmannschaften*, attempted to influence and direct the actions of the larger organisations. The intimidation within the *Landsmannschaften* was amplified by the fact that regulations and discipline for contravening the organisation's rules appear to have been almost totally *ad hoc* and not set down in a written form. This gave the executive of a *Landsmannschaft* the opportunity to impose a virtually arbitrary reign of terror on its members. In contrast to this, the student orders introduced the practice of written constitutions which incorporated within them that order's chivalric code. The code in turn defined the behaviour expected by the members of the order and determined the punishment to be imposed for infractions of the constitution. According to Laukhard the order Amicitia stated its rubric as follows:

> Friendship is the fundamental precept of our society and it is the duty of every member to obligate himself with the task of endeavouring to be on good terms and understanding with all other members.[36]

However preferable the student orders were in comparison to the *Landsmannschaften*, they also had some less savoury aspects. From their secretive vantage point within the *Landsmannschaften* the student orders attempted to recruit those new students whom they felt were best suited for their fraternal organisations.[37] Bitter conflict often erupted when more than one order sought to recruit new members within the same *Landsmannschaft* or university community. This of course was intensified by the fact that the orders adhered to a cavalier code of honour which demanded that their members, and by convention all other scholars as well, were required to demand and give satisfaction on points of honour. These instances quite often were merely *Losgehen* or provocation for the sake of a fight, and took place at almost any time or place: 'in cellars, in taverns and even in the open'.[38] But conflicts did not exist merely between the student orders. Strife was also caused by the orders within the *Landsmannschaften* through their continued attempts to gain control by placing their own members in executive positions.[39]

The problems caused to the *Landsmannschaften* by these internal power struggles reached such proportions by the 1790s that most *Landsmannschaften* required their new members to take an oath solemnly swearing that they were not, nor would they become, a member of a student order. The orders also disrupted the student community as a whole by their intimidation of non-members and by using not only the university precincts but whole towns for their running frays. One such incident between Constantia and Harmonia in Heidelberg is reported to have been of almost battle size proportions.[40] Non-members, scholastic and otherwise, did not readily accept the existence of secretive orders in their midst, and the rowdiness and breaking of the peace proved vexing to university and civil authorities alike. But when, following 1790, the majority of the orders enthusiastically adopted the ideas of the French Revolution and pledged themselves to cosmopolitan revolution, the student orders advanced in the eyes of state authorities from merely suspect societies to potential insurrectionists.[41] Furthermore, they were suspected of having connections with the clandestine and revolutionary organisation known as the *Illuminati*, which had been founded in 1776 by a rather disputatious professor of religious law at the University of Ingolstadt named Adam Weishaupt.[42] Although Weishaupt's group, the Bavarian Illuminati, were suppressed in the mid-1780s,[43] the easy association of secret lodges among university students, with the disruptive behaviour of the student orders within society as a whole, and their open acceptance of the French Revolution, made the orders appear as a potentially revolutionary force which needed to be dealt with by both the civil and university authorities.

Ernst Röhlke contends that the goal of the orders was to establish a free, Protestant empire under a Protestant emperor in opposition to the Roman Catholicism of the Holy Roman Empire,[44] a plan reminiscent of the Union of German Protestant Princes in the previous century.[45] Due to their small numbers the student orders hoped to achieve their aims through evolution rather than by an outright test of force. They were none the less greatly disappointed when Frederick the Great did not try to gain the Holy Roman Crown following the Seven Years' War.[46] But regardless of what their motives actually were, the student orders were viewed as treasonous organisations, and as such were banned.

On 1 June 1792, Duke Karl August von Weimar issued a *Conclusum Corporis Evangelicorum* against the orders. This was followed by an imperial report in June 1793, which was presented to the Holy Roman Emperor. The report was issued by the chancellory of the Elector of Mainz regarding the orders and other secret societies for the purpose of acquiring imperial support to implement uniform and binding regulations in the matter.[47]

Needless to say, a society which had existed at least partially in secret, would not dissolve itself at the mere wave of the imperial sceptre. The accolade cross worn at the throat by order members symbolised the Protestant, Christian aspects of their society and the ribbon supporting the cross indicated the binding of the order's brothers to the cause, and of the cause to them, for life.[48] However, their strength at the universities slowly began to wane even though reports exist of activity among the members of the Constantia order as late as the winter of 1804–05.[49] But the suppression of the orders was not uniformly enforced as the Kaiser chose not to give the previously mentioned imperial report ascent to imperial law, thereby making it difficult for regional rulers to use the report against the orders.[50] None the less it was felt that the villains needed to make recompense and the regional rulers in conjunction with the university authorities, imposed punishment on the orders for their terrorism of both the academic and municipal communities. However, the sentences imposed tended to be fines and short terms of incarceration as both professors and the citizenry of the university towns realised their financial dependence on the students and did not wish to lose this source of income.[51] This, then, allowed the student orders to die a somewhat more natural death than would have been the case through their outright persecution by the authorities. It also allowed the student associations which replaced them a period of time in which to adopt some of their principles and practices without being proscribed for similar unlawful activities and beliefs.

The orders had offered their members brotherhood for life, a less parochial outlook, and written constitutions, whereas the *Landsmannschaften* had given their members little more than *ad hoc* intimidation imposed by their compatriots. The internecine conflicts between the orders and the *Landsmannschaften* on the one hand and between the various student orders on the other caused the downfall of both groups.

THE *KRÄNZCHEN*

During the 1780s, a new type of hybrid student society slowly began to appear at certain of the German universities under the name of *Kränzchen*; a term used in the eighteenth century to denote a small social group.[52] Perhaps the best example can be drawn from the student community of the University of Frankfurt on the Oder which became the leader in the development of student *Kränzchen*. The student orders at Frankfurt on the Oder, as elsewhere, had continued to be so blatantly detrimental and injurious to the academic laws, the disciplinary practices and the well-being of the university in general,[53] that they were forbidden by the university senate as of 12 January 1786.[54] Freed from the terror of the orders, a group of conscientious students formed a new association known as the *Neue Gesellschaft*. This 'New Society' and its written constitution were approved by the university authorities on 3 July 1786.[55] With that mandate the society set out to improve academic life through the uniform application of codified regulations for all students at the Viadrina (University of Frankfurt on the Oder).

The society's founders realised that it would soon become too large to function with amicability and therefore decided to subdivide the society into smaller groups known as *Kränzchen*. Eventually in this way there developed the Selesian, Pommeranian, Prussian and Brandenburgian *Kränzchen* at the Viadrina.[56] In the New Society there was a fusing of both *Landsmannschaft* and student order practices. The division of the New Society into autonomous subsections composed of compatriots harkened back directly to the traditional recruiting demarcations of the *Landsmannschaften*. However, each of the regional canton-like subgroups of *Kränzchen*, was a separate but equal member of the New Society. Each of the cantons had its own *Senior*, but all adhered equally to the Society's codified rules for the behaviour of its members, which was known as a *comment* (taken from the French 'to know how'). The individual *Kränzchen* held their own *convent* or meetings, to ensure the observance of the *comment* by their own members.[57] The *Senioren*, in addition to presiding over their own individual *Kränzchen*, represented their particular canton at the council of seniors or *seniorum conventum*, later known as the *Senioren-Convent*, where they worked together to enforce a uniform implementation of the *comment* by the New Society as a whole.[58]

The New Society was a synthesis of previous practices taken from the orders and the *Landsmannschaften*, but with a new type of application. The *Senioren-Convent* and the admission of compatriots as members, were both practices taken from the *Landsmannschaften*, while codification and writing down the Society's constitution in the form of a *comment* had been adopted from the student orders. But the application of one *comment* to all students at the same university was a new and unique development of the *Kränzchen* at Frankfurt on the Oder.

The popularity of the *Kränzchen* spread and similar organisations soon were formed at other universities, the earliest being at Halle and Erlangen. In 1791 the King of Prussia suggested to the Prorector and Senate at the University of Erlangen that student societies should be authorised rather than forbidden. This led to a special letter of royal consent in 1798 and the subsequent founding of the Ansbacher Kränzchen at Erlangen, which took the Roman name for Ansbach, Onoldia.[59] Landsmannschaft Guestphalia, on the other hand, was the product of a reform movement among the *Landsmannschaften* at the University of Halle in 1789, which sought to combat a concerted effort on the part of the student order Constantia to destroy the local *Landsmannschaften*.[60] Guestphalia adopted a written constitution, with the result that it, and similarly reformed *Landsmannschaften*, became known as 'constitutional' *Landsmannschaften*, thereby differentiating them from similar fraternities. Later a number of this new denomination of *Landsmannschaften* also moved towards the practices of the *Kränzchen*.[61] But Onoldia and Guestphalia were single *Kränzchen*, not part of a larger society as was the case with the *Kränzchen* at the Viadrina. This difference, however, soon began to disappear. In 1798 Onoldia was the first student fraternity to adopt the prefix 'corps' to its name, a practice which came into use in the early 1800s to designate constitutional *Landsmannschaften* or *Kränzchen*. The term 'corps' also referred to fraternities which had formed themselves into a *Senioren-Convent* by means of a contract or *Cartelgesetz* which bound the member fraternities to one common and codified *comment*. In writing on the Heidelberg Comment which was adopted in 1806, Wilhelm Fabricius observes that the work became a prototype and therefore has special significance in that many other university communities adopted this *comment*; some took it up almost verbatim as, for instance, at Tübingen and Freiburg, while others made use of the content.[62]

The *comments* was not identical at each university nor was there any attempt to set up an affiliation between the *Senioren-Conventen* of the various universities, as the student orders had done with their networks of lodges. But regardless of their autonomy in application, the various *comment* were uniform in their purpose; that of regulating the deportment of students. This is borne out by the subtitles and rubrics of the different *comments*. The preamble of the Heidelberg *comment* describes it as the general and binding regulations for the deportment of all students at the University of Heidelberg. The older and less pedantic *comment* at Frankfurt on the Oder is simply described as the general regulations of the four respective *Kränzchen* at the University of Frankfurt on the Oder.[63] This latter somewhat more laconic work goes on to define the boundaries of the geographical cantons of the four *Kränzchen* and their relationship to one another. The draughtsmen of the document wasted little ink before setting down their enmity to the student orders by stating, that should an altercation arise between a *Kränzchen* and an order, the affair would automatically become the responsibility of all four *Kränzchen*, which were mutually obligated to support each other against the common enemy.[64] This was followed by the manner in which matters involving insults and points of honour were to be carried out and settled. But perhaps the most significant aspect regarding the *Kränzchen* and the *Senioren-Convent*, was their assumption of responsibility for the student body as a whole. Any student who was not a *Kränzianer* and who found himself in a dispute, whether with a *Kränzchen* member or an order member, would be given assistance by the *Kränzchen* members of his particular geographic canton. This was a significant departure from former practices whereby 'free' or unattached students were considered virtually open sport by both the orders and the *Landsmannschaften*. This new jurisdiction applied not only to students who contravened the *comment*. Merchants could also find themselves placed under specific periods of ban by the local *Senioren-Convent* for unfair trade with students. During such a period of ban any student found trading with a proscribed merchant would be required to give satisfaction at arms to the senior of all the four *Kränzchen*.[65] The question of what constituted satisfaction will be dealt with later.

A further point emphasised in the *comment* of the New Society was the solemn pledge by each of the *Kränzchen* never to become a student order. Should it ever occur, the renegade *Kränzchen* was to be struck down with the combined vengeance of the other three *Kränzchen*.[66]

The Viadrina Comment ended with Section XXII which charged each *Senior* with the responsibility of introducing each new member of his *Kränzchen* to the other three *Senioren* so that they might get to know one another and thereby the cause of friendship would be better served.[67]

Although the original impetus for the New Society grew out of a wish for collective security, the legality of the *Kränzchen* and the resultant comradeship, built a loyalty and respect within the student community for the New Society which eventually sounded the death knell for the student orders. The orders deteriorated internally and disappeared quietly and without notice by 1813.[68] Similarly, it was the open, constitutional and egalitarian practices of the *Kränzchen* which commanded the respect and allegiance of the scholastic community as a whole.

Needless to say, there was great bitterness and resentment on the part of the student orders during their demise and Friedrich Ludwig Jahn, who later became a driving force in the nationalist German student movement, and who himself was a member of the student order Unitas, stated: 'Nothing will improve at the universities until the last *Kränzchen Senior* is strangled with the intestines of the last *Kränzchen* member.'[69] With the Battle of Jena in 1806 and with the final defeat of Napoleon, an important point was reached in the development of German student history as well as for German unification in general.[70] This new development brought nationalism into student life at German universities, a factor which found its apex in the Third Reich, intimidating and dividing the academic community through political directives and bigotry.

THE RISE OF THE *BURSCHENSCHAFTEN*

The Napoleonic Wars helped to accelerate the growth of German nationalism and gave focus to youthful patriotism through groups such as Major Ludwig von Lützow's Free Corps. This notorious band of irregulars was composed predominantly of students and university trained professionals. Following Napoleon's retreat from Russia, Jahn and other reformists strongly supported the King of Prussia's appeal to the educated youth of Germany, to help drive out the French. Von Lützow's Free Corps was comprised of three to four thousand volunteers who counted among their members Jahn himself, Friedrich Friesen his associate, and the poet Theodor Körner.[71] Germany having been liberated, many student Free Corps members were inspired by Jahn, who 'marshalled and led university students in a challenge to the neo-authoritarianism of Restoration Germany'.[72] His purpose was to forge German students into one national federation, with the express purpose of hastening the arrival of German unification. It is interesting to note the teachings of Jahn in the light of his having been a member of a student order; of which they possibly were merely a later manifestation.

The new association of all German students as advocated by Jahn and his associates was known as the *Deutsche Burschenschaften*. This organisation developed very quickly but differed considerably at various universities. The *Burschenschaften* of Halle and Jena perhaps serve as the best examples, since they both were in the vanguard of the movement but differed in their evolution. In Jena in 1815, the members of Landsmannschaft Vandalia, which was composed predominantly of Mecklenburg Free Corps volunteers, managed against considerable opposition to manipulate the dissolution of the local *Senioren-Convent*.[73] This was done in order to establish a separate single association for all students who had a more nationalist orientation. However, in Halle, where the movement centred around Burschenschaft Teutonia, it differed from Vandalia in that only those students who were thought to be suitable and useful to the movement were allowed to join. In both cases the *Burschenschaften* were founded on pan-Germanism, but Teutonia envisaged a movement encompassing all German students, while Vandalia, which was pro-Prussian, envisaged an organisation for the reforming of the existing *Landsmannschaften* into suitably nationalistic units.[74] Shortly before Teutonia was forced by the civic authorities to disband because of duelling in 1817, the *Burschenschaften* of Jena and Halle managed to establish a *Kartell*. The idea of forming a pan-German

Kartell and putting it into general practice at all universities, was promulgated at the Wartburgfest of 1817. This festival had been promoted fervently by Jahn to celebrate, as a national commemoration, both the Victory of Leipzig and Luther's Reformation. The speeches and discussions held on the Wartburg emphasised and widened the differences between the *Landsmannschaften* and the *Burschenschaften*. The latter group was both adamant and convinced of the necessity for the growth of a single nationalist organisation of German students.[75]

The organisational shift from local *Senioren-Conventen*, which bound the individual *Landsmannschaften* to the *comment* at their own universities, to that of a national *Kartell* of all students under one disciplinary code, had a certain appeal to many students at the Wartburgfest, including the members of several corps. Furthermore, the differences between the corps and *Burschenschaften* were not as quickly definable in some instances, as was the case later in the century.[76] There was also a further complication in that a numebr of student fraternities attempted to synthesise the new and the old forms, hoping to maintain their appeal regardless of what might develop. The result was that no clear picture arose as to what the future might hold for the *Burschenschaften*.

In the following spring fourteen *Burschenschaften* met and adopted the nineteen points of the 1818 constitution as proposed by the Jena *Burschenschaft* thereby pledging their membership to the ideals of equality, unity and freedom as well as to a Christian-German physical and intellectual education for the service to the Fatherland.[77] This new association of *Burschenschaften* took as its colours black, red and gold, for which there are several alleged symbolic reasons: one being that they were in the first version of the old Reich's colours, another that they had been the colours of the uniforms of Lützow's Free Corps. Egbert Weiss states that recent research would indicate the colours adopted were those of Vandalia, Jena, which had presented the constitution to the 1818 conference, thus discounting the traditional case put by Franz Schnabel for the *Freikorps* colours.[78]

As with most movements, although the goal was agreed upon, the *Burschenschaften* lacked unanimity as to the method of achieving it, and factionalism soon arose. One of the most notorious and radical of the groups was the 'Blacks' at the University of Giessen, led by the Follen brothers.

The name was derived from the plain black, old-fashioned dress of the members, which symbolised their ideal of a Germany stripped of frills and decadence. Ideologically they developed the concept of a Christian, German *Burschenschaft* in which Christianity and German nationalism were inseparable.[79] It is this group that is said to have inspired Karl Sand to assassinate the writer August von Kotzebue in Mannheim for his allegedly conspiring with Russia against the Fatherland. The blame for much of the student unrest in this period was attributed to the *Burschenschaften* and this dispraise eventually prompted the implementation of the Carlsbad Decrees in 1819.[80] This edict forced the *Burschenschaften* to function in much the same arcane fashion as had their antecedents, the student orders, only a few decades earlier. Central *Burschenschaften* tenets – some of which continued to command a following well into the Third Reich – began to evolve and can be seen in the 1821 Streitberg Amendments to the original constitution. Paragraph III of the amendments stated that *Burschenschaft* education was Christian and German and that foreigners and Jews, since they were not part of the Fatherland, should be excluded from membership because their presence would disrupt the education and awareness of the Fatherland within the *Burschenschaft*.[81]

The young movement showed a great deal of tenacity, for neither the so-called *Jünglingbund* plot nor the subsequent arrests in 1821–4 seem to have greatly weakened the *Burschenschaften*.[82] At the *Burschentag* of 1827 in Bamberg the representatives were able to recreate temporarily the *Allgemeine Deutsche Burschenschaft* which had been previously proscribed. But dissension arose and factionalism struck again. *Germania*, which was numerically much stronger and much more nationalistic than its rival faction *Arminia*, took an active political stand on the issue of national unity.[83] The rivalry which emerged between these two wings of the *Burschenschaften* reached outright enmity and at certain universities duelling between the members of the *Germania* and *Arminia* movements became a common occurrence.[84] This internecine conflict was settled indirectly by the civil authorities through the 204 subsequent arrests and trials of *Burschenschaft* members following the abortive *Vaterland* plot of *Germania* at the *Frankfurter Wachturm* in April 1833.[85] As a result of the abortive coup in Frankfurt the *Burschenschaften* were not allowed to reappear at the universities until 1848 following the advent of political reform in Germany. The restoration of the *Burschenschaften* to a legal status was celebrated by a second *Wartburgfest* in Eisenach on 13 June of that year and a student parliament was held in conjunction with the festivities. However, it was only after Bismarck and the foundation of the empire that the *Burschenschaften* became a unified association like their contemporary associations of fraternities and finally joined together to form the *Allgemeinen Deputierten-Conventen* on 20 July 1881.[86]

THE *ALLGEMEINE SENIOREN-CONVENT*

Although the growth and development of the *Burschenschaften* had in many cases overthrown unreformed *Landsmannschaften*, the suppression of the *Burschenschaften* for their political and social indiscretions only served to strengthen and legitimise the corps.[87] They soon were viewed both within and outside of student communities as the one legitimate organ for student government. The *Burschenschaften* could do little other than sit quietly observing the corps gaining a continually stronger foothold at the universities during their proscription. But not all *Burschenschaften* members wished to remain passive and in order to protect themselves from reprisals on the part of the *Burschenschaften*, the *Senioren-Conventen* of the three Saxon universities, Halle, Jena and Leipzig, entered into a contract in March 1821 which excluded *in perpetuum* the goals and beliefs of the *Burschenschaften* from their membership.

The *Landsmannschaften* of the three *Senioren Conventen* pledged to support each other through mutual friendship and assistance in dealing with their common enemy, the *Burschenschaften*, just as in all other *comment*-related matters, in as far as location and circumstances allowed. Fraternities which embraced the *Burschenschaft* spirit and purpose would always be excluded from the agreement and from the three *Senioren Conventen*.[88] In order to aid in this collective stand against the *Burschenschaften*, the three *Senioren-Conventen* agreed to a biannual exchange of membership lists and other information pertinent to their own particular university communities. In addition the corps of the three Saxon universities pledged to send representatives to assist each other should a situation arise in which one of the other corps was implicated or needed auxiliary physical support.[89] The agreement was expanded in September 1831 when the representatives of the three *Senioren-Conventen* met at Köstritz to adopt the statutes and formally inaugurate their new *Kartell* known as the *Allgemeine Senioren-Convent (ASC)*. As part of the new cartel statutes the three *Senioren-Conventen* agreed to recognise judgements such as rustication pronounced by the *Senioren-Convent* on students at the other *Kartell* universities and to enforce the same measures should the students in question appear in either of the nearby academic communities. Matters arising between the *Senioren-Conventen* of the *Kartell* were to be referred to, and dealt with only by the *Allgemeine Senioren-Convent*. Paragraph IV of the statutes requested that a regular meeting place, roughly equidistant from all three universities be established and Bad Kösen was adopted.[90] This town subsequently gave its name to the association of corps known as the *Kösener Senioren-Conventen Verband (KSCV)* which eventually succeeded the *ASC* of the Saxon universities.

THE *KÖSENER SENIOREN-CONVENTEN VERBAND*

After the violent attempts in the year of revolution, 1848, a discernible atmosphere of apathy manifested itself amongst university scholars as much as with other sections of the German people. But at the same time people tried to preserve and maintain seminal thoughts of an earlier time as well as to gather new strength.[91] As a direct result of the new rights granted there was a blossoming of student societies, the majority of which attempted to outbid one another with variations of resuscitated nationalism and traditional academic forms. Most such groups enjoyed a fairly short life-span and departed from their respective university communities without leaving much evidence of ever having existed.

The few survivors of the movement tended to be those with pious predispositions and formed the foundation for what later became the *Schwarzburgbund* (Christian *Burschenschaften*) founded in 1885, *Unitas* (Roman Catholic) founded in 1855 and *Wingolf* (Lutheran) founded in 1841. These fraternities and others with strong religious affiliations gained the general designation, in student circles, of confessional fraternities.[92]

This proved to be a critical period for the various *Senioren-Conventen*. Their structure, previously developed to deal with student matters, had few, if any, of the diverse political precepts or nationalist tenets of unification to serve as an emotive lure to attract new members. They found themselves inert and vulnerable, as the main thrust of the *Burschenschaft*, with its goal of unifying all student groups into one large general movement, left the locally organised *Senioren-Conventen* with very little strength to combat the momentum of such a widespread organisation. The *Allgemeine Senioren-Convent*, as seen above, was established to strengthen the corps against the ardent nationalism of the *Burschenschaft*. But the *Allegemeine Senioren-Convent* had been envisaged and initiated on an almost parochial framework for the protection of the corps in Saxony, not to combat the *Burschenschaft* on a national scale. The period of proscription prior to 1848 kept the *Burschenschaft* from mobilising the nationalistic sentiments of their many adherents. Realising that if the *Burschenschaften* were allowed time to gather their forces, there would almost certainly be bitter struggles for control of the universities, the crops considered collective action of their own. The necessary initiative was taken by the *Senior* of Corps Vandalia in Heidelberg, named Friederich von Klinggräff. In May 1848, the *Senioren-Convent* of Heidelberg, under his leadership, undertook to invite representatives from all German university *Senioren-Conventen* to meet in Jena on 15 July 1848. The purpose and objectives of the meeting as given on the invitation were the protection and encouragement of *Landsmannschaft* interests, the discussion of mutual regulations and the draughting of a general *comment*.[93] Each *Senioren-Convent* was requested to send representatives and the agenda as given on the invitation to attend was,

1. To mark the position occupied by the corps *vis-à-vis* the general membership of student associations.
2. to draught a general corps *comment*.
3. to introduce correspondence among the member *SC*'s on a regular basis.[94]

Prior to the meeting in Jena the term 'corps' had no specific use when referring to student fraternities, and as noted above, was used interchangeably as a synonym for both *Kränzchen* and constitutional *Landsmannschaften*. The Heidelberg *Senioren-Convent*, however, gave instructions to its delegates that the meeting should recognise as corps only those student fraternities which excluded all political inclinations and goals, which accepted and allowed the practice of the specialised student duel among like-minded scholars and which did not accept as a full member of their society any person who had not fenced at least once. They were also charged with the task of initiating the creation of a *Schiedsgericht* or court which would hear disagreements between parties.[95] The establishment of a *Schiedsgericht* was in the first instance for the arbitration of disputes between different corps and in that way to solve issues which might otherwise splinter a *Senioren-Convent* or the whole federation. In the second instance it gave all students the opportunity to have their complaints heard by their local *Senioren-Convent*. Members of student corps were required by the *Kösener* statutes to give unquestioned satisfaction through armed combat in affairs of honour. Other students, whether fraternity members or not, were expected to give 'relative satisfaction'. This meant that they had the choice of seeking redress either through duelling or by submitting their case to the *Schiedsgericht* for arbitration. If the court found in the plaintiff's favour he would be entitled to *Revokation*, which was a public apology and withdrawal of any contentious statement by the accused party.[96]

The first congress of the *Kösener Corps* dealt with many other matters, but in essence it extended the cartel formed by the corps of the *Allgemeine Senioren-Convent* to encompass the *Senioren-Convente* of all German universities which were willing to adhere to its statutes and to comply with the definition of a corps as set down by the corps of Göttingen and ratified by the congress. The following definition, along with a communique declaring the congress as the only authentic and legitimate student organisation, was forwarded to the Frankfurt Assembly and directly contradicted statements which emerged from the Wartburg addresses of the *Burschenschaft* held only a short time previous. 'We, that is to say, the corps, the *Senioren Conventen* and the federation of corps as such decline from active participation in politics and do not allow ourselves to become involved in the everyday affairs of party politics'.[97]

There were, as one might expect, several *Senioren-Convente* and *Kränzchen* which were slower than the majority to join the new association, but after the first three annual meetings at the Rudelsburg in Bad Kösen, the machinery was well set into motion, so that when the federation was finally founded as the *Kösener Senioren-Conventen Verband* in May 1855, it began a chain of annual congresses that ran unbroken until 1914. There were seven *Senioren-Convente (SC)* which were the signatories at the federation's inauguration in 1855, thirteen covenanters by the congress in 1858 and sixteen of the possible eighteen were parties to the agreement in 1861; the last two being Königsberg in 1865 and Munich in 1862.

All of the numerous decisions of the various annual congresses are not necessarily germane to this study, but several of the more salient issues should perhaps be mentioned at this point. The most far reaching in terms of the twentieth century was the statement made in 1848 by the corps that party politics had no place in the structure of either a corps or a *Senioren-Convent*. As will be seen later this was what separated the corps from other student fraternities and set them in juxtaposition to the heavily politicised Nazi Students' Association. The corps defined themselves as fraternal associations which, without regard for any or a particular political direction that would bind its members, held the general aim on the basis of a special constitution, to uphold German studentdom and the *comment* set up by the *Senioren Convente*.[98] This allowed corps members to have whatever beliefs they wished privately and thereby contrasted greatly with the political nationalism of more radical student groups such as the *Burschenschaften*.

In 1858 and 1859 the congresses decided that all candidates for membership in a corps were required to fence at least one *Bestimmungsmensur* prior to being received as a *corpsier*.[99] The *Bestimmungsmensur* will be dealt with in some depth later, but for the moment let us be laconic and merely describe it as fencing with sharp edged swords. The introduction of this regulation demanded that each corps member be blooded and thereby prepared to accept his responsibility for giving unquestioned satisfaction as prescribed by the statutes of the *Kösener* corps. The introduction of a *Schiedsgericht* initiated a means whereby arbitration between corps within a *Senioren-Convent* or different *Senioren-Convente* could be affected. The idea of exchanging membership lists and records of any subsequent honours or discipline, as begun by the *Allgemeine Senioren-Convent*, was expanded to include all corps of the *Kösener Verband* and is still practised today.[100]

Prior to 1868, corps alumni generally played very little part in the life of their own fraternity, and less with others, after the completion of their studies. They were considered to have become part of the extra-academic world or realm of the Philistines and their passing beyond the pale of academe was referred to as entering *Philisterium*. In the meantime over-zealous adherence to the *Kösener* statutes which demanded unquestioned satisfaction, frequently fired the personal and parochial pride of young corps members and provoked heated disagreements between various corps. The concept of unquestioned satisfaction was extended to include a given number of members from one corps matched against an equal number of members from another corps, in a series of rather fierce fencing matches. Such exchanges came to be called *pro patriae* and by the 1860s it became a common practice for whole *Senioren-Convente* to be matched against one another.[101] The related extravagant costs to both the physical and fiscal resources associated with staging such events brought many corps close to the brink of dissolution. Eventually a *corpsier* named Leonhard Zander, interceded at the 1881 congress of the *Kösener* corps by presenting a petition from 4000 corps alumni, including the signatures of Otto von Bismarck, himself an avid duellist, and the Crown Prince Wilhelm of Prussia. The petition requested that the literalism in interpreting the statutes and the bloodletting be tempered. Amendments were made by the congress to the statutes as proposed by the alumni, forbidding *pro patriae* between *Senioren Convente*, but left the choice open to individual corps themselves regarding the practice of inter-fraternity matches. Zander apparently had not intended to form an alumni association, but as a result of the intervention regarding the *pro patriae* the corps alumni began to form an organisation, which later became known as the *Verband Alter Corpsstudenten (VAC)*. It eventually developed both local and federal aspects to its organisation, but was established with the purpose of serving cumulative corps interests rather than those of individual fraternities or *Senioren-Conventen*.[102] This organisation, as will be shown later, played a significant role in the corps' stand against the *NSDAP* during the 1930s.

By the 1860s certain factions of the various student communities which belonged neither to the *Burschenschaft* for political reasons, nor to the *Senioren-Convent* through lack of the social position necessary for students to join a corps, grew discontented with their excluded status and formed a new organisation at Coburg in 1868, known as the *Allgemeiner Landsmannschaftlicher-Convent (LC)*. This new association of fraternities was neither political nor confessional and adopted a number of practices typical of corps, such as organisation around a local *Landsmannschaftlicher Convent* at each university and the creation of a written *comment*.[103] This in itself is not of great significance, but it does illustrate that the corps were being paid the very high compliment of emulation and were much revered by younger student fraternal associations.

It evolves that, as intimated earlier, the corps became the student fraternities for the sons of the higher echelons of society.[104] A very quick glance at the lists of corps alumni show Otto von Bismarck in Corps Hannovera while studying in Göttingen and Kaiser Wilhelm II as a member of Corps Borussia in Bonn.[105] But not all students restricted themselves to universities and as technical post-secondary education developed in the latter half of the nineteenth century, associations of corps other than the *Kösener Senioren-Conventen Verband* were formed. These fraternities evolved their own *Senioren-Convente* and modelled themselves on the *Kösener* corps. When the four new *Senioren-Convente* of Karlsruhe, Zurich, Hannover and Stuttgart met in 1864, they chose Weinheim on the Bergstrasse as the most equitable point at which to meet and adopted its name for their new organisation.[106] The *Weinheimer Senioren-Convent (WSC)* continued to grow so that just prior to the First World War its original dozen corps had swollen in number to 59 within an organisation of 14 *Senioren-Convente*. An agreement was reached between the *Kösener* and *Weinheimer* corps whereby the older federation of corps would function only at the universities and the latter would restrict its activities to the technical institutions of higher learning.[107]

Two additional and smaller organisations of corps also developed during the nineteenth century. The *Rudolstädter Senioren-Convent (RSC)* was first formed in the 1850s by students at colleges of veterinary medicine and later expanded to include fraternities at forestry and mining schools as well.[108] It eventually joined the *Weinheimer* corps in the 1930s hoping for security within a larger organisation.

The second group was the *Naumberger Senioren-Convent* which developed at the agricultural colleges and was, for the most part, absorbed by the *Weinheimer* corps following the Second World War.[109]

KARTELL AND *KREIS*

The federation of corps established at Bad Kösen in 1848 was in essence a cartel of *Senioren-Convente* much like the *Allgemeine Senioren-Convent* of the Saxon corps or the *Kartell* between the *SC* of Erlangen and *SC* of Würzburg for the corps in Frankonia.[110] These regional organisations were initially formed to serve as a united front against the *Burschenschaften* at the universities of specific territories. The founding of the *KSCV* superseded the need for regional organisations and although they were not eliminated by the Kösener statutes, they slowly disappeared as the need for them diminished. However, following the founding of the *KSCV*, another type of *Kartell* which was based upon patriality, became more popular among the corps. The practice of a corps admitting as members only those students from a specified geographic canton, much like the mediaeval academic nations, was known as the *Landsmannschaft Prinzip*. This dictated who was eligible to join which corps and regulated a certain amount of regional homogeneity in the various fraternities. Following this line, compatrial cartels blossomed after 1848. For example, the Rhineland corps; Corps Rhenania of Bonn, Corps Rhenania of Heidelberg, Corps Rhenania of Erlangen and Corps Rhenania of Würzburg formed one such compatrial *Kartell*, as did Corps Bavaria of Munich and Corps Bavaria of Würzburg.[111] This practice was in no way in opposition to the *Kösener* federation, but rather was an embellishment as it reflected the natural provincial affinity between the corps within such a *Kartell*, which exceeded normal inter-corps relationships.

By 1855–60 the term *Kartellkreise* was in common use among the corps to denote inter-corps cartels, but the term later literally split so that by 1870 each of the words composing the compound took on a more specific meaning of its own. *Kartellcorps* indicated a very strong bond between corps whereby a member of one corps *eo ipso* was extended membership in other corps of the *Kartell*. This quite often had a compatriate base, as with the *Kartell* between Corps Baruthia of Erlangen and Corps Bavaria of Würzburg with the result that a *corpsier* was expected to treat an insult to his *Kartellcorps* as one to his own corps.[112]

There also developed groups of corps known as *Kreise*, which generally adopted a colour, usually the one which was the most common in the tricolours of the member fraternities, so that terms such as *Blauer Kreis* or *Roter Kreis* also became a part of *Kösener* corps vocabulary. These groups were not merely a product of *Verhältnispolitik*, serving to extend social interaction and convention, but rather factions within the *Kösener Verband* which attempted through *Kreispolitik* and associated conferences, to manipulate the whole of the *KSCV* towards their own conceptions and interpretations of the statutes and principles which should be fostered within the *Kösener* federation.[113] But the problem experienced by the *Burschenschaften* whereby two pugilistic and strongly competitive coteries attempted to seize control, was not a threat to the corps, if for no other reason than that most *Kreise* contained less than a dozen corps and the eight or more *Kreise* afforded no faction a significant footing to shift the whole federation in its direction. The high point of *Kreispolitik*, according to Wilhelm Fabricius, was in the 1870s and 1880s.[114] The intervening years prior to the First World War witnessed a reduction in the number of *Kreise* and by the time of the Weimar Republic only a handful remained; some corps having no *Kreis* at all. The last major point of contention involving the *Kreise* was between 1928–33 when the corps were faced with the decision of whether to centralise following the spirit of the times or to remain autonomous according to their traditions.[115] This issue tended to align itself along the lines of *Kreispolitik*, but to the German republic in general there was very little if any indication of factionalism within the *KSCV*.

We have seen that the corps developed from a synthesis of post-Reformation philosophy and academic traditions into self-regulating scholastic communities which became the arbiters for student behaviour. To a certain extent, these fraternities and their federation were formed initially for the mutual protection of their members. But what was the central percept around which the corps functioned and how was it translated into everyday deportment of their members within the municipality in which the university was located? It is this question that we shall turn to next.

2 Students, Law and Codes

As mentioned briefly above, the German universities received a certain amount of legal attention and reform from their state authorities during the eighteenth century. Prussia, often the leader in legal codification during that period, introduced regulations on 5 September 1750, whereby the discipline of students was to come under the jurisdiction of the universities.[1] Only a few decades later such autonomy might well have not come to law, as the latter part of the century so rife with widespread fears and allegations accused secret societies with fomenting discontent and revolution. In the midst of these perceptions, activities of the student orders were viewed with suspicion and classified as subversive. But the spirit of alarm which brought about the Imperial verdict of 6 June 1793 calling for the proscription of clandestine societies and fraternities does not appear in the codification of Prussian Law. This contrast serves as an indication of the tolerant disposition on the part of the Prussian crown toward student associations.[2] The *Allgemeine Landrecht für die Preussischen Staaten* of 1794 as cited by Herbert Kessler in his work on the law and the German universities, states that the existing stance of the law in Prussia was merely codified, nothing more. Under the codification, universities were declared institutions of the state, having their own corporal constitutions, with all the rights of privileged corporations and their academic senates were given jurisdiction over all teachers and students alike.[3]

The new legal code for the Prussian states did, however, go much further than its precursor of 1750 in that it outlined the bounds of academic legal responsibility and jurisdiction. The new statutes empowered the academic courts to act in cases of civil dispute and disorder within the university community, through the right granted them to implement and enforce the legal code generally used for police and criminal matters.[4] In addition, special reference was made to the academic community under the statutes by such paragraphs as 84 and 85 which dealt with academic life in general. It could be argued that what the universities gained in terms of legal autonomy was bought at the individual student's loss of self-determination, for Paragraph 97 dictated specifically how a student's financial and legal affairs were to be conducted. Whether or not personal autonomy was forfeited by the students is difficult to assess, but the regulations were definitely an effort to protect the interests of both 'town and gown'. In matters such as the inheritance of property, a student came under the jurisdiction of the law enforced in the state from which he held his citizenship, rather than under the codex of his university. In most other matters a student was a ward of the university and his dealings with citizens of the municipality in which the university was situated were to be tempered with that in mind. Most contact between scholars and the citizenry was with merchants and victuallers, which almost immediately would have raised the very contentious point of giving credit. The academic courts were therefore charged with the task of regulating student credit with great scrutiny and even students over the age of majority were not to have extended credit nor could they act as guarantors, without the express sanction of the academic court.[5] Merchants and other citizens who neglected to observe these regulations had no recourse if they sought reparation from a student to whom they had given unauthorised credit. This, of course, did not remove all disputatious situations but it did remove the foundation for many of the more basic types of disagreements.

In Baden the legal code allowed the academic courts to deal with all civil law matters which concerned student discipline. This covered a wide range of infractions which included insults, bodily assult and even duelling in some cases, as long as death or serious maiming were not a result of the fray. If grave injury occurred the case was referred to the civil authorities for prosecution under the criminal code. The senate of the university interceded only in the more solemn aspects of student discipline such as rustication. All other matters came under the jurisdiction of the academic court's *Amtsmann* who, aided by a small policing force of beadles or bulldogs, such as those at Oxford or Cambridge, was responsible for the apprehension of offenders and the enforcement of legal discipline within the student community.[6]

In the case of duels, which was interpreted to include the intention of duelling without necessarily crossing blades, or the firing of shots, the matter was no longer a case for academic jurisdiction and the university magistrate bound the parties over to the civil authorities for trial. Anyone having knowledge of an intended duel was required by the university regulations to report the matter so that the persons involved could be confined to their quarters, or if necessary, placed in the student gaol. Following an investigation of the incident both parties to the quarrel were required by the university to sign a declaration of reconciliation. They were also required to give a solemn promise, on their word of honour, that they would not fight for the remainder of their period of studies. Those students who did not comply with the regulations, even medical students offering assistance to a fellow student wounded in a duel, were also liable to be given a *consilium abeundi*, which broadly speaking, was strong advice to leave the university. Such expulsion could quite easily mean the end of a student's academic pursuits and it was considered very much the ultimate discipline (*ries ultima*) of the university authorities.

The student's most valued asset was his word of honour, for it was that which allowed him access to the university when taking his oath at matriculation. It was his word of honour which allowed him to have credit authorised by the university. The student was honour bound to keep his word, for it was his only negotiable possession and his word of honour was seen as the outward indication of his true character and worth. Again this followed the idea of the student as a knight errant.

In his interesting and informative article on the application of honour to everyday student life, Gerhard Neuenhoff notes that in all situations, whether the administering of an oath or a legal matter before the courts, a student ritually and solemnly gave his word of honour. Those who refused to do so were punished for insubordination. Similarly the giving of his word through a handshake gave both the understanding and assurance to the other party that a student was committed to keep his promise. Failure on the part of the student to honour such an obligation could result in the enforcing of very severe punishment under the university's regulations as well as from student society.[7]

Herbert Kessler makes mention in his work on the student orders and secret societies, that the regulations set out in the academic laws of 1803 and 1810 were first and foremost measures for implementation against the orders and only secondarily applied to the *Kränzchen*. In that way the legislators made a fine distinction and the arcane fraternities were more severely punished than the *Kränzchen*.[8] This preferential treatment before the law, enabled the corps to establish themselves as legitimate organistaions, particularly during the period up to and following the Carlsbad Decrees of 1819. Further reform of the laws affecting universities moved slowly, but after 1848 the cumbersome dictates imposed on student organisations by the Carlsbad Decrees were removed. A special assembly of university officials in 1849 expressed the opinion that the universities needed no special disciplinary bodies and recommended the dissolution of academic courts. The matter took somewhat longer to settle in some principalities than in others and in Baden, for instance, the academic judicial system was not reformed until almost twenty years later, in 1868.[9]

Much of the argument for dissolution of the special academic legal courts and related laws, came from members of the *Burschenschaften* who argued that such independent legal status for academia was undemocratic and not consistent with the spirit of the new political freedoms granted in the previous year. In Leipzig, where the universities' residue of mediaeval legal privilege remained unchanged until 1868, the corps and most other fraternities fought for its retention. Their main argument was that the youthful misconduct of students should be disciplined by university courts in the context of academe rather than by state courts where punishment could give young scholars a criminal record and damage their possibilities in later professional life. Today, when decentralisation is often considered very progressive, the position of the *Burschenschaften*, that the academic courts were undemocratic, could seem the more antiquated argument, but apparently won over the authorities who found in favour of reform.[10]

The *Gerichtsverfassungsgesetz* of 1877 made no reference to the existence of special powers assigned to academic courts and thereby placed students under the jurisdiction of civil courts in all but strictly academic matters.[11] The change of status held by the academic courts altered the relationship of students to the civil authorities and society in general, but it made little if any change within the realm of student interaction or their code of behaviour.

After 1815 the student orders were almost gone from the universities, and the corps also referred to during that period as both *Landsmannschaften* and *Kränzchen*, were the only legitimate student organisations at the universities. This greatly aided the establishment of a local *comment* by the various *Senioren-Convente*.[12] The enforcement of law by the academic courts based on the honourable deportment of students, had been reinforced by the *comment* of the *Senioren-Convente* at the various universities. Corps members were required to conduct themselves in accordance with the local *comment*, which demanded that their honour be intact and defended through giving unquestioned satisfaction if it were called into question. In fact, the *Handbuch des Kösener Corpsstudenten* defines the term *comment* as 'The "How" that is to say the way in which an "honourable student" was expected to deport himself at university.'[13]

The earlier forms of *comment*, as drawn up by the *Kränzchen*, had a predominant bias towards the protection of *Kränzianer* and the students of associated cantons in order to guard them from attacks and intimidation by members of the proscribed student orders. As the dangers posed by the orders slowly died out, the corps took over leadership and control of the universities. The *comment* then became much more an instrument for regulating the behaviour of the student body in general. It was still based on the concept of student honour, but unlike the academic authorities which could, if needed, bring the weight of the state to their aid in cases of unruly scholars, the *Senioren-Conventen* used the weapon of *Verruf* or ban, which excluded an offender of the *comment* from the society of all honourable students. The constitution of one Leipzig fraternity stated that every member must consider his word of honour as sacred. Whoever broke his word was to be given a friendly warning the first time, a severe reprimand the second time and should it occur a third time he was to be expelled from the fraternity. The 1791 constitution of Landsmannschaft Marchia at the University of Halle was not as patient with offenders of its constitution. Anyone who was found guilty of misconduct and who did not undertake to rectify matters in the proper manner would not be tolerated in the fraternity and the breaking of his word of honour was considered grounds for his expulsion.[14]

A member's word of honour not only bound him to his personal obligations to society in general, but also served as the currency upon which his membership and interactions within the fraternity were based. This is seen in the constitution of Guestphalia at the University of Göttingen in 1812 where the members reciprocally swore on their honour to observe and conduct themselves within the regulations of their constitution.[15] Therefore a student who broke his word of honour broke it not only with the party to whom the promise was originally made, but broke it with his fraternity and each of its members as well. This indicated that he was without honour and thereby did not qualify for the society of honourable persons; hence his expulsion from the fraternity.

The enforcement of *Verruf*, sometimes more poetically referred to as the *Bannenstrahl*, could be enacted for short periods or in cases of extreme dishonourable behaviour, *in perpetuitum*; later known among the corps as *i.p. Dimission* from the latin *dimittere* to dismiss.[16] A student sentenced with perpetual ban by the *Senioren-Convent*, was well advised to leave that particular university and seek out a new Alma Mater where news of his ignominy was not likely to follow him.[17] As mentioned above, merchants and landlords could also find themselves placed under *Verruf* by the local *Senioren-Convent* for unfair treatment of students.

However, the attitudes which eroded the status of academic courts also altered the relationship between the *Senioren-Convente* and the citizenry of their particular municipality. The loss of segregated legal privileges effectively removed the power of the *Senioren-Convente* to invoke bans within the community at large and partially undermined their position as leaders and figures of authority within studentdom. However, the *comment* was still applicable to the members of corps and the concept of the honourable student remained the strong foundation upon which the corps continued to exist and develop.

THE *CORPSSTUDENT* AND HONOUR

By the late nineteenth century each of the federations of fraternities, the corps, *Burschenschaften*, *Turnerschaften*, etc., had established their own criteria and particular orthodoxy regarding the meaning and bestowal of honour. The corps enjoyed a position of unquestioned high prestige due to their history of legality and their register of well placed and powerful alumni. The various federations of fraternities functioned almost as mutually exclusive organisations having very little in common socially, except with other fraternities of their own federation. Therefore the corps and the new *Landsmannschaften*, which had been constituted at the Coburg Convention in 1868, regardless of the fact that they had many of the same views on the ideal organisation of student communities, actually interacted very little at an official level. The *Burschenschaften*, on the other hand, were neither silent nor passive about their jealousy of the privileged status enjoyed by the corps. In fact, the demise of the corps was considered almost imperative if their goals were to be achieved. Through the years, a long embittered history of ban and counter-ban had existed between the two federations and the situation only began to reconcile itself with the founding of the Empire under Bismarck.

The ideal of honour as held by the corps of the *Kösener* federation was multifaceted. It was not seen simply as a given privilege according to social status which served as a justification for arrogance. Honour was held to be the reflection of the inner person. The arrogant student was analogous to silver plating, while the honour of the *corpsier* was pure hallmarked silver; the external appearance being equal in value to the internal man. The corps self-consciously attempted to produce members of sterling quality through their stringent demands of honourable conduct and unquestioned answerability. Corps education sought first and foremost to establish the student as an educated, refined gentleman and to assist him to develop the qualities of self-reliance and answerability for his actions at all times. This was encouraged by the three pillars of *Corpsstudententum* namely; self-observation, self-answerability and unindulgent self-control.[18] Fencing offered an excellent opportunity for the corps to implement these concepts of training and deportment. An article in the *KSCV* periodical dealing with the purpose and objectives of *Corpsstudententum*, pointed out that in practice the corps did not make the irrational pugnacious demands of other fraternities. Corps did not force their fencers to stand *auf Mensur* until, through loss of blood and being thrashed to pieces, they collapsed from fatigue. The corps expected their members to exercise self-control, and to fence well regardless of where the blows might fall.[19] To the corps it was an exercise in self-discipline, not unlike what we know today of the relationship of Zen and the oriental martial arts.

Fencing was seen by the corps and their *Alte Herren* as an exercise to train their student members for later life and to prepare them for situations of all types which would need to be faced with confidence and courage. Students were therefore encouraged to savour and enjoy their golden years of youth, but also were to keep in mind that soon duty and responsibilities would await them. Their training therefore sought to teach them observance of themselves, self-control and the strength of character to answer for their own actions, so that they could honourably face the challenges and struggles of professional life which lay ahead.[20]

By the beginning of this century this approach to training young academics for professional life in the world of Philistines was apparently not shared by a number of groups within German society. The Social Democrats of the *Reichstag* were led by August Bebel in an attack on the fencing fraternities in general, and more particularly on the *KSCV* and the *comment* of its affiliated *Senioren-Convente*. The corps appear to have received the brunt of the attack, more because of their highly placed alumni and the prestigious positions which they had enjoyed during much of the nineteenth century rather than because of any particularly contentious aspects of their *comment*. Actually, the much less enlightened general *comment* of the *Burschenschaften* or those of the other federations would have made much easier targets for attack. But it appears to have been the persons rather than the actual practices of the *comment* to which the Social Democrats objected, and by associating those persons with duelling in general, it was hoped that it would go some way towards undermining their hold on key positions within government departments and commerce. The corps' periodical, *Die*

Akademischen Monatshefte of 1902 made the point that honour cannot be legislated or controlled by governments. The article agreed with Bebel's criticism of the duel as evil, but argued that it is an evil, much like war, which cannot be avoided. One does not wish it, but when it looms ahead it must be faced and met. The article goes on to point out that, contrary to popular opinion and conjecture, it was the students who did not belong to fraternities which demanded satisfaction of their members, who were the quickest to demand satisfaction with heavy sabres or pistols. On the other hand, students who belonged to such *Satisfaktionsfähig* fraternities, because of their strict codes, self-control and courts of honour, seldom found it necessary to answer demands for satisfaction (*schwere Forderung*).[21] This may or may not have been the case, but it should help to clarify things if we turn briefly to examine fencing as actually practised by the fraternities, in order to explain the application of honour.

THE *MENSUR*

The term *Mensur* originally referred to the measure of the boundaries within which a duel took place and later came to mean the actual match as well. But the *Bestimmungsmensur* is essentially different from a duel as seen in the definitions given to the two practices by Friedrick Hielscher in his interesting and illuminating work on student fencing. The *Mensur* is a sport engaged in by two participants for the enjoyment and camaraderie of both parties. In contrast, a duel is armed combat with the malicious intent of killing, or at least rendering the adversary unable to continue fighting.[22] These two practices which are generically the same, that is to say the wielding of swords, therefore prove quite divergent in their approach and objective. The one sees the opponent as a friendly competitor, while the other views him as an adversary and enemy who must be at least in part destroyed.

Hielscher explains the divergent *raison d'être* of the Romantic and Baroque duels by tracing their descent in previous centuries through the ritual of the Germanic *Thing*, trial by combat and the mediaeval tournament. The duel of the Renaissance, as practised in the lands of the Romance languages, was condemned and punished through excommunication by the Roman Catholic Church in accordance with *Codex Juris Canonici*, canon 2351, of the Tridentine Council of 1563. This Romantic duel was seen to have originated with atheists and nihilists, who in following their own personal inclinations, cast down those ancient pillars of Christian morality which contradicted their personal whims.[23]

The Baroque duel on the other hand, from which the *Mensur* descends, is prefigured by examples taken from the *Wormser Rosengarten* and the fight between Lohengrin and Telramund. As Hielscher illustrates, using the mediaeval text, the purpose of combat in the *Wormser Rosengarten* was not a question of victory or defeat, but rather the establishing and fostering of true friendship by bringing the participants together. The *Wormser Rosengarten* demanded no price to be paid.[24] The Baroque duel, which continued to be practised in northern Europe until into the eighteenth century, was actually a form of trial by combat. It viewed the opposite number in the match not as an honourless creature for butchery, as was the case in the later Romantic duel, but rather saw him as an honourable opponent and equal whom one did not wish to kill but with whom one sought reconciliation after the combat.[25]

The *Mensur* therefore was viewed as a friendly exercise with weapons that descended from a practice which espoused competition for the enjoyment of the contest and the camaraderie gained through the testing of skill. It also became a means of exhibiting inner qualities through outward indications of honour. Damaged outward honour was to be rectified by the duel, but the *Mensur* afforded the opportunity to demonstrate inner qualities through the self-control demanded during the *Mensur*. The actual and true character of a person was thought to be seen outwardly through constant observation of one's self, the constant acceptance of responsibility for one's own actions and constant self-control. These qualities formed the harmonious outer shell for the inner values of the *Corpsstudent* and facilitated the necessary elegant and harmonious combination of form and content necessary for a man of true worth and character.[26]

The student orders struggled long and hard to eventually put academics on an equal footing with both the noble and officer classes. Along with their post-Reformation adoption of Italianesque dress, the orders also took on a more romantic or Renaissance approach to armed combat and the settling of personal differences. This was done through the introduction of codes of honour which in turn served as a foundation upon which the *Kränzchen* later developed the *comment* as mentioned above.

This equality of rights was recognised in that an insulted nobleman or officer would meet a student with cold steel. Consequently this student duel fully achieved its purpose within the German-speaking countries, and brought about a certain egalitarianism between university scholars.²⁷ The purpose was for the two disputacious parties to face each other and bring the matter to an end rather than promote a long-lasting quarrel or intense engagement. To that end the student duel was restricted to a certain number of rounds. This practice of rather short encounters can be seen in the old *Senioren-Convent Comment* from Marburg dated 1807. It stated that after three rounds the insulted party could take satisfaction from the fact that his challenge had been adequately answered and after nine rounds he was obliged to take such satisfaction.²⁸

The Göttingen *SC Comment* of 1809 also gave three rounds as sufficient for the injured party to take satisfaction and stated that no one should be called upon to stand for more than twelve rounds, at which point it was mandatory for satisfaction to be taken.²⁹ Tübingen's *SC Comment* of 1808–15 shows a similar approach and attitude, and changed only the minimum number of rounds to six before the challenger could take satisfaction.³⁰

The *Mensur* offered an opportunity to demonstrate honour while honour also served the *Mensur*. Honour served the *Mensur* in that it taught participants to stand their ground but without the goal of vanquishing one's opponent. With its objective of self-mastery in the face of cold steel, the *Mensur* became an experience shared by both fencers rather than the egocentric goal of the duel – to overpower the adversary. The duel was self-centred and sought to demean the opponent, while the development of bearing and control as fostered by the Mensur was focused towards comradeship and concord engendered through a commonality of experience with an opposite number.³¹

In the *Festschrift zum Kösener Congress 1960* it is noted that the conflict of trial by combat (*Gottesurteil*) is a dispute regarding the law whereas the issue of conflict in a duel is a point of honour. Competition at arms as embodied in the practice of the *Mensur* acknowledges both the rights and honour of both parties.³² The *Mensur* offered an opportunity to demonstrate honour and vice versa.

But student fencing practices and attitudes towards fencing changed so that by the early twentieth century it became common for corps members to fence both *Mensuren* and duels. Regarding the development of student fencing prior to this century, Hielscher notes that the student duel was heavily influenced by the Romantic duel. This resulted in the *Mensur* alone retaining the elements of formal combat and it could be seen as a return to the practices of the *Rosengarten*.³³

The universities of the eighteenth century were notorious for the many rough and often fatal brawls with blades known as *Rencontres* engaged in by their scholars. Student behaviour became only slightly more refined than previously through the adoption of very basic codes of honour. In fact, the remark has been made that their general practice of duelling was only another form of the sixteenth century Italian *alla marchia*, employing the arms and venue which first came to hand.[34] The student orders did, however, limit themselves to the use of swords, that being the weapon used by the upper classes. Previously the use of cudgels, whips and daggers were not uncommon in student armed frays.

In writing on the *Rencontre* of the student orders, Wilhelm Fabricius notes that a challenge, as in knightly contests, needed a cause other than a direct insult in order for a duel to be correctly set. About 1736 there were two methods commonly used to provoke a challenge. The first, called the 'light method', occurred when the light from a window or lantern was said to give offence to a would-be pugilist. If it were not extinguished upon demand, and lucent object was pelleted with stones and/or broken, which usually gave sufficient annoyance to provoke a quarrel and the requisite armed brawl. The other commonly used method was known as the *Kontra-Wessen*. Upon approaching his chosen adversary a student would call out '*Pereat*', to which the reply was '*Pereat Contra*', thereby clarifying that both the student and his adversary were prepared and willing to fight. That being established, the first party would reply with '*Contra*', and coupled it with any of a number of colloquial insults.[35] This was considered to be sufficient and the quarrel could progress to armed combat without any further preliminaries. Members of a student order who did not answer such challenges, were considered not to have given satisfaction and were liable to receive harsh discipline from their confrères. As mentioned earlier these *Rencontres* or *Balgereien* were not necessarily limited to one pair of opponents and it was not uncommon for the numbers to be uneven and the alarm cry, '*Burschen heraus*', would be given, to which all students in the vicinity were to answer under pain of ban.[36]

The *Rencontres* gradually died out after 1780 with the student orders when they were replaced by the *Kränzianer*, who introduced much stricter regulations regarding fencing and the deportment of students. The *comment* of the *Kränzchen* were also based upon honour and the giving of satisfaction. Anyone who fell into ill-repute stood the chance of expulsion from the company of his compeers until such time as he proved himself worthy by giving unquestioned satisfaction.[37]

The *comment* of the *Kränzchen* decreed that no *Mensur* was to take place without just cause and that it must be in accordance with the grounds and regulations governing affairs of honour as set out in the *comment*. As mentioned above, the maximum and minimum number of rounds which could be fenced were codified and the whole practice took on a much more formal mode. Furthermore, the required fixing of a venue and time at a later date for the affair to be settled, hampered extemporaneous clashes between the parties.[38]

The weapon generally used during the mid-eighteenth century was the *Stossdegen*. This sword was not unlike today's fencing foil but had a guard of larger diameter and a trifid rather than a four-cornered blade. The tactics employed were a point attack, as the blade edges were not sharpened. The object was to skewer one's opponent in the upper arm, thigh or rump.[39] Puncture with this weapon could cause severe internal bleeding, and following the particularly gruesome death of a student at Göttingen in 1767, efforts were made to develop a sword which did not produce such agonising and gory results.

The new weapon which evolved was the *Schläger*; a modified rapier which took two divergent forms. Most of the universities east of the River Elbe adopted the *Glockenschläger* named after its bell-shaped guard and which incorporated an obliquely pointed blade. The majority of the *Senioren-Conventen* took up the *Korbschläger*, which had a large basket guard and a blade with a squared (i.e., non-piercing) tip. This new weapon was adopted because point attacks, with the aim of skewering, were rendered ineffectual. As a direct result, the style and methods of fencing were also forced to adapt in order to employ, and parry, the edge attack of the new *Schläger*. The distance between the back boundaries of the *Mensur* decreased with time, which also demanded adjustments and changes in style, as well as techniques and tactics.[40] The reduction of distance between the opponents was compensated for by restricting their movement as seen in the *glacé* stance, where a fencer's left foot remained stationary allowing extended steps only with the right.[41] Also, particularly vulnerable parts of the fencer's body were given added protection through the gradual adoption of leather leggings, padded gloves which extended to shield the right forearm and elbow, and a thick scarf to guard the throat. The cylinder hat or fraternity cap, originally worn in order to protect the eyes, was replaced by specially constructed goggles which were developed for that purpose in 1857 by Dr Immisch of Heidelberg.[42]

Between 1848 and 1870 the duel and the *Mensur* diverged and assumed their own characteristics and meanings. The meaning of the duel is clear. Its form remained more or less static with the *glacé* stance, leather leggings, throat bandage and elbow-length glove. However, the rapier blade of the *Schläger* was replaced with a curved sabre blade and this new student style of sabre, also unpointed, was adopted for cases of redressing honour. The *Mensur* developed in what Hielscher has described above as a *Waffenspiel*, using the *Schläger* as its weapon. The distance between the opponents gradually diminished to one sword length measured from chest to chest. The target for attack in the *Mensur* also decreased to include only the opponent's head which was partially protected by eye goggles. This is reminiscent of practices in the Middle Ages as described by J. Huizinga:

> It is not always furious anger which urges people to acts of violence in pursuit of vengeance; amends for offended honour are sought according to a well-regulated plan. It is, above all, a question of shedding blood, not of killing; sometimes care is taken to wound the victim only in the face, the arms, or the thighs. The satisfaction sought for, being formal, is symbolic.[43]

The *Mensur* as *Waffenspiel*, exposed a small vulnerable and usually unfatal area, thereby echoing symbolic retribution as in mediaeval and ancient practices. On the other hand, the academic duel in its demand for vengeance, exposed both the head and torso to fatal blows; illustrating it to be a product of the Romantic idea of redress.

As stated above, both the duel and the *Mensur* required a reason for fighting. Prior to the divergence of the duel and *Mensur*, students before the late 1850s visited *Kontrahierkneipen* which were formalised soirées, held for the express purpose of providing would-be fencers with a chance to give sufficient provocative wit and insult to other like-minded scholars as to furnish themselves with adversaries for the *Mensur*. The *Senioren-Convente* eventually managed to irradicate the *Kontrahierkneipen* by removing the need to insult. Each corps appointed a member, who, working with his opposite numbers in other corps of the *Senioren-Convente*, was charged with the duty of finding suitable opponents for his fraternity brothers who wished to fence. This practice began the separation of the *Mensur* from the vindictive nature of the duel. The duel then parted from the *Mensur* as it was employed to redress honour which had been called into question through insult or injury. According to tradition the duel was regulated by a court or council of honour, which decided if, in accordance with the *comment*, sufficiently grave damage or offence had occurred to warrant the risk of maiming or death.

The other development, in addition to the court of honour, which made the practices of the corps very different from the *Rencontre* of the student orders, was the mandatory attendance of witnesses and seconds, who were to ensure that the affair was carried out in accordance with the *comment*. The modern conception of seconds views them very much as passive observers rather than participants. This interpretation would appear to have led certain modern authors to refer to illustrations of a *glacé Schläger Mensur* as 'double duels'. In actual fact, the second pair with swords in such an illustration, each standing to the left of one of the principal parties, are the seconds.[44] As such, seconds were generally experienced fencers and took an active part in the match by protecting their man from premature and delayed strokes by his adversaries, through deflecting such strokes with the second's own sword. The silhouette on the jacket of this book offers an excellent illustration of such *Mensur* positioning.

As well as seconds, a referee or *Uniparteiische* was required to be present. He was a senior member of a third corps and therefore represented neither of the parties involved in the match. His function was to serve as an unbiased neutral party, interpreting the *comment* when called upon by the seconds, and empowered to nullify the match and expel fencers for infractions of the rules. The referee's position developed out of necessity, insofar as many matches ended with disagreements between the seconds and subsequently resulted in the seconds themselves duelling to settle their dispute as well. The third neutral party helped to avoid the development of further confrontations.

We have seen how the *Senioren-Convente* regulated the interaction of their own individual member corps and that the federation was established in order to facilitate liaison between the *SC*s. But what apparatus, if any, existed to assist relations between the federations of corps; all of which shared very much the same attitudes? And what means were there even further afield for *entente* with the non-aligned federations such as the *Deutsche Burschenschaft*? It is this inter-federation rapport which will be examined next.

THE ERLANGEN AND ERFURT AGREEMENTS

Prior to the First World War it became apparent to the larger federations of student fraternities that their influence as leaders within the academic community was dissipating and this was due to a great extent to their quarrels regarding fraternity jurisdiction over students. Central to the disputes was the reluctance of each federation to recognise the codes employed by the other federations in regulating their members' activities. As a result of this segmented behaviour, critics of student fraternities in general, and *Waffenstudententum* in particular, were given a firm toehold in their climb towards recognition as a tenable alternative power within German academe, which for so long had been the bailiwick of the fencing fraternities. This had the result for the corps that the power of the *Senioren-Convent Verruf* declined as an instrument for regulating student interaction. The erosion was partially precipitated by the establishment and expansion of other student federations within the academic community. These federations, such as the *Deutsche Burschenschaften*, attempted to enforce their own right to pronounce and impose ban upon their members, and other persons whom they felt had contravened the collective interest of their fraternities. But the practice arose, and quickly spread, whereby one fraternity would invoke a ban on all members of another fraternity. By the second decade of this century the situation appeared critical to the *Korporationen*. The free students, that is to say, those who did not belong to fraternities, and those students critical of the *Korporationen* on political or other grounds, had grown in number so that if the authority and legitimacy of the fraternities were to survive as the predominant mode of student life and behaviour, they somehow needed to be reorganised.[45] For some time before the First World War there were attempts among the student federations to develop a uniform means by which to control cases of assault, and the practice of ban and counter ban among their fraternities.[46]

Professor Dr Wilhelm Fabricius of Marburg took the initiative in trying to rectify the situation in favour of the federations. At his suggestion, discussions took place in Marburg intermittently from 1912 to 1914 between what were described as the 'four old fencing federations': the *KSCV, Deutsche Burschenschaft, DC-Verband der Turnerschaften* and the *Deutsche Landsmannschaft*. These talks resulted in an agreement on 15 July 1914 known as the *Marburger Abkommen*. The purpose of the Marburg Agreement was laid out in its preamble and introduction: 'The four undersigned federations give their united voice in the hope that their example will be taken to heart and adopted by all student circles and thereby bring about active opposition to assault and the lifting of bans between fraternities.'[47]

The first section of the agreement set out five basic rules to limit and discourage assault on the part of their members. Verbal as well as physical abuses were to be disciplined by the offender's own fraternity, regardless of whether a duel was fought subsequently in connection with the incident. Furthermore, any persons found guilty three times of casting aspersions on the honour of, or alleging cowardice on the part of, a *Waffenbruder* would be denied the right to give or receive satisfaction from the fraternities of the four signatory federations to the Marburg Agreement.[48]

Section Two of the agreement, which dealt with *Verruf*, called for the immediate lifting of all bans between fraternities of the four federations and the establishment of a local autonomous cartel at each university. The primary function of these cartels, or *Waffenringe*, was to regulate and standardise the use of weapons in their particular local setting. If contested, the right of a party to demand or give satisfaction at arms, *Satisfaktionsfähigkeit*, could only be ruled upon by the appropriate body of his own federation. Such a decision was conclusive and unassailable. In cases where satisfaction at arms followed a case of assault, the injured party was to receive automatic advantage; that is, first sword stroke or in the very rare case when pistols were employed, first shot.[49]

Situations which proved difficult to settle under the provisions of the local cartel were to be referred to the executive branch of the association in order that an appropriate committee be struck and a decision taken. In no sense were the local cartels to take action against one another and their disputes were similarly to be referred to the association's executive for arbitration.[50]

Bearing in mind the long history of attacks made by the *Deutsche Burschenschaft* against the corps, entering into the Marburg Agreement with the *DB* was a great concession on the part of the *KSCV*. Apparently it was felt that when compared with the free students, the two federations had much more in common to protect than they had differences to dispute. However, it soon became apparent that the *DB* wanted to use the new organisation formed by the Marburg Agreement, not only to undercut the influence of its opponents, but also wished to extend the work of the local cartels to that of active political confrontation with the free students' association, the *Finkenschaft*. The *KSCV*, both by tradition and statutes, excluded its corps and their membership as such, from involvement in party politics and was supported by both the *Deutsche Landsmannschaft* and the *Turnerschaften* in its adamant rejection of the political attitude exhibited by the *DB*.[51] However, the matter was never resolved as the First World War intervened and with the universities closed for the duration of the war, the issue became, at least for the moment, irrelevant.

Following the First World War the corps found themselves in a position which had been weakened both numerically and socially. The corps of the Weinheim federation had lost 426 members out of 3506 who had served in the war,[52] while the *Kösener* corps lost a total of 2360 *corpsier*.[53] The defeat of Germany brought with it the demise of the old political and social structures which had been its mainstays. The enemies and critics of the old regime saw the student *Korporationen*, and particularly the corps with their connections to most of the aristocratic families of Germany, as remnants of the old system which needed to be weakened and purged from the republic.[54] In order to strengthen and protect themselves from the attacks of their critics, the corps entered into two agreements: one was an expansion of the Marburg Agreement which established the *Allgemeinen Deutschen Waffenring* and the other was a formal undertaking between the Bad Kösen and Weinheim corps which offered reciprocal status to the other federation.

Following the war, the development of the many new and highly politicised student groups took differing forms. One such organisation, which later played a large role in German student politics during the Weimar Republic was the *Hochschulring deutscher Art*. Founded in 1919 by members of the *Fichte Hochschulring*, the *Kyffhäuser Verband* and several of the Berlin *Burschenschaften*, it was structured initially as an amalgam of nationalistic and *völkisch* groups, rather than as a political party. But it soon entered into the melee of university politics, backed by the nationalistic fraternities and to a lesser extent by free students. By 1921 the *Hochschulring* managed to gain a majority in many of the elections at larger German universities, thereby securing a platform from which to preach its doctrine.[55] The *Deutsche Wehrschaft (DW)* was another of the post-war groups which sprang up. However, the *DW* was a strange hybrid in that it injected rampant *völkisch* politics into the form of the traditional student fencing fraternity and took retroactively the date of the Treaty of Versailles, 28 June 1919, as its official founding date.[56] Needless to say, the principles of political and religious neutrality on the part of the corps contrasted sharply with the *Deutsche Wehrschaft* and its vehement pulpitry for *völkisch* politics.

Prior to the signing of the *Allgemeinen Deutschen Senioren-Conventen Verband (ADSCV)* agreement between the corps of the *Kösener* and the *Weinheimer* federations, there had been a reluctance on the part of the *Kösener* corps to recognise their *Weinheimer* counterparts as equal. This was due in part to the difference in age of the two federations; the *WSC* being founded in 1863 and the *KSCV* in 1848. However, the fact that the *KSCV* corps were to be found only at universities, while the *WSC* corps centred their activities around the technical institutes of higher learning, also played a part in the question of mutual recognition. In most instances there was little reason for members of the two organisations to come into contact with each other as municipalities tended to have only a university or a technical institute. However, in centres such as Berlin and Munich where both universities and technical institutes existed, there was confusion as to the proper protocol and the degree of recognition which was to be extended to the other federation of corps. To remove this confusion, the *KSCV* and *WSC* corps of Berlin set up a combined council on 15 October 1920.[57] The following year negotiations began between the two federations and moved quickly towards establishing a similar relationship for all corps of the *WSC* and *KSCV*. On 25 June 1921, the two federations extended mutual recognition to each other and entered into an agreement which created the *Allgemeinen Deutschen SC-Verband* for the purpose of protecting and promoting interests of the corps in both federations.[58] The associated document set out regulations to govern etiquette, correspondence and the settling of affairs of honour between *corpsier* of the two federations. It was hoped that by co-operating in the many aspects which they held in common, it would present a united and stronger front with which to rebuff their critics and enemies. However, the above agreement did not include the corps of the *Rudolstädter Senioren-Convent (RSC)*, which existed at institutes of veterinary medicine. In 1922 the *Senioren-Convent* of Dresden, a member of the *WSC*, forwarded a statement to the executive of the *ADSCV (KSCV-WSC)* reporting that the *RSC* corps in Dresden were attempting to gain a foothold at the technical institute, in addition to their traditional activities at the veterinary school. This apparently was not a singular incident and a meeting between the *ADSCV* and the *RSC* was called in order to discuss the matter of operational jurisdictions. An understanding was reached whereby each corps would remain attached to, and recruit new members only from, the institute of higher learning with which it was originally associated. This followed the same basic principle agreed upon by the *KSCV* and *WSC* regarding the universities and the technical institutes, leaving the veterinary colleges to the *RSC*, and thereby theoretically removed any further demarcation disputes between the three federations.[59] Although the *RSC* did not become a party to the *ADSCV*, it did act in close co-operation with the other two federations in their front against the politicisation of the German universities.

When the second *Waffenstudententag* was held in 1918, for the purpose of giving form to the Marburg Agreement through establishing the *Allgemeine Deutsche Waffenring*, the *Deutsche Burschenschaft* issued a statement declaring that on constitutional grounds it declined any further affiliation with the organisation, but hoped to continue to work in co-operation with *ADW* fraternities at the local level.[60]

The Marburg Agreement of 1914 had only encompassed university fraternities and thereby had excluded the corps of both the Weinheim and Rudolstadt federations. However, the *Allgemeiner Deutscher Waffenring (ADW)*, which was formed at the two *Waffenstudenten* conferences of 1918 and 1919, expanded to include *WSC* and *RSC* corps as well and thereby extended the influence of the *ADW* to all the technical institutes. This meant that despite the withdrawal of the *Deutsche Burschenschaft*, there were five *ADW* federations; all of which demanded that their members fence a minimum of one *Bestimmungsmensur*. The *KSCV* congress of 1918 stated that it was in favour of an expansion of the *ADW*, but emphatically affirmed that an enlarged *ADW* was in no way to become a *supra* federal structure, and entitled to make policy for the *ADW* member federations which it represented.[61] The corps of all three federations held relentlessly to the tenet that the *ADW* was to remain only a commission, acting for the protection and representation of *Waffenstudententum*'s interests.

At the same time the *Deutsche Burschenschaft* attempted to build a separate association of like-minded federations which were interested in active participation in political and *völkisch* activities. By 1922 the corps felt that their case for political neutrality had been made abundantly clear and with the understanding that their position in politics would be respected, they expanded the *ADW* membership regulations to include federations which were prepared to abide by the Marburg Agreement and require that their members give satisfaction at arms when demanded. Previously only federations which had required that their fraternity members fenced mandatory *Bestimmungsmensuren* had qualified for *ADW* membership. The new agreement which founded the expanded *Allgemeinen Deutschen Waffenring* was signed by no less than eighteen *satisfaktionsfähige* federations and was known as the *Erlanger Abkommen*. The purpose of this agreement was to resolve differences between *Waffenstudenten* in the spirit of the Marburg Agreement of 15 July 1914. Of special importance under the agreement were the preservation and care of the basic principles of German student fraternities and unquestioned satisfaction. These were to be expressed through the creation and observance of a general honour codex for *Waffenstudenten* and the establishing of regulations to deal with instances of ban and common assault.[62] This was accomplished by expanding the local cartels established previously through the Marburg Agreement, to incorporate the fraternities of the federations which had signed the new accord. Each local cartel (*Waffenring*) created the administrative machinery necessary to deal with matters occurring between members of different federations in its own particular academic community. Matters to be settled between different *Waffenringe* came under the jurisdiction of the executive of the *ADW*. Matters of honour were not to be settled by duelling unless the responsible *Waffenring*'s court of honour ruled that sufficient grounds had been given and the parties obviously did not wish reconciliation through an apology. This then would leave an honourable student no other avenue for restitution but to demand satisfaction at arms. Interestingly this method was in many ways identical with the *Schiedsgericht* established by the early corps for settling disputes.

In May 1923 the *KSCV* extended its influence even further by entering into an agreement which established the form and etiquette for settling affairs of honour between its members and members of the *Deutschen Offiziersbund* and the *Nationalverband deutscher Offiziere*. Interestingly there were actually four signatories to the agreement as the *KSCV Alte Herren (VAC)* association also was a party to the accord. This occurred because corps alumni in their professional life could well have more instances of interaction with officers than their younger fraternity brothers. The agreement gave the *KSCV* a virtual exclusivity on the handling of matters of honour between fraternities and members of the officers' associations. Paragraph 10 of the agreement stated that entry of additional federations into the agreement would require the approval of all the original parties to the agreement. However, admission to the accord stood open at any time to such organisations as the Association of Naval Officers, the Order of St John and the Society of German Nobles.[63] The agreement and the relationship which it established between the corps and the officers' associations was the basis for an important interchange between the Munich *Senioren-Convent* and Baldur von Schirach of the Nazi Party in 1931. As will be demonstrated below, the enmity which resulted from the incident only served to intensify the heated exchanges already extant between the corps and the Nazis, and which lasted well into the Third Reich.

At the annual *Waffenstudententag* of the *ADW* in 1923, the representative of the *Deutsche Landsmannschaft* proposed that the *ADW* follow the precedent set by the *KSCV* earlier in the year and enter into a similar agreement with German officers' associations. The idea does not appear to have come to fruition. But further proposals made to the conference in 1923 regarding the establishing of a code of honour for the whole of the *Deutsche Studentenschaft*, started a discussion and the subsequent exchanges plagued the *ADW* until its own dissolution early in the Third Reich. The first motion called for the implementation of a national code of honour which would include all *Volksdeutsche* as well as *Reichsdeutsche* students. As a corollary to this it was decided that foreign fraternities which were associated with a *Reichsdeutsche* federation, such as the *KSCV*, when dealing with fraternities of the *ADW*, were to abide by the *comment* of their associate. However, should no such affiliation exist, it was agreed that as a general convention, the matter would be settled in accordance with the *comment* of the challenged party.[64] This was later developed into arguments for the existence of *völkisch* honour which, as will be seen, eventually was responsible for rupturing the strength of the *ADW*.

In the same year, the *Kösener* congress of 1923 affirmed its strong affiliation and willingness to work closer and cooperate with the *WSC* and *RSC* corps, but the *KSCV* also expressed great concern and disapproval of the complicity which had grown up between the *Deutsche Hochschulring* and certain student corps members. This was felt to be a slackening of 'corps student neutrality'; placing the *KSCV* in a position of vulnerability relative to the *Deutsche Hochschulring (DHR)*. In order to eliminate any further problems of a like nature, the *KSCV* passed a resolution and there was unanimous agreement by the members of the congress to reject any meddling of the headquarters of local offices of the *DHR* in the fields of responsibility of individual student fraternities. A similar rejection was also expressed regarding any one-sided public comments made by the *DHR* leadership concerning cultural matters or matters with respect to party politics.[65] However, several of the more nationalist federations of the *ADW* openly and actively supported the *DHR*. For that reason the *KSCV* congress of 1924 again felt obliged to draw attention to the fact that the work of *corpsier* at the universities when functioning in conjunction with the *ADW*, was to be in strict accordance with the Marburg and Erlangen Agreements. Therefore the *KSCV* requested that the individual *Senioren-Conventen* make themselves responsible for regulating the type of involvement entered into by their local *Waffenringe*, as the *KSCV* in keeping with its statutes, could not be a cooperative member of a 'supra federal organisation'; especially one which engaged in political activities.[66]

Shortly before the *KSCV* congress of 1926 the *Reichsgericht* confirmed the decision of 1883 and ruled that the student *Schlägermensur* was not a sport but was considered to be assault with lethal weapons. With the *Mensur* ruled illegal, a mainstay of corps structure was called into question; as was that of the other federations of the Marburg Agreement and many of the signatories to the Erlangen Agreement as well. If members of those fraternities were required to fence the *Bestimmungsmensur*, and the *Mensur* was ruled by the national courts to be illegal, then the fencing fraternities demanded that their members break the law. Particularly for the corps, which before the First World War had been the epitome of German respectability, this decision was viewed not at all favourably and the *KSCV* congress accepted that measures would need to be taken toward confronting and removing this threat – not only to *Corpsstudententum*, but to *Waffenstudententum* as a whole. A special committee known as the *Zehnerausschuss* was set up for the purpose of promoting communication and the implementation of measures which would either defeat and/or circumvent the problems created by the new court ruling.[67]

The *ADW* conference later the same year, adopted the suggestion that all issues pertaining to honour should be heard in a court of honour and that only extreme cases should progress to an actual duel in order to achieve satisfaction. It was felt that this would reduce the number of incidents and thereby minimise the chance of confrontation with the authorities.

The *Zehnerausschuss* reported to the *KSCV* in 1927, that thanks to the cautious handling of *Mensuren* and duels by the *Senioren-Conventen*, the threat to *Waffenstudententum* did not appear as grave as it had in the previous year. Furthermore, the new court of arbitration which had been built into the statutes of the *ADW* had helped to reduce the number of cases demanding satisfaction through duelling. This in turn had reduced the number of cases which had been heard in the civil courts and sanctioned with stringent sentences. The availability of satisfaction at arms had not been completely removed, but rather students were limited to only one instance in which they could demand armed combat during their university studies. In that way they had been encouraged to act with prudence and not waste the option.[68] This meant that most issues of honour between students could be settled through satisfaction by arbitration, rather than satisfaction at arms and thereby opened the door for yet another set of student agreements, known as the *Erfurter Abkommen* of 1931, which will be looked at shortly.

In 1928 the *Zehnerausschuss* was able to report to the *KSCV* that 27 393 *Mensuren* had been fought since the end of the First World War despite the political climate which was less than favourably disposed to *Waffenstudententum*. Strong sentiment was expressed at the congress that perhaps the *KSCV* should embark upon the political education of its younger corps members. This suggestion was declined in favour of developing patriotism through the establishment of the *Ausschuss für Grenz- und Auslandsdeutschtum*.[69] The energy and resources channelled into this commission were invested in the building of a school for the instruction in handwork skills and technology at Windhoek, in the former German colony of South West Africa. The school was completed and handed over to the local board of education in 1931.[70]

But what was the attitude of the corps towards Jewish students and their fraternities? This later became a central issue of contention between the Nazi hierarchy and the *KSCV*, and the background of this dispute should be looked at briefly in order to understand the position taken by the corps.

JEWISH STUDENTS AND THE *KÖSENER VERBAND*

The question of Jewish members in corps is a topic that has been given very little attention by fraternity historians, but which is central to the eventual proscription of the corps after Hitler's assumption of power in 1933. In order to gain a proper perspective of this issue we must briefly return to the nineteenth century.

The *Burschenschaften* with their very nationalistic and political inclinations were not long in adopting racial criteria for membership within their fraternities. For more *völkisch* orientated groups, such as the *Deutsche Wehrschaft*, the acceptance of Jewish students as members was completely out of the question, regardless of the fact that according to the Prussian Emancipation Act of 1812 Jews were to be treated as indigenous Prussian citizens, to whom the institutions of higher education were open.[71]

Following the passing of the above act there was an influx of Jewish students to the univerisities; particularly between 1825–1830. The *Burschenschaften*, as well as the corps, had Jewish members, since religious persuasion seems not to have played a major role, if any, at that time, in accepting new members for student fraternities.[72] By the 1840s, the corps had many Roman Catholic and Protestant students of theology as their members. Despite this, the problems associated with denominationalism did not arise since each university tended to be either Protestant as at Erlangen, or Roman Catholic, as at Würzburg. As an example, the 1814 constitution of Corps Moenania of Würzburg stated that any political purpose was forbidden to its membership and thereby avoided the problems associated with the corps being involved in causes or movements.

Prior to the founding of the *Kösener* federation in 1848, there was no uniform policy concerning the acceptance of Jewish students as corps members. However, the adoption of the *KSCV* of the Tolerance Principle as its primary precept at the federation's formal founding in 1849, allowed student corps membership, regardless of their religious persuasion or citizenship.[73]

In his 1897 description of the corps earlier in that century Moldenhauer writes:

As to a confessional [religious] inclination on the party of corps it is out of the question. In earlier times Jewish corps brothers were not uncommon and they were outstanding and excellent members. I myself was a member with such corps brothers and regarded them highly as I did those whom I met in other corps.[74]

He also noted that the corps did not promote political activity. They expected and encouraged their members, while at university, to develop their own political ideas which could be advocated in later life, after maturing and reflection.[75]

Early anti-Semitism among the fraternities seems to have entered Germany from the east. The Austrian corps, which originally were organised as a single unit, rather than a federation of *Senioren-Conventen*, recorded a number of Jewish members who were accepted in Graz about 1883. Prague and Vienna also seem to have had some Jewish members within the corps and little, if any, attention appears to have been given to the religious profession of potential new members even as late as 1900. The Austrian *Burschenschaften*, on the other hand, were heavily influenced by Georg von Schönerer and his *völkische Politik*. This is seen in their defining Jewish as racial rather than religious in nature. Certain elements within the Austrian *Burschenschaften* were not merely converted to the more extreme *völkisch* stance, but took up positions in the vanguard of the movement. The Viennese *Burschenschaften* Silesia and Olympia, for example, had by 1865 and 1867 respectively, excluded Jews on religious grounds from their membership.[76] A decade later, in 1878, *Burschenschaft* Libertas of Vienna went so far as to state in its first by-law that not even baptised Jews could be considered German and were therefore excluded from the ranks of its membership, as were all non-Aryans.[77]

The non-Austrian *Burschenschaften*, in line with the Prussian Emancipation Act of 1812, initially accepted Jewish students as members. However, that was altered at the first anniversary of the *Allgemeinen*

Deputiertenkonvent when the *Burschenschaften* revised their constitution and indicated strong anti-Semitic tendencies much like their Austrian counterparts. In fact, when their federation's periodical, *Burschenschaftliche Blätter*, went into regular publication in 1887, it soon became a forum for discussing *Burschenschaft* orthodoxy. It quickly became apparent through the views expressed, that the idealistic alumni were struggling to counter the strong anti-Semitic tendencies of their younger fraternity brothers.[78] When Prussian Jews were denied the right to hold reserve officer's rank and were barred from district magistrate positions, the *Burschenschaften* introduced a new requirement in 1893, whereby all its new members had to produce verification of their religious profession. By the following year the federation declared itself *judenrein*.[79]

At the same eleventh *Bundestag* of the *Burschenschaften* in 1894, all but the most liberal faction of the federation, the *Allgemeine deutsche Burschenschaften*, had accepted and carried out the edict of the conference by refusing to accept Jews as members. In 1921 the *Allgemeine deutsche Burschenschaft* also succumbed to implement the exclusion of Jews after the Eisenach Resolutions of 1920 were adopted by the conference. The Eisenach Resolutions combined the existent political anti-semitism which was strongly endorsed and sponsored by *Burschenschaft* Franconia of Bonn, with the Waidhofen Principle, which had been imported from the Austrian *Burschenschaften*. The Waidhofen Principle,[80] which was not adopted outside of Austria until after the First World War, was initiated by a Viennese student assembly in 1896. The edict set out the premise that in the fullest evaluation of the facts, there existed a deep moral and physical difference between Aryans and Jews. This was seen in the Jews' lack of appreciation for the national individuality of Aryans and found expression in Jewish students' characterless and honourless nature. The resolution of the Waidhofen Principle stated that henceforth no Jewish student was to be given satisfaction as he was proclaimed unworthy, since the German concept of honour was totally foreign and unattainable for him.[81] But the Eisenach Resolution went further and declared that 'Jewish' could only be defined as racial and therefore could not be altered through the sacrament of baptism. Furthermore, the acceptance of Jewish students, or students with partially non-Aryan antecedents, was constitutionally discouraged. The extent to which this precept of 'new members free of Jewish and coloured blood'[82] was to be enforced was left open to the individual fraternity. But some factions were able to take the idea even further and the *Burschenschaft* conference charged the individual chapters to educate their members so that marriage with a Jewish or coloured female would not occur. Should such a case arise, the member involved was to be expelled.[83]

The *Burschenschaften* were not alone in their political anti-Semitism at the German universities. The *Verein Deutscher Studenten* appears to have been in the vanguard of German student anti-Semitism by uniformly adopting the Waidhofen Principle for all its fraternities in 1920. It was followed in a kind of racial one-up-manship by the *Kyffhäuser Verband*, which demanded not only the adoption of the Waidhofen Principle, but also that all prospective new members were required to produce genealogical proof of an acceptable Aryan familiy tree.[84]

In the face of growing anti-Semitism and social consciousness, several associations of Jewish students were formed, each indicating a separate and differing view of the role of Jewish students in German society as a whole. Possibly the best known group was the *Blau-Weiss* association of Zionist students founded in 1912, but its membership and activities were not restricted to the university community. The *Blau-Weiss* was an offshoot of the German Youth Movement and shared its ideology as well as its actions – the emphasis on nature rambling, on learning to live in nature and on 'view[ing] it with one's soul'. The hope, as one leader put it, was that this sharing of a foreign experience would lead to the realisation of a Jewish goal.[85]

Of the strictly university centred Jewish student groups the following three organisations should be mentioned: the *Kartell Jüdischer Verbindugen*, which was founded in 1914, and had as many as seventeen individual fraternities representing it at the various universities, technical colleges and polytechnical institutes in Germany and Latvia; and the *Bund Jüdischer Akademiker* founded in 1906 was represented by eleven fraternities at universities in Austria as well as Germany. However, the most important of the Jewish students' federations for the purposes of this work, was the *Kartell-Convent: der Verbindungen deutscher Studenten jüdischen Glaubens* (*KC*) which was established in 1906. The major significance was that this federation, unlike the other Jewish fraternities mentioned, stood on the principle of unquestioned satisfaction and the wearing of fraternity colours. However, members were not obliged to fence *Bestimmungsmensuren*.[86] It should be mentioned that the practice of *Mensur* fencing was observed in some individual fraternities, such as the federation's founding fraternity Viadrina in Breslau, while in many others, such as Badenia of Heidelberg, the practice was generally not observed. The fraternities of the *Kartell-Convent* were founded with the objectives of establishing self-confidence and resilience among Jewish students in order to combat the anti-Semitism encountered at the universities; much of which radiated directly from the *Vereine Deutscher Studenten*. The students of the *KC* sought equality with other student *Verbindungen*, particularly the fencing fraternities, and to that end concentrated on sabre fencing in order to guarantee that they could also give unquestioned satisfaction when required.[87] They saw themselves, as their name stated, students of the Jewish faith, following German academic traditions. This is further illustrated by the fact that *KC* fraternities had, in addition to the usual *Fuchsmajor* or member charged with instructing the new members in the traditions and practices of the fraternity, another member whose duty it was to act much like a chaplain and see to the instruction and observance of Jewish customs by the members. Prior to the First World War the Jewish fencing fraternites seem to have been well accepted by the majority of the *satisfaktionsfähig* fraternities. As an illustration of this, at the extravagant *Bismarck Kommers*, which was held at Würzburg in 1909 as a national celebration for the centenary of Bismarck's birth, the festivities were presided over by the Jewish fencing fraternity Salia of Würzburg.[88]

Following the First World War, the *KSCV* Congress of 1910, adopted a motion made by the representatives of the Austrian corps,[89] that the aims of the federation as set out in the statutes should be expanded to encompass 'Service to the *Vaterland* through cultivation of "*vaterländische*" morality and by the avoidance of everything immoral and un-German'. The term 'un-German spirit' was meant to exclude the membership of Jews. It was not decided until the congress of the following year that the definition of 'Jewish' was to refer to the ancestry rather than the religion of prospective student members. However, admittance of members was the jurisdiction of the individual corps and could not be legislated by the federation. Furthermore, the Waidhofen Principle was not adopted by the Congress of 1920, and it was left to the individual *Senioren-Convente* to determine the question of the *Satisfaktionsfähigkeit* for the Jewish students within their own locality. Jewish corps members were automatically *satisfaktionsfähig* without question, by virtue of their being corps members. This practice was also followed by the corps of the Weinheim federation.[90]

The corps of the Rudolstadt federation struck a compromise on the racial question in the 1921 amendment to their statutes. Under the new wording of the regulations all persons seeking membership in a *RSC* fraternity were required to give a declaration that to the best of their knowledge and conscience they had no Jewish ancestors.[91] Jews were therefore barred from joining a *RSC* fraternity, but it was the attitude of the *RSC* towards Jewish fraternities which is interesting. The new *RSC* regulations set out that Jewish fraternities would not be given recognition in their own right for the purpose of giving satisfaction at arms. But a very interesting aspect was adopted by the *RSC* at this point. *RSC* fraternities would recognise the right of Jewish students to give and demand satisfaction as long as the affair was conducted in line with the guidelines of the local *Waffenring*.[92] In other words, a Jewish student having a point of honour to settle with a *RSC* member would follow the traditional practice of non-fraternity students and request to *Beleg Waffen* (the use of weapons and a second) from another *RSC* corps, or another fraternity which was prepared to sponsor him in the affair. Following convention, this latter fraternity would maintain a neutral role in the affair, merely providing the vehicle through which the matter could be resolved. This attitude contrasts quite markedly with the practice adopted by the *Deutsche Burschenschaften* in its implementation of Waidhofen Principle, which refused to recognise or give satisfaction in any way, to Jewish fraternities, Jewish students, or any other non-Aryans. This stance adopted by the *RSC* narrowed its guidelines to exclude racial Jews rather than the more general category of all non-Aryans as practised by the *Deutsche Burschenschaften*. Interestingly, the *RSC* indicated that its members would give satisfaction to members of any Jewish fraternities which fenced *Bestimmungsmensuren*. As this was a demand made by all corps upon their own members, it shows that the corps of the *RSC* were perhaps not willing to accept Jewish students as members, but were willing to partially accept Jewish fraternities and offer them recognition with status almost equal to other corps.

Oskar Scheuer, in his extensive article, *Burschenschaft und Judenfrage*, makes the point that even though the *KSCV* did accept the Austrian corps' racial definition of 'Jewish', the Austrian proposition for the future exclusion of Jewish students was viewed only as a guideline to be enacted if the individual *Senioren-Conventen* and corps saw fit.[93] In sharp contrast to this the *Deutsche Burschenschaft* had adopted the confessional *(Glaubensbekenntnis)* interpretation of Jewry in 1893 and enacted exclusion of Jews as members retroactively from that date.

The *KSCV* corps remained firm to the commitment of their original statutes, that the federation and its corps, were to refrain from political activities or involvement. This was reasserted regarding the *Allgemeinen Deutschen Waffenring (ADW)* in 1919. The *ADW* had been established as a federation of cartels, each in a separate student community and organised for the one task of protecting the interests of fencing fraternities in general; not for the development of an association which would act as a superstructure over all the fencing federations. It was only in that form that the *KSCV* corps could be asociated with the *ADW* and remain true to the conviction of their federal statutes which would not allow either the *KSCV* congress, nor any other organisation, the jurisdiction whereby it could adopt policy that would bind the individual *Senioren-Conventen*. The *KSCV* later agreed to an expansion of the *ADW* to include the fraternities of all the federations which gave unquestioned satisfaction. But as mentioned above, agreement from the *KSCV* for the expansion held with it the proviso that the *ADW* was to restrict ifself purely to a policy of collective bargaining for the protection of *Waffenstudententum*.[94] According to Adolph Asch, many of the Jewish fraternities saw the establishment of the local *Waffenring* as taking the place of traditional academic *Ritterlichkeit*, whereby all students were allowed to defend their honour. The new organisation was thought by some to ostracise those students who did not belong to *Waffenring* affiliated fraternities, thereby denying them *Waffenfähigkeit*.[95] This, however, depended upon local situations which varied from one university to the next. As seen in the *RSC* statutes of 1921, the corps did not deny any student the right to fence, as long as he was a member of, or acted through, a fraternity which was recognised by the local *Waffenring*.[96]

As mentioned above, the *Allgemeine Deutsche Waffenring* had no mandate to make policy for its member federations, particularly with regard to sweeping ideas such as racial anti-Semitism which were decided upon strictly within the federations themselves. For this reason it was a great breach with tradition and practice when the *Deutsche Wehrschaft* proposed a motion to the *Waffenstudententag* of 1931, demanding that the *ADW* immediately adopt what was in essence the Waidhofen Principle.[97] The *DW*'s motion called for the immediate exclusion of all Jews and those with Jewish antecedents from *ADW* affiliated fraternities. In addition, such persons were to be refused satisfaction.[98] The *ADW* refused to consider or adopt either the urgency, or the essence, of the *Deutsche Wehrschaften* proposal. In response to this rebuff, the representative of the *Deutsche Wehrschaften* withdrew both himself and his federation from the conference and the *ADW*. As an isolated incident, the event perhaps appears merely as an exercise in theatrics, but in terms of German student history it was a milestone along the road towards institutionalised anti-Semitism within academe.

It also indicated the beginning of factionalism among the various federations, brought about by the introduction of *völkische* ideology – a contentious issue which had not previously arisen among the *ADW* federations.

THE *NSDStB* AND THE STUDENT FRATERNITIES

When the *NSDStB* appeared at the German universities in the late 1920s, it was merely yet another political group attempting to capitalise on the youthful zeal of politically and socially disaffected students. Within the complex genealogy of student fraternities and federations, which stretched back into the eighteenth century, the lack of a suitable pedigree left even the best intentions of the *NSDStB* without respectability when seen in the light of the older and more prestigious student corporations. As yet another admixture to the nearly fifty federations of student fraternities, the *NSDStB* found itself merely one more organisation competing for members. The corps had a history of great social status, due predominantly to their many august members over the years, while the *Deutsche Burschenschaften* (*DB*) had gained a reputation for their contribution to the cause of German unification during the nineteenth century. The *DB* from its beginnings, borrowed not only the basic fraternity structure developed and used by the corps, but embellished it by draping it with political nationalism. The *NSDStB* in its search to achieve broad appeal among German students, borrowed from both the corps and the *DB*, intensifying the latter's nationalism to the level of *völkische* doctrine. Following that same tack, the *NSDStB*, prior to the Nazi assumption of power in 1933, attempted both to ingratiate itself with the traditional student corporations and to present itself as an alternative student organisation. To achieve that, it sought to cater to those students already orientated towards *völkische* nationalism and also to those barred from membership in the highly class structured hierarchy of student fraternities.

As regards the corps, although individual corps members could be counted among enthusiastic nationalists, the corps and their local *SC*s had always maintained a non-sectarian and cosmopolitan stance in such matters. As previously pointed out, interest and participation in sociopolitical and religious issues were considered personal pursuits and were not the reason for the existence of the corps. Furthermore, the corps were based purely on a local structure around the *SC*, to serve a particular university community and not as an all-pervading national organisation pursuing a cause, as was the case of the *Deutsche Burschenschaft*.

Following the First World War the structure of student political institutions changed in compliance with popular sovereignty promised in 1918 and student councils were organised on democratic lines which often were very close copies of the Weimar Constitution. This effectively removed the previous system, whereby the student corporations had directly controlled the students' councils, but it did not erase the great prestige accumulated by the student corporations over the years. The scope of student government had expanded from that of self-regulating communities based on personal and collective honour, to a broader base which encompassed the tenets of the Weimar Republic and allowed student councils sufficient latitude to pursue their activities along the lines of political philosophy. Extending and widening the trend, the *NSDStB* offered an even further expansion of student ventures into the extramural world; the realm of mass oriented *völkische* ideology. The idea of forming the Nazi *Studentenbund* came from a *Burschenschaft* member in 1926. Hans Glauning, himself a Nazi student, saw a great potential for using the revolutionary traditions of the *Deutsche Burschenschaft* based on nationalism and comradeship, to draw students, who were disenchanted with the discouraging socio-economic climate, into the vanguard of National Socialism. According to Anselm Faust's work on the early *NSDStB*, the organisation had no specific party affiliated programme, but rather grew out of Nazi *Weltanschauung* and a strange pot-pourri of contemporary views for educational reforms. The membership strongly criticised the university system on the ambiguous grounds of not serving the needs of the German *Volk*, and called for the protection of academic freedom against hostile government officials. Further to that, the *NSDStB* demanded a *numerus clausus* for Jewish students. This was seen primarily as a measure to safeguard the purity of the universities against the 'Disintegration of German cultural values' by Jewish thinkers, and as an economic precaution, to preserve for Aryans the few positions available to university students upon graduation. These tenets were reinforced by the *NSDStB* through its general physical fitness programme, which sought to make all its members strong and fighting fit for service to the German *Volk*.[99] As a result, this new organisation soon won many sympathisers within the *Deutsche Burschenschaft* and such great popularity among members of the *Deutsche Wehrschaft*, that whole chapters of the *DW* were recorded to have joined the *NSDStB en bloc*.[100]

Despite the *NSDStB*'s appeal to *völkisch* nationalist students, it could only be regarded as another political group, since it had neither traditions nor a place within German history. For those and a number of other reasons, the *NSDStB* did not thrive under the guidance of its first leader, Wilhelm Tempel, and it was only after Baldur von Schirach was appointed *Reichsstudentenführer* in 1928, that the organisation began to gain any significant footing in its attempts to recruit new student members. Schirach changed tactics and gave a new and clearer focus to the group. A number of differences could be seen between Schirach and the naive beliefs of Tempel. For although Schirach could never disavow his obvious fanaticism, and continued to appear like an immature student of literature with lyrical ideals, he nevertheless possessed a sound instinct for politics and was a smart, calculating tactician.[101] It has been suggested that Schirach had belonged to a corps, but in fact this was not the case. He apparently sought membership in a fraternity while studying in Munich, but was rejected for refusing to fence.[102] And it possibly goes a great way in explaining his antics regarding the Munich corps which will be seen later.

The main thrust of attack under Schirach's leadership was changed from that of a social revolutionary organisation, opposing, as Tempel had attempted, *Bürgertum* and the whole system in general, to a focused position, opposing the social and political hierarchy. These oppressive institutions were felt to be reflected in the bourgeoisie, whose members, according to *NSDStB* allegations, refused to recognise the *Not des Volkes*.[103] This gave the *NSDStB* a chance to recruit many anti-bourgeois students. For these students such sentiments were fostered and motivated by the prospect of unemployment and economic uncertainty at the conclusion of their studies – sentiments which were anti-government and anti-civil service, rather than anti-society. It was the switch from anti-society to anti-government that the *NSDStB* effected under Schirach's leadership and its ranks grew as a result of the change.

However, this did not solve the question of respectability. Put most simply, any reputable student fraternity possessed a code of honour to which all its members adhered. It was the fraternity's codes which gave it recognition by the local *Waffenring*. A code of honour was considered by the established and prestigious fraternities to be the essential requirement for recognition, despite the illegality of *Mensur* fencing during the Weimar Republic. The traditional fraternities could not begin to think of the *NSDStB*, with its many non-fraternity members, as their social equal, as long as the *NSDStB* did not subscribe to the minimum requisite of giving satisfaction in affairs of honour. Schirach realised that without respectability in the eyes of the established fraternities his fledgling group stood little chance of being considered anything more than a collection of nationalist extremists and with the goal of respectability in mind, he set out to court favour with the older and more revered of the student corporations.

As seen above, the *ADW* federations had tried repeatedly to have the *Mensur* removed from its status of armed assault under German Law, but with little effect. In an attempt to gain a new area of support, the Nazi members of the *Reichstag* turned their attention to this issue during the debate on the *Mensur* in 1930 and supported the fencing fraternities by speaking in favour of legalising the *Mensur*. However, this was later shown in 1935, to have been little more than a wooing tactic on the part of the Nazis in the hope to ingratiate themselves, and especially their student organisation, with the fencing fraternities and their alumni. This point has subsequently led to a great deal of misunderstanding regarding the relationship between the student corporations and the *NSDStB*, by giving the impression that the Nazis and *satisfaktionsfähige* student federations embraced predominantly the same tenets and *raison d'être*. This was not necessarily the case as will be seen below.

In spite of the efforts on the part of the *ADW* federations, and the unsolicited assistance of the previously mentioned Nazi members of the *Reichstag*, the draft of the penal code (*Strafgetzbuch*) of 1930 still listed the *Mensur* as armed assault and thereby punishable under the law.[104]

True to its independent and autonomous nature, the *KSCV* congress of 1930 answered the continued opposition from the *Reichsrat* on the one hand, and the ineffectiveness of the *ADW* on the other, by establishing its own committee to promote legalisation of the *Mensur*. The campaign was strengthened with a report from the German Society of Surgeons which outlined that the *Mensur* was not a deadly sport, and therefore not a duel, when as with any other sporting activities, proper precautions were taken. At the same time, the *SC* of Berlin was given a severe reprimand for contravening accepted corps policy and jeopardising the campaign. Apparently certain corps members had made pictures from a *Mensur* available to an American press representative, with the result that the task of lobbying for legalisation of the *Mensur* had been made more difficult.[105]

The *Kösener Congress* also promised financial support for the work undertaken by the chairman of the *Deutsche Studentenschaft*, who, as a *corpsier*, expended great energy in trying to steer the attention of the *DSt* back to student related problems rather than following the general trend towards the arena of party politics.[106] It was also recommended by the

KSCV that the *Allgemeine Deutsche Waffenring* and its local chapters remain free from party politicisation – an issue not easily controlled.

In order to keep the support of its allies within the *ADW*, such as the *Deutsche Wehrschaft* and *Deutsche Burschenschaft*, and to advance the *NSDStB*'s struggle for acceptability among the student 'establishment', Schirach announced in *Die Bewegung* of 8 July 1930, that retroactive from 1 July 1930, there existed a code of honour for all *NSDStB* members.[107] This appears to have been merely a manoeuvre towards recognition on the part of Schirach and other *NSDStB* functionaries but it did remove some of the apprehension on the part of some federations regarding the acceptability of the *NSDStB*. Other federations doubted whether or not members of the *NSDStB* would conduct themselves as 'honourable students' and if they were worthy of recognition by members of *ADW* fraternities. Actions indeed spoke louder than words, for as will be seen, Schirach himself reneged in an affair only months later in early 1931.

The bold words of his code of honour for the *NSDStB* began with instructions to all *NSDStB* members to observe their own personal honour as closely as they would that of others. The preamble assured them that groundless insults could not touch their inner honour, but if such insults were ignored it could give the impression that they had no sense of integrity.[108]

The code then went on to say that as a political organisation the *NSDStB* had within its ranks both proponents and opponents on the issue of giving satisfaction at arms. The *NSDStB* did not take a stance on the question of how satisfaction was to be given, but it did require that every member, without exception, be prepared to give satisfaction when called upon. The *NSDStB* itself accepted the practice of *Verbriefte Satisfaktion*, whereby the matter would be given to an appropriately formed court of honour for a ruling. This placed the *NSDStB* within the later provisions of the Erlangen Agreement and gave its members no option other than the traditional academic mode for settling differences.

Point 5 of the *NSDStB* code made it clear that affairs of honour between its members and fraternity students, fraternity alumni or members of an officers' association, were to be conducted in strict adherence to the regulations of the academic codex. The matter could only proceed to arbitration after full particulars of the incident had been reported to the *Reichsführer* of the *NSDStB* by the leader of the local *NSDStB* group.[109] However, the *NSDStB* code of honour did not assume competence to carry out the handling of affairs of honour, which if it had, would have most certainly swept away the association's chances of acceptance by the *ADW*. On the contrary, the drafters of the code wisely left the handling of any such disputes to the fraternities of the *ADW* as described under Point 12 of the new code. If a *NSDStB* member also belonged to an *ADW* fraternity, his corporation would take responsibility for the regulating and settling of the affair. The *Ehrenwart*, or *NSDStB* local officer for such matters, was to execute the responsibilities of his office only if the fraternity were unable to conduct the affair properly or if the member did not belong to a fraternity.[110]

As a safeguard for the *esprit de corps* of the *NSDStB* and in order to maintain jurisdiction over its members, especially those who also belonged to fencing fraternities, Point 16 stated that *NSDStB* members of the same university group, would not settle their internal disputes externally through the mechanisms of the local *Waffenring* and those who insisted upon satisfaction at arms to settle disputes with fellow *NSDStB* comrades would be expelled from the association.[111]

After citing the code of honour (*Ehrenordnung*) to this point verbatim as it appeared in the *Die Bewegung*, Anselm Faust, in his very comprehensive history 'Der Nationalsozialistische Studentenbund' omits the remainder of Point 16 and Point 17 completely.[112] These omitted points declared the obligation of all university *NSDStB* leaders to inform every new member of the association's code of honour and they were obligated to read the code aloud at the first meeting of their group, each university semester. The leader was further charged to inform the *Reichsleitung* immediately of the cause and manner of settlement of all affairs of honour which involved *NSDStB* members within his jurisdiction.[113] Not long after their publication, these lofty words were called into question in Munich where an incident brought both the local *Senioren-Convent* and the *NSDStB* into direct conflict over a point of honour involving Walter Lienau and Baldur von Schirach himself.

In the following four months of 1930 the *NSDStB* made sufficient inroads so that the *ADW* accepted a motion to open negotiations with the *NSDStB* with the purpose of reaching an agreement of recognition, eventually known as the Erfurt Agreement. Through this agreement both parties, the *ADW* federations and the *NSDStB*, consented to free their members from the obligation of voting for a specific list of candidates in student elections. As there were students who belonged to both the *NSDStB* and an *ADW* fraternity, they previously had been placed in a position of divided loyalty when it came to voting. This was the substantial gain made by the *NSDStB* in the Erfurt Agreement with the *ADW* federations. In future elections, the Nazis would in all likelihood be able to glean a few votes from despondent fraternity members, while there was little chance of their losing the votes of their own members, as the *NSDStB* was a student association formed for the purpose of propagating a specific political ideology. This unfortunately is the point upon which most of the very brief existing analyses of the Erfurt Agreement dwell. Some mention has also been made of the fact that following the Erfurt Agreement members of the *NSDStB* were allowed to fence against members of *ADW* fraternities, but the significance of this arrangement should not be underestimated. The *ADW* obviously would not have made the electoral concessions had it not received something which it wanted in return. In actual fact, the terms agreed to by the *NSDStB* were quite substantial. The *Ehrenordnung des NSDStB*, which was presented to the *Erfurt Waffenstudententag* in January 1931, had been expanded from the 17 paragraphs issued by Schirach in July 1920, to a document of 24 paragraphs which began:

> The *NSDStB* Code of Honour is equally binding for all its members. It serves to regulate affairs of honour between members of the *NSDStB* as well as outside students, academics and officers. . . .
> To a person of Germanic extraction, honour is the greatest good. The basis of the Germanic concept of that which constitutes honour, is the respect and recognition of a person acting honourably.[114]

Point 5 stated definitively that the *NSDStB* commanded its members to give or to demand satisfaction as the situation demanded. But of even greater significance it included the Waidhofen Principle whereby those students declared racially Jewish were to be refused the courtesies of honour or satisfaction by the *NSDStB*.[115]

Under Paragraph 6 of the Erfurt Agreement the *NSDStB* promised not to impede *ADW* members from attending fraternity functions and to release *NSDStB* members who were also members of fraternities from their *NSDStB* duties in order that they could give precedence to their fraternity obligations. The *NSDStB* also undertook not to present itself in any way as another association of fraternities nor to adopt colours, heraldry or any other types of insignia which might be construed to represent it as such. However, it is Subsection C of Paragraph 6 which is most significant and under which the *NSDStB* agreed to recognise the jurisdiction of *Verrufe* declared by *ADW* fraternities:

> The *NSDStB* acknowledges those bans which are correctly declared by the undersigned federations, and persons and such scholars as

whom find themselves under such a ban will be excluded from membership in the *NSDStB*.[116]

Members of the *NSDStB* who were also members of *ADW* associated fraternities were of course expected to give and demand satisfaction by means of edged swords and the mechanics for settling such affairs of honour were to be conducted by those members' fraternity under *ADW* Regulations, Section 31. Members of the *NSDStB*, who were not also members of an *ADW* fraternity, were expected to approach a fraternity of the associated federations and ask for *Waffenschutz*, which would be extended by the fraternity, thereby allowing the *NSDStB* member the opportunity to settle the matter through the good offices of the *ADW*'s local *Waffenring*. However, the Erfurt Agreement also made allowances for those *NSDStB* members who did not wish to wield cold steel. Such members were to list themselves in the *NSDStB* records as not prepared to give satisfaction at arms and were required to give *Verbriefte Satisfaktion* as outlined in the Erlangen Agreement. This, as with *Waffenschutz*, was to be carried out through the good office of a fraternity which was a signatory of the Erlangen Agreement (*Erlangen Verbände Abkommen*).

The Erfurt Agreement was considered valid from the date of signing in January 1931, but required ratification by the various federations of the *ADW* at their annual conferences, most of which fell during the spring months of each year. The agreement was then to have its rough edges smoothed and to be reaffirmed at a meeting with the *NSDStB* in October of the same year; validating it for three years. However, there were several intervening incidents which stopped the corps from ratifying the agreement and which set the stage for a bitter animosity between the *KSCV* and the *NSDStB*.

As can be seen from the sections quoted, the Erfurt Agreement gave the *NSDStB* some political concessions, but when seen from the standpoint of the fencing fraternities, the *NSDStB* had submitted itself to the traditional student codex of honour and to the giving of satisfaction. The traditional student stance, particularly for the corps, was that party politics had little legitimacy within the universities. This meant that the making of political concessions to the *NSDStB* was not seen as giving ground. The *NSDStB* showed itself willing to submit, not only to the conventions, but also the discipline of the fraternities, therefore placing itself under the jurisdiction of the *ADW*, even after having been granted the compromise on student election procedures.

Scepticism regarding the seriousness with which the *NSDStB* signed the Erfurt Agreement soon grew on the part of the *KSCV*. This mistrust proved well grounded, and later justified, by the actions of the *NSDStB* leadership; the prime examples being Baldur von Schirach, and Walter Lienau, who was elected chairman of the *Deutsche Studentenschaft* at Graz in 1931. In order to better understand how the precepts and covenants of the *KSCV* were translated into events, let us look at an incident that occurred in Munich in the autumn of 1930, which not only illustrates the workings of corps apparati, but also set in motion a bitter animosity between the *KSCV* and the *NSDStB*, only partially resolved by the corps dissolution five years later.

3 The Corps versus the *NSDStB*

AN AFFAIR OF HONOUR

When setting down his memoirs in 1965, Baldur von Schirach dated his initial role in the following incident as early in 1930.[1] However, according to both Nazi and *KSCV* primary documents, the affair began late in 1930 and carried through until the autumn of 1931,[2] by which time it had set into motion a contentious interaction between the *NSDStB* and the corps, an interaction which continued well into the Third Reich and through the Second World War.

In late September 1930, Leutnant d.R. Freiherr von Holzschuher, who was at that time personal secretary to Major Buch, the Chairman of the *NSDAP*'s *USCHLA* (the Investigation and Adjustments Committee) received a letter which requested that he settle a three-year-old debt of 3600 RM with his former fellow officer Oberleutnant von Scanzoni. In the letter Scanzoni apologised for his break with usual decorum, but the request was prompted by the embarrassment of his dire financial situation. Shortly afterwards the two men met in public and in front of witnesses, Holzschuher accused Scanzoni of having been drunk when he wrote the letter. When Scanzoni replied that his request had been both earnest and sober, Holzschuher stated: 'Then with all the consequences which might arise from it, I declare you a previous regimental comrade who at present has neither honour nor integrity.'[3] This grave insult was delivered to Scanzoni in front of Holzschuher's superior, Major Buch, whose fear for being tainted by the incident – as will be seen later – was perhaps the single most important issue in the dispute and gave fuel to the initial stages. Correspondence between two uninvolved corps alumni regarding the affair stated: 'The whole thing is explained through the self interest of von Holzschuher, who before the war was released from the army with unceremonious dismissal. During the war he reformed himself somewhat and now serves as secretary to Buch.'[4] On two later occasions Holzschuher refused the requests of persons representing

Scanzoni that he withdraw his remarks. Scanzoni then passed the matter to the officers' association of his regiment, which in turn referred it to the Munich chapter of the *Deutsche Offiziersbund (DOB)* for action. The court of honour which was called sat three times and their findings stated that Scanzoni's honour was intact and that Holzschuher was not required to withdraw his remarks.⁵ Apparently this ambivalent verdict was given because the covenant between Scanzoni and Holzschuher had been an oral agreement, and Scanzoni was unable to produce either witnesses or documentation to substantiate his claim against Holzschuher for the overdue debt.

However, the *DOB* court of honour had found that Scanzoni's honour was intact despite Holzschuher's remarks. Bearing in mind the agreement of the *KSCV* with the *DOB* and *Nationalverband Deutscher Offiziere (NDO)* in 1923, Scanzoni, on 1 December 1930, sought assistance to settle his dispute with Holzschuher at arms and *Belegte Waffen* with Corps Franconia of Munich. On 2 December 1930 Holzschuher was visited by members of Corps Franconia acting on behalf of Scanzoni.⁶ They asked Holzschuher to withdraw his remarks regarding Scanzoni, but he refused and he also refused to accept a challenge in answer to Scanzoni's demand for satisfaction. Furthermore he insulted the deputation from Corps Franconia by telling them that they would make themselves a laughing-stock by representing Scanzoni.⁷ This was a rather curious remark to come from someone who refused to honour either his debt or any obligation to give an account of his actions to his creditor. The delegation from Corps Franconia took note of Holzschuher's attitude and received documentation the following day in the form of a lengthy letter from him in which he defended his actions. His claim was that any person who could allow such a grave insult to remain unchallenged from 30 September until 3 December must be without even the most primitive grasp of the concept of honour. He therefore could not take Scanzoni's demand for satisfaction seriously.⁸ He did not dispute the fact that he had given grounds for Scanzoni to demand satisfaction; his contention was that Scanzoni was not *satisfkationsfähig* and therefore was not in a position to demand satisfaction of him.

Holzchuher's approach to the affair was incorrect both in points of fact and in procedure. In the first place, a court of honour of the *DOB* had ruled on 26 November 1930, on their dispute and had declared that the honour of Scanzoni was unsullied and intact. Secondly, in accordance with the *KSCV–DOB* agreement of 1923, only a court of honour struck for the specific purpose would be qualified to judge whether or not one of their members was without honour and therefore unqualified to give or demand satisfaction. The proper and effective method for Holzschuher would have been first to accept the challenge and then to request that a court of honour be struck for a ruling on the status of Scanzoni. By his outright refusal to accept Scanzoni's challenge, Holzschuher placed himself in danger, as a former officer, of being proven forsworn. Furthermore, as he had confirmed in writing his rejection of Scanzoni's demand for satisfaction and implied that Corps Franconia was laughable for representing Scanzoni, his actions were ruled censurable by Corps Franconia. Therefore, Holzschuher was declared a man without honour and banned from the right to demand or give satisfaction at arms as from 21 December 1930.[9] It was later argued by Dr Adolf Wagner, in the *NSDAP* memorandum summarising the incident, that the handling of Holzschuher's case was not true to the regulations of the Munich *SC Comment*. He claimed that under Paragraph 158 of the *comment* the party in question could not be declared under ban unless they twice refused to meet a challenge.[10] But Holzschuher had refused the challenge given to him by Scanzoni's representative and furthermore had confirmed in writing his intentions to ignore Scanzoni's demands for satisfaction. His assertions were not supported since as one of the parties to the dispute, and especially as the offending party, he was by definition unqualified to judge on his opponent's honour.

The declaration of *Waffenverruf* against Holzschuher not only brought his character into question, but also was apparently interpreted as having cast aspersions on both his superior, Major Buch, and the *NSDAP* leadership as well. On 12 December 1930, one week after the *Verruf* against Holzschuher had been declared, Corps Franconia received correspondence from Major Buch, as well as from Baldur von Schirach acting in his role as *Reichsleiter* of the *NSDStB*. Buch's letter began with a rather opaque but minatory undercurrent. He related that he was in the midst of organising the Nazi faction in the *Reichstag* to move an amendment to Paragraph 205 of the *Strafgesetzbuch für das Deutsche Reich May 15, 1871*, whereby the *Mensur* was seen as armed assault; the sentence for which could carry incarceration. Buch claimed that out of his deep affection for the fencing fraternities and his conviction that it was from their ranks that the future leaders of Germany would come, that he was arranging for the law to be revoked.[11] Major Buch then spent several paragraphs praising Holzschuher's valour and unfamiliarity with cowardice while he had served as Buch's ordnance officer during the First World War. The correspondence cited above, which mentions Holzschuher's discharge from the army, would seem to call Buch's accuracy, as well as Holzschuher's deportment, into question. Buch then went on to state that he intended to press charges and have Scanzoni expelled from his regimental association.[12] If they had actually expelled him, Scanzoni would have indeed stood the chance of being ruled *unsatisfaktionsfähig*, but it appears to have been yet another lie in what was to become a rather complicated proliferation of untruths issued by Nazi functionaries during this incident.

Through correspondence with the officers' association of Scanzoni's regiment, the Baden Sixth Infantry Regiment, the Munich *SC* established that the charge by Major Buch against Oberleutnant a.D. Scanzoni was 'Endangering of the profession's honour' (*Gefährdung der Standesehre*). However, the maximum punishment for the charge, according to the agreement between the *DOB* and the officer's associations, was never expulsion, but a strong reprimand, which in no way would alter the previously declared intact and unquestioned *Satisfaktionsfähigkeit* of Scanzoni.[13] Furthermore, on 7 January 1931, Major Buch's allegations against Scanzoni were heard by the annual meeting of the regiment's officers' association and no action was taken regarding Scanzoni's status. This calls both Buch's accuracy and integrity into question. But perhaps more significantly, Holzschuher appears to have made no attempt to seek redress, protection or a decision through the offices of the *DOB* to strengthen his case. This indicates Holzschuher's total reliance on Major Buch and the Nazi Party to shield him from the consequences of what would seem a case which went more and more in favour of Scanzoni. However, this merely explains how the Nazi Party got drawn into the dispute, while the major action took place between the *NSDStB* and the *KSCV* corps of Munich.

The other letter which Corps Franconia received on 12 December 1930, that written by Schirach, began a new phase of the incident and reflected a rather haughty and arrogant stance on the part of Schirach: 'I hereby command you in the name of the *NSDStB* and in the name of the national leadership of the *NSDAP*, to send a representative to the apartment of Freiherr von Holzschuher by 9 pm December 20, 1930 for the purpose of retracting the ban and also to offer the apologies of Corps Franconia for the same.'[14] The very high-handed tone of Schirach's letter, as well as the threat of publication of the incident in the Nazi press if Corps Franconia did not comply with his demands, would indicate either an exceedingly inflated opinion of his own position on the part of Schirach or a great zest for bluffing. Either way, it would seem to have been a great over-reaction on the part of the Nazi hierarchy, particularly in the case of Major Buch and Schirach. It also shows a definite lack of knowledge on the part of Schirach regarding the procedures surrounding affairs of honour. The *Waffenverruf* against Holzschuher was not proclaimed, nor could it have been proclaimed, by Corps Franconia alone, as it was by definition a collective decision of the whole Munich *Senioren-Convent*. Corps Franconia had merely represented the interests of Scanzoni and had Holzschuher accepted the challenge, he in turn would have been represented in the affair by another corps of the Munich *SC*.

The date of his ultimatum to Corps Franconia was extended in a subsequent communication by Schirach to 18 January 1931 in order to make allowance for the university Christmas recess. In the same letter of 13 January 1931, Schirach also made the statement that due to the charges brought against him, Scanzoni's regiment had decided to expel him at their meeting on 7 January 1931. Schirach then went on to say that in view of Scanzoni's expulsion from his officer's association Corps Franconia had given *Waffenschutz* to a man deemed unfit for membership by his regiment and therefore unable to give satisfaction.[15] In light of the correspondence from the *DOB* to the Munich *SC* mentioned above, the charge against Scanzoni could not result in his being expelled from the officers' association even if Major Buch's allegations against him were found substantiated. However, the association's annual meeting did not find against Scanzoni. Schirach's statement meant either that he was very ill-informed regarding the findings of Scanzoni's regiment or that he purposely ignored the facts when writing to Corps Franconia on 13 January. The result was the same. Schirach lied to Corps Franconia. Upon receipt of the letter, an extraordinary meeting of the Munich *Waffenring* was held which verified that the *Waffenverruf* against Holzschuher was justified. This meant that all *satisfaktionsfähige* fraternities within the Munich *Waffenring* supported the action against Holzschuher.

The affair at this point begins to diverge into two different cases, one dealing with Holzschuher and the other with Schirach. Holzschuher's case was summarised as follows by Corps Hubertia, then the presiding corps of Munich, in a letter to the *NSDAP* on 17 January 1931. Holzschuher had refused to give satisfaction to Scanzoni on the grounds which he set out in his letter to Corps Franconia on 3 December 1930. The grounds were not acceptable, since the court of honour established by the *DOB* to deal with the matter had ruled that Scanzoni's honour was intact. Holzschuher had therefore refused to give satisfaction to a gentleman and fellow officer to whom he owed money and whom he admitted to having gravely insulted. Because of this, the *Waffenverruf* against Holzschuher was to remain until such time as he either accepted the challenge and gave Scanzoni satisfaction or sought dispensation through his officers' association.[16]

Because of the insult expressed in the letter of 13 January 1931 to the *SC*, Corps Franconia was compelled to demand from Schirach on 14 January, that he retract his comment which alleged that Corps Franconia was guilty of allowing an obvious blunder to occur.[17] Schirach requested until three o'clock the following day in order to confer with the *Reichsleitung* of the Nazi Party before committing himself to the challenge. During that period Schirach threatened both to disclose the incident to the press and also to take the matter to the *Waffenstudententag*, which was to be held in Erfurt later in the month. His eventual reply to the challenge was to appoint Walter Lienau as his representative, but he refused to give satisfaction on ground that Corps Franconia was, in his eyes, not *satisfaktionsfähig*.[18] This behaviour was somewhat puzzling, and representatives of the Munich *SC* met Nazi Party authorities on the following day to clarify the matter. Despite assurances on the part of the Nazi representatives that the incident would not reach the press, the following notice appeared in the *Völkischer Beobachter* on 19 January 1931:

> The *Untersuchungs- und Schlichtungsausschuss* [*(USCHLA) NSDAP* disciplinary court] hereby declares that members of Corps Franconia refused to give satisfaction to members of the *NSDAP* and are hereby refused to demand the same.
> Grounds:
> The Corps Franconia, in a frivolous and unacceptable manner, declared and implemented a ban against Freiherr von Holzschuher, denying him the right to satisfaction at arms. Furthermore in defiance of the demand made both by Party Member Major Walter Buch and *Reichsführer* of the *NSDStB* Party Member Baldur von Schirach, an apology has not been made by Corps Franconia.
> The ban on Party Member Freiherr von Holzschuher has been falsely placed.
>   Signed Buch, Head of the *USCHLA*
> Munich, 19 January, 1931[19]

The question naturally arises, when was the membership of Corps Franconia called upon to give satisfaction to members of the *NSDAP*?

The only apparent answer to be drawn from the information available would come from wording of Schirach's letter to Corps Franconia which demanded they send a deputation to Holzschuher, to proffer their apologies. Schirach used the verb 'auffordern' which generally would mean to request, call upon, ask, demand, etc., but which under certain circumstances could also mean to challenge. If used in the latter sense, the fact that Corps Franconia did not comply with his demand for an apology to Holzschuher, could have been twisted by Schirach to mean that Corps Franconia refused a challenge and therefore had refused to give satisfaction, both to him and to Holzschuher. This point of the affair is rather hazy but it has little bearing on the ignoble behaviour on the part of the *NSDAP* members associated with the incident. It does, however, give an indication how hollow Nazi preaching on duty and honour actually was when tested. The picture painted by Schirach of himself in his memoirs is considerably braver and brighter than documentary evidence affords. According to his account of the incident, Corps Franconia challenged him and he accepted on condition that the matter be settled with pistols; at which point Corps Franconia supposedly withdrew.[20] However, the corps records already cited state clearly that it was in fact Schirach who refused the challenge based on the strength of Buch's notice in the *Völkischer Beobachter*. According to a private account of the affair, Hitler learned of the matter while reading the *Völkischer Beobachter* in a cafe and went into a rage regarding Schirach's actions. As mentioned earlier, Schirach's accuracy in this particular chapter of his memoirs is less than vigilant, but one thing does seem certain – Schirach countermanded orders given by Hitler and came close to falling from the favoured position which he held near his *Führer*.[21]

On 19 January 1931, the Munich *SC* also received a letter from Walter Lienau, who was acting on behalf of Schirach. The letter charged Corps Franconia with improper procedure under the regulations of the *SC Comment* and restated Schirach's opinion regarding the honourless status of Corps Franconia. Lienau had distinguished himself already while holding a number of executive positions both in the *Deutsche Studentenschaft* (*DSt*) and the *NSDStB*. However, perhaps his greatest notoriety was to come, when in July 1931, he was elected chairman of the *DSt* at its annual international conference at Graz. The position gave him the distinction of being the first Nazi to hold the chairmanship of an international, non-party organisation. In acting for Schirach, in January 1931, Lienau placed himself into a conflict of interests. As a member of Corps Isaria of Munich, Lienau was required to abide by and uphold the decisions of the Munich *SC*, but his position within the national leadership of the *NSDStB* also demanded that he act in the interests of the Nazi movement.

The *SC* answered Lienau's letter by stating that charges against a corps of the Munich *SC* could be brought only by such persons or organisations which were recognised by and which accepted the basic tenets of *Waffenstudententum* and not by a political party. The *NSDStB* was not recognised by the *ADW*. Furthermore, the *Verruf* against Holzschuher had been imposed by the whole of the Munich *SC*, not by a single corps. And finally, there were means by which Holzschuher could vindicate himself from the ban; means which had already been made clear in the *SC* s letter to the *NSDAP* of 17 January 1931. Lienau then personally visited the presiding Corps Hubertia on 21 January, and attested that improper procedure, rather than the status of Scanzoni's honour, was the reason for Holzschuher's refusal to give him satisfaction. To this new tactic, the *SC* replied by sending a letter with the charges against Schirach to Hitler, with copies of the letter to the *Reichsleitung* and the *NSDStB*. The letter pointed out that Holzschuher had not appealed against the charges through the channels open to officers and students, either on the grounds of wrong procedure or false information, and could therefore not substantiate either claim.[22]

The letter then turned to the allegations made against Corps Franconia in the *Völkischer Beobachter* on 19 January. The Munich *SC* demanded that a retraction under the same column, *Aus der Bewegung*, was to appear in the *Völkischer Beobachter*, declaring the ban on Corps Franconia unfounded and that its *corpsiers* were of unquestioned honour. If the retraction did not appear, the *SC*, with the support of the Munich *Waffenring*, was prepared to have the matter discussed in full at the *Waffenstudententag* in Erfurt on 24–25 January 1931. In addition, all *NSDStB* members would be placed under *Verruf* and all federations of the *Allgemeiner Deutscher Waffenring* would exclude from their ranks any student who was a member of the *NSDStB*.[23]

As seen above, the *NSDStB* was to present its code of honour for approval to the Erfurt *Waffenstudententag* and a presentation by the Munich Waffenring of the case regarding Schirach's questionable behaviour could seriously damage the chances of the *NSDStB* gaining recognition by the federations of the *ADW*. This was driven home by the letter's third section which pointed out that even under the *NDStB Ehrenordnung*, which was to be presented at Erfurt in several days' time, the actions of both Holzschuher and Schirach had been incorrect. A challenge was to be accepted when given and the honourability of opponents would be ruled upon by a court of honour only after the challenge was taken up – not before. Therefore, according to the *NSDStB* code of honour, members of the Nazi *Reichsleitung* and even the *Reichstudentenführer* of the *NSDStB*, Schirach himself, who had been responsible for publishing the code in *Die Bewegung* on 8 July 1930, were in breach of the very code which they were obligated to uphold. Accordingly, the *Reichsleitung* was obliged to take action against itself and against Schirach if he refused the challenge offered him by Corps Franconia.

Schirach also received a communication from the Munich *Senioren-Convent*, informing him that Corps Franconia, as a member corps of the Munich *SC*, was by definition of unquestionable honour. It stated further, that should his political party forbid him to give satisfaction to Corps Franconia, such a move would not be an admissible reason; as the basic assumptions would be incorrect and would show grave ignorance of all military and student etiquette and tradition. He was further informed that a court of honour would be held on 27 January 1931, to rule on his case and that either Schirach himself, or his representative, was expected to attend. Negligence to attend would be dealt with accordingly.[24]

On the evening of the same day, 21 January, the corps of the Munich *SC* presented the details of the affair to the other fraternities of the Munich *Waffenring*. Although not of the same proportions, other *Waffenring* fraternities also had grievances against the *NSDStB* and it was unanimously decided that their disapproval of the less than valourous behaviour exhibited by both Schirach and the *NSDStB*, should be presented to the *Waffenstudententag* in Erfurt by the Munich *Waffenring*.[25]

Hitler's apparent displeasure with the situation made itself felt very quickly and by 23 January, the *NSDAP* proposed to the *SC* that an unofficial commission be formed to deal with the problem. The representatives put forward to represent Nazi interests were General von Epp, Major a.D. Hühnlein, Oberstleutnant Röhm,[26] and Direktor Fürholzer. The *SC* appointed three representatives, one from each of the corps Hubertia, Suevia, and Franconia, and agreed to have no dealings with the *NSDStB* until the matter was settled. On that same day the representatives of the *SC* met Fürholzer who, as a alumnus of Turnerschaft Ghibellinia in the *ADW*, officiated over the commission. At the conclusion of a thorough three-hour discussion, Fürholzer gave his assurance that the *SC* had been completely correct in its handling of the matter. On 26 January, further discussions were held with Fürholzer, and Rittmeister Beurer and K. A. Reichel, who functioned as proxies for the other two non-corps members of the commission. The following two points were fully agreed upon by all present. Holzschuher, in ignorance of correct form and the resultant consequences, had refused the challenge issued by Scanzoni and was to accept it. The second recommendation was that Major Buch print a retraction of the allegations made against Corps Franconia. This notice was also to include an explanation of Holzschuher's situation, namely that the *Verruf* against him would be lifted as soon a he accepted his obligation to give Scanzoni satisfaction.[27]

The commission as a whole then met with Major Buch and Rudolf Hess, in his capacity as Hitler's private secretary. The negotiations had, during the first two sittings, moved ahead without any hindrances, but they then met a major obstacle in the form of an emphatic demand on the part of the Nazi *Reichsleitung*. The commission in turn insisted that the new condition was unrelated and lay outside its mandate. Walter Lienau, who had acted as Schirach's representative in the affair with Corps Franconia, had been placed in a position of divided loyalties between the *NSDStB* and its leader whom he represented on the one hand, and his oath as a member of Corps Isaria to abide by the comment of the Munich *SC* on the other. Lienau had been required to account to his corps for the support which he had given Schirach against the *SC*. It appears that his answers were rather unconvincing and so the direct question was put to him: would he honour his obligation as a *corpsier* of Corps Isaria and, if it were demanded of him, give satisfaction to a member of Corps Franconia? His answer was no – thereby following the edict of the *NSDStB* rather than his corps and proving himself forsworn to Corps Isaria. He was therefore dishonourably expelled from his corps as of 23 January 1931.[28] He did, however, make a lengthy appeal for readmission to Corps Isaria in late April, but the ruling stood and he remained permanently ostracised. It was the readmission of Lienau to Corps Isaria on which Buch and Hess were adamant in their negotiations with the commission mentioned above.

The two factions parted without having reached a final recommendation, but the general impression was that the deadlock was not insurmountable. The commission had no power to make demands or regulations as to the membership of a corps. None the less, it was felt that further discussion would produce an acceptable solution. However, the next day the *SC* representatives were informed that, since the function of the commission had been unofficial, those persons previously acting on behalf of the Nazi *Reichsleitung* had been relieved of their responsibilities for the case and that regotiations in the future were to be conducted through a Herr Swoboda. It was subsequently learned that Major Buch had left Munich for a holiday and could not be reached for consultation until his return.[29]

At this point it was decided to write directly to Hitler in the hope that he could bring his underlings into line. The letter drew the fact to his attention, that the appointed commission had been in agreement regarding the matter and that, whereas the *SC* previously had been consulted as to the acceptability of the Nazi representatives on the commission, they had not been requested to accept Swoboda's credentials and therefore did not recognise him as the representative of the *NSDAP*. The letter went on to say that in light of the fact that the representatives of both parties were in 99 per cent agreement as to the resolution of the matter, the Munich *SC* respectfully suggested that perhaps Hitler's aides had not correctly or adequately informed him regarding the affair.[30] Hitler's reply of 31 January stated that Swoboda was to act as the representative of the *Reichsleitung* and, as he was a *Waffenstudent*, it was hoped that the Munich *SC* would not question his credentials. The letter also indicated that the commission had been purely of an investigative nature and the *SC* should also feel free to change its representatives for future negotiations if it so wished. Hitler took exception at the intimation made by the *SC* that he had not been briefed properly by his aides but stated:

> Although I strongly reject the claim that the *NSDAP* or one of its affiliated branches has because of its political stance caused conflicts to occur between itself and *Waffenstudententum*, I am still willing to do my best to eliminate or clarify differences of opinion or misunderstandings between *Waffenstudenten* and the *NSDAP*. I am therefore also prepared to send members and form a commission to deal with and find a solution for such issues.[31]

As will be seen later an organisation was established under a directive from Hitler, but it functioned as a Nazi sponge to draw as many fraternity students as possible into the *NSDStB*. Swoboda was an alumnus of the fraternity Apollo in the *Rothenburger Verband Schwarzer Schlagender Verbindungen*, which was a recognised federation of the

Allgemeinen Deutschen Waffenrings. His credentials were accepted by the Munich *SC* and in a meeting with him on 3 February 1931, it was agreed that the *Völkischer Beobachter* should print an announcement stating that both the ban against von Holzschuher and the proclamation against Corps Franconia were nullified. The reasons to be given were that Corps Franconia had acted properly in conducting the matter so that the ban pronounced against its members was incorrect and unjustified. The ban against Holzschuher had been lifted as he and Corps Franconia had come to an agreement. This verbal understanding was reached between Swoboda and the *SC* representatives and the matter was thought finally to have been laid to rest. The following day the *SC* received a letter from Hitler's private secretary stating that Swoboda had not been empowered to act on behalf of the *Reichsleitung*, only to represent its interests to the Munich *SC*. The agreement reached between Swoboda and the *SC* was therefore not binding for the *Reichsleitung*. At this point the *Senioren-Convent* of Munich decided that negotiations with the *NSDAP* were impossible and broke off relations. Ironically the memorandum written by Adolf Wagner for the *NSDAP* concerning the case ends with an expression of hope that all *Waffenstudenten* would avail themselves of the memorandum in order to properly inform themselves regarding the incident.[32]

The denouement of the affair was as follows. In order to give credibility to the code of honour which he had authored and published, Schirach presented himself to a court of honour held by the Munich *SC* on 28 February 1931, and formally retracted the remarks he had made regarding Corps Franconia and asked to be pardoned for his actions against the *Senioren-Convent* in general.[33]

The dispute between Scanzoni and Holzschuher, on the other hand, did not end until September of that year. Holzschuher apparently was also required to fall in line and, in order that the Nazi *Reichsleitung* might not lose further face in the affair, he accepted Scanzoni's challenge in accordance with the officer's code of honour. However, the adversaries never met. Holzschuher *Belegt Waffen* with Corps Suevia of Munich, thereby conforming with the *DOB–KSCV* agreement of 1923. But before the two men could meet, Corps Suevia received a communique from his officers' association that Scanzoni had been excluded from it and that he was therefore no longer *satisfaktionsfähig*. That having been established the corps of the Munich *SC* had little choice but to drop the whole matter despite the great efforts and aggravation which it had caused them during the previous nine months.[34]

THE ERFURT *WAFFENSTUDENTENTAG* 1931

The conference began with a flair when the *Deutsche Wehrschaft*'s representative insisted on an emergency change of the agenda to enable the immediate adoption and implementation of the tenets found in the Waidhofen Principle. The *DW*'s resolution called for the exclusion from all *ADW* fraternities and the denial of satisfaction at arms to Jews, persons with Jewish relatives and baptised Jews.[35] The urgency of the motion was not accepted by the conference, and the motion was defeated. Upon the rejection of the motion, the *Deutsche Wehrschaft* delegate withdrew from the conference. 'The representative of the *Deutsche Wehrschaft* emphatically stated that the *DW* would only acknowledge a *Waffenstudententum* which embraced *völkisch* doctrine.'[36] The question of *völkisch* honour was temporarily dismissed from the *Allgemeinen Deutschen Waffenring* but, as will be seen below, became a central problem to the *ADW*, and the cohesion of its membership, during the next few years.[37]

However, in 1931 the more immediate issue dealt with at the *Waffenstudententag* was the presentation of the *NSDStB*'s code of honour for recognition and acceptance of the *NSDStB* by the federations of the *ADW*. The actual tenets of the document have already been looked at in the previous section on the *NSDStB*, but the negotiations should also be examined briefly in order to help explain the stance taken by various of the *ADW* federations regarding the acceptability of the *NSDStB* both at and following the Erfurt conference. Furthermore, it will help to put into perspective and explain relationships between the *KSCV* and the *NSDAP* in the years immediately following.

It becomes very clear when looking at the incident between Schirach and the Munich corps, that the Nazi *Reichsleitung* would seem to have entered into negotiations only as a tactic in order that the *NSDStB*'s code of honour would not be blocked by the Munich *Waffenring* at the Erfurt conference. Just several days prior to the conference, the matter was still at an eruptive stage and the *NSDStB* could not afford to take the chance that its proposed code of honour, which had been openly breached by its author Schirach, might be blocked. As the incident between the *NSDStB* and the Munich *SC* was unresolved, but none the less under negotiation on the date of the conference, it was not raised by the corps, obviously in the expectation that it would be settled amicably in the very near future.

The only point affecting the *NSDStB* and raised by the Munich *Waffenring* at Erfurt was a motion obligating all *Waffenstudenten* to vote for the list supported by their local *Waffenring* in university elections. The motion was not adopted by the conference and was particularly unacceptable to the corps, which insisted that the role of the *Waffenring* was non-political. The result, whereby both the *NSDStB* and federations of the *ADW* released their members from voting for a specific list, has been examined above.

The motion for recognition of the *NSDStB* by the *ADW* was made on the strength of its code of honour published by Schirach in July the previous year. The motion put on behalf of the *NSDStB* indicated a rather compliant stance on the part of the Nazi students, but in view of the friction in Munich with the *Waffenring*, there was little choice left open if the *NSDStB* hoped to be successful in achieving recognition by the *ADW*. The *NSDStB* promised to remain uninvolved in *ADW* matters and not to employ the *Deutsche Wehrschaft* as a vehicle for *NSDStB* propaganda within the *ADW*. It further promised that it would make no attempt to extend the jurisdiction of its code of honour to other *Waffenstudenten*, asking only that if any of its members were involved in an affair of honour, that the matter be communicated to the executive of the *NSDStB*. But perhaps the most significant point at the time was that the *NSDStB* stated it would recognise only expulsion from its ranks as punishment for its members if they were found in contravention of its code. Furthermore, it would not attempt to exercise bans, although it would recognise any such ban proclaimed by the *ADW*.[38] This last concession was perhaps the greatest, for had it been proposed and accepted only two months sooner, Schirach would have been obliged to comply immediately with the Munich *Senioren-Convent* demands.

Neither the conference as a whole, nor the *ADW*, were empowered to adopt or approve policies which would be binding on its member federations. This meant that the Erfurt Agreement had to be ratified by the various federations of the *ADW* at their respective annual conferences, which for the most part were held in the spring of each year. The point which is usually emphasised in connection with the Erfurt Agreement is that a truce was called between the *ADW* and the *NSDStB*, whereby neither group obligated its members to vote for a specific list in student government elections. For the corps this was not a concession, as corps members were, in accordance with corps statutes, free to hold or adopt any political or religious beliefs they wished. On the other hand, the *NSDStB* was by both constitution and name a political student group and its members could almost certainly be counted on to vote for any list backed by the *NSDStB* in student council elections. The releasing of members from mandatory backing of a certain list was most advantageous to federations of the *ADW* such as the *Deutsche Burschenschaft* and *Deutsche Landsmannschaft* where fraternity brothers might well also have been members of the *NSDStB* and had previously been forced to choose between loyalty to their fraternity (and the list which it supported) and their political inclinations expressed through the *NSDStB*. This arrangement freed the fraternities from the possibility of being torn apart through the heterogeneous interests of their members.

The actual document of the Erfurt Agreement was drawn up in April 1931, and was adopted by the annual conferences of the *Deutsche Burschenschaft, Deutsche Landsmannschaft*, Weinheim *Senioren-Convent*, Rudolstadt *Senioren-Convent*, Naumburg *Senioren-Convent* and *Akademischer Turnbund (ABT)*. The *Sonderhäuser Verband akademisch-musikalischer Verbindungen (SV)* and the *Miltenberger Ring (MR)* did not adopt the agreement. The *KSCV*, in accordance with its statutes, was not empowered to take a decision on the agreement, and the matter was referred to the individual *Senioren-Convente* for action.[39]

The agreement, if adopted by the various federations, was valid until 31 October 1931, at which time a revised version was to be produced and sanctioned if all parties concerned were satisfied with the results of the April 1931 document.[40] But the interaction between Schirach, Lienau and the *ADW* federations was far from finished, and several rather important developments occurred in the meantime.

THE *DEUTSCHE STUDENTENSCHAFT (DSt)* CONFERENCE, GRAZ, 1931

In July 1931 the *NSDStB* swept into the leadership of the *DSt*. According to participants at the conference, a bitter battle was fought by many of the student corporations, which had previously dominated the *DSt*, particularly the corps, to prevent the organisation from becoming politicised. Schirach explained it away in his memoirs by claiming that the dissenting corps representatives were merely carrying out the wishes of their alumni, upon whom their fraternities were financially dependent.[41] However, as has already been shown, the *NSDStB* had not endeared itself to the corps and particularly to those of Munich. It is therefore not terribly surprising that the corps tried to move against the *NSDStB* at Graz, first in keeping with their statutes by discouraging political involvement in student groups and secondly as part of what was to become something approaching a running battle between the *KSCV* and *NSDStB*. For this reason Lienau's election as chairman of the *DST* in Graz added insult to injury for the corps; particularly those of the Munich *SC*. However, nothing overt of any great magnitude occurred until the autumn of that year, when the winter semester commenced; presumably this quiet resulted from the fact that the universities were on vacation.

The charges that were eventually laid against Lienau came from the representatives of five *ADW* federations and a faction of the *DSt* as well. Among other things, Lienau had written an article under the pseudonym L. Retlaw entitled *Der Pfahl im Fleisch*, which appeared in the first November issue of *Die Sturmfahne* published by Gerhard Krüger's *NSDStB* university group. The article contained several statements such as: 'Which are you first, a fraternity student or a member of the *NSDStB*?'[42] The article, along with charges of heavy-handed and unconstitutional tactics, called into question Lienau's ability and readiness to act without bias while serving as chairman and chief representative for all interests within the *DSt*. This fact had apparently been brought to Lienau's attention a number of times, but each time it had been met with equal indifference on his part.[43] The authors of the paper *An die studentischen Verbände* outlined the case against Lienau and strongly intimated in that memorandum their disillusionment at the retrogression in negotiations with the *NSDStB*. Their sense of betrayal was due, in great part, to Lienau's performance and the general attitude exhibited by the *NSDAP* towards the majority of *ADW* federations through the *NSDAP*'s disregard of the purpose outlined in the Erfurt Agreement. The 4 November 1931 had been set as the date from which a new era of co-operation and comradeship was to begin between the student fraternities and the *NSDStB*, and thereby putting to rest its dispute with the majority of student federations.[44] The appearance of Lienau's article at about the same time as the truce and the co-operation were to begin, brought his ability further into question. With the *Waffentag* of 1932 planned for less than a month later at Goslar, the report on Lienau ended with the observation that the full extent to which he had sabotaged the agreement would still have to be assessed and any further decisions would be left to the conference at Goslar.[45] The significance and disappointment felt regarding the situation are well reflected in the fact that the first signature on the report against Lienau was that of the same representative who, less than a year before, had presented the original motion to the Erfurt *Waffentstudententag* of 1931 which opened negotiations with the *NSDStB* and was responsible for the first edition of the Erfurt Agreement.

THE LINES ARE DRAWN

Lienau was called upon to account for his actions before representatives of both the *ADW Verhandlungsausschuss* led by Fritz Hilgenstock and the Nazi Party represented by Gerhard Krüger and Oskar Stäbel. Anselm Faust in his history of the *NSDStB* names this group as the *Erfurter Verhandlungsausschuss* which must be an error as the *KSCV* was clearly represented by Dr Johannes Heinricht of Corps Teutonia Berlin and the *KSCV* had refused to ratify or consider the Erfurt Agreement. The same document and further material dealing with the incident refer to the committee as representing the *Erlangen Verbände (ADW)*.[46] That aside, the price extracted by the *ADW* representatives for Lienau's indiscretions was his removal as *DSt* chairman and the publication of a statement in the December issue of the same *NSDStB* periodical in which Lienau admitted responsibility for the article published under the pseudonym, coupled with an apology and retraction of the inflammatory remarks. He claimed that it had not been his intention to insult any of the federations or their members and expressed his regret at the fact that his article had caused problems. The declaration, he said, was made in answer to questions raised by Gerloff, Heinricht and Sikorski.[47] Lienau was replaced as chairman of the *DSt* by Gerhard Krüger, who ironically was *Kreisleiter* of the *NSDStB* group which had published Lienau's article against the federations of the *ADW*, ultimately causing his removal from office. The reason given for Lienau's dismissal was 'for internal reasons' and 'because of behaviour detrimental to the party'.[48] At the same meeting on 1 December 1931, a *corpsier* named Hans-Heinrich Schulz, who had been Lienau's predecessor as chairman of the *DSt*, was, as a means of compensation to the *KSCV* for the aggravation caused them by Lienau, nominated and heartily endorsed for election to the post of elder of the *DSt*. As well as serving as chairman prior to Lienau's installation, Schulz had served (and continued to serve after stepping down) as head of the *DSt* Langemarck Fund. Langemarck had been the scene of a battle in the First World War in which many German student volunteers had lost their lives. It therefore took on an emotional as well as a militaristic and almost sacred symbolism to student groups of the late 1920s and 1930s. Schulz distinguished himself as a fund-raiser for the Langemarck Fund, and Krüger in his own new role as *DSt* chairman strongly supported Schulz's nomination for the post of *DSt Ältester* in the elections to be held in the following week.

Several of the *ADW* representatives were sceptical about replacing

Lienau with Krüger and the results of the elections held by the *DSt* on 8 December proved their premonitions to have been well founded. Schulz's candidacy for *Ältester* was not supported as promised, and in his place Krüger manipulated the election of Lienau to the position. The *ADW* representatives were understandably livid when they learned of Krüger's double dealing and raised the following questions. Had Krüger informed the *NSDStB* of Lienau's dismissal and the reasons for it? Were the *NSDStB Kreisleiter* aware that Krüger and the six other members of the *DSt* executive had supported the nomination of Schulz for the post of elder? As pointed out in the previously mentioned *ADW* publication *An die studentischen Verbände*, which dealt with the incident, how was it possible for Lienau to be elected an elder of the *DSt*, supported by the *NSDStB*, when only one week previous he had been removed from the executive and membership of the *DSt* by the *NSDStB* for dangerous misrepresentation of the Nazi Party? In effect Lienau was, through Krüger's manipulation, made an elder of an organisation of which he no longer was a member.[49]

It appears that Schulz had become the target for reprisals by the *NSDStB* against the *KSCV* for forcing the removal of Lienau from the *DSt*. But for Schulz, insult was added to injury. Krüger also orchestrated his removal from the position of head of the Langemarck Fund. This was the final straw for many of the federations, and Krüger quickly realised that if the Erfurt Agreement was to survive the *ADW Waffenstudententag* at Goslar, he would need to do some very extensive fence mending with the federations. His actions stood to discredit the *NSDStB* with all the federations, for if the *NSDStB* hierarchy was not prepared to abide by the tenets of an agreement which it had helped to conclude, or to bargain in good faith for less than one week, what trust could be placed in its political aspirations? The *KSCV* had refused to consider adoption of the Erfurt Agreement because of the problems encountered with Schirach and Lienau in Munich and it held firm to that conviction at a meeting with *NSDStB* executive members on 10 October 1931, which attempted to improve relations between the two groups. In an effort to curtail the growing enmity toward the *NSDStB*, Krüger met with the *Verhandlungsausschuss* of the *ADW* in Goslar the day prior to the *Waffentag* of 9–10 January 1932. His olive branch was the promise that Lienau would be removed from his new post as elder within the *DSt* and that those dislodged from their positions by the elections held on 8 December 1931, would be reinstated. The *ADW* representatives accepted this and presented it for the approval of the various federations at the conference the next day.[50]

THE *WAFFENSTUDENTENTAG* IN GOSLAR, 9-10 JANUARY 1932

The *Waffenstudententag* held at Goslar in January 1932 was every bit as heated and dramatic as that of the previous year at Erfurt. The second version of the Erfurt Agreement between various of the *ADW* federations and the *NSDStB* had been ratified by the majority of the *ADW*'s member federations, with the previously noted but not suprising exception of the *KSCV*, which had abstained. The two principal reasons were as follows. In the first instance the *KSCV* congress in accordance with its statutes was not empowered to make decisions for its various *SC*s or corps. But the more significant reason was the ongoing dispute between the corps, especially those in Munich, and the leadership of the *NSDStB*.

The general assembly of the *Waffentag* was informed by its special commission formed to deal with public relations for the *Waffenstudentent* federations, that political attitudes towards the *Mensur* and *Waffenstudententum* in general had improved in comparison with previous years, a trend which it was hoped would continue through the influence of the *Reichsjustizminister* who was an alumnus of the *Deutsche Burschenschaft*. Furthermore, with the growing interaction between the Nazis and the Italian Fascists, Mussolini had spoken in laudatory terms of the worthy training offered by German fencing fraternities to their members.[51] The *Deutsche Wehrschaft (DW)*, which the year before at Erfurt had demanded the immediate adoption of the Waidhofen Principle by the *ADW*, was featured again on the agenda of the 1932 conference by petitioning for readmission to the ranks of the *ADW*. Its representative pleaded the *Deutsche Wehrschaft*'s case on the grounds that the previous representative had not been empowered to withdraw the organisation's membership from the *ADW*. However, the *DW*'s case had been greatly weakened by an article published shortly before in its monthly periodical, which had been subsequently quoted by other federations, notably the *Deutsche Burschenschaft*. In the article the *ADW* was attacked for its short-sightedness and inertia regarding the tide of true German *völkischer* nationalism. The reaction of the Goslar conference was to demand that the *Deutsche Wehrschaft* indicate its sincerity of intentions by offering an apology and retraction of the previously published remarks. The *DW* bluntly refused, whereupon the conference unanimously adopted a motion calling for the formal withdrawal of the *DW* from the *Waffenstudententag* and the *ADW*.[52]

This then dealt with most of the inter-federation matters which needed to be discussed at Goslar, but the situation which had arisen regarding Schulz and the implanting of Lienau as an elder of the *DSt* had not been resolved and a number of the federations threatened to withdraw their signature from the Erfurt Agreement until such time as the *NSDStB* could satisfactorily explain Krüger's actions.[53] Disintegration of the *DSt* threatened to deprive the *NSDStB* of its powerful and central position within the German student community. Therefore on 10 January, the *NSDStB* issued a statement in appeasement, but which also merely repeated what Krüger had promised the *Verhandlungsausschuss* on 8 January – Lienau was to withdraw from the *DSt*. In addition Krüger endorsed the reinstatement of those representatives who had been removed from their positions in the *DSt* through his manipulations at the 8 December elections. Krüger had also manoeuvred the ejection of other members of the *DSt* executive from their positions along with Schulz, by abrogating the agreement reached on 1 December. Hilgenstock and Welte, both elders of the *DSt*, Gierlichs an executive member and Kraak the press officer, had all four been ousted in the 8 December elections of the *DSt*. It was their reinstatement to their former positions which the *NSDStB* underwrote in its attempts to damp down the potentially volatile situation with the *ADW* federations. But the retrieval of Schulz's position as head of the Langemarck Fund was not as easily accomplished. Krüger had made several accusations against Schulz which, if found substantiated by the *Oberster Ehrenrat* of the *DSt*, would bar him from resuming his office.[54] Despite frequent requests by Schulz that Krüger formally state the allegations so that they could be refuted, Krüger delayed and then, having stated them, assumed the charges proven and felt excused from honouring the agreement made in Goslar between himself and the *ADW Verhandlungsausschuss*.[55] His accusations were that Schulz was not capable of filling the position of elder satisfactorily because, while in office as head of the Langemarck Fund, Schulz had pursued an economic policy which was unacceptable to the *NSDStB*. The alleged proof was that he had neglected his responsibilities to the German National Association for the Care of War Graves and Krüger also insisted that there had been discrepancies regarding the accounts which were directly traceable to Schulz. On the basis of those allegations Krüger insisted that Schulz could not be reinstated.[56]

The *Verhandlungsausschuss* of the *ADW* established that the charges brought by Krüger were totally unfounded. Schulz had performed in an exemplary fashion while administering the Langemarck Fund, both as a fund-raiser and steward of its finances. His predecessor had managed in the year previous to Schulz's tenure to raise RM 6000, while Schulz in the two years which he held the position raised RM 100 000. Furthermore, correspondence from the German National Association for the Care of War Graves stated clearly that Schulz's relationship and work regarding their organisation were above criticism.[57] Further vindication was given Schulz when the books of the Langemarck Fund were inspected by Professor Dr Kloss and the *DSt* accountants, and both parties commented on the good order in which they found the accounts. The point which Krüger insisted upon terming an irregularity had in fact been explained and clarified to Krüger to his satisfaction by Hilgenstock prior to his first allegations against Schulz. In summation the *ADW Verhandlungsausschuss* stated that Krüger's attack on Schulz was the most tenacious and defamatory it had ever witnessed in a student dispute, and it awaited with interest for the results of the *NSDStB* leaders' meeting on 24 February 1932.[58]

Hilgenstock, presumably for his efforts in clearing Schulz of the charges made by Krüger, was caricatured and maligned in the February issue of *Deutsche Revolution* published by the Nazi press in Munich. Krüger wrote to him on 7 February, apologising for the insults and promised to take action against those of his people who were responsible. It later emerged from discussion that, following his letter, the incident was virtually ignored by Krüger.[59]

Following the *NSDStB* leaders' meeting on 24 February, Krüger requested that the *ADW Verhandlungsausschuss* meet the members of the *NSDStB* executive. Although sceptical as to whether anything other than further aggravation would result, the *ADW* representatives agreed to meet in the hope of perhaps finally having peace within the realm of the student federations. Krüger then, after having requested the meeting, informed the *Verhandlungsausschuss* that he refused to negotiate with them, as a representative of the Roman Catholic *Cartellverband der katholischen deutschen Studentenverbindungen (CV)* was a member of the committee. The representative, Welte, was one of the *DSt* elders whom Krüger had jettisoned in the December elections and whom he had been forced to reinstate. However, Krüger's objection went further than the personal level, for he went on to say that he would continue to refuse to negotiate with the *ADW* as long as the *CV* federation of fraternities was a member of the *ADW*. The *Verhandlungsausschuss* and the *ADW* in general resented Krüger's attempt to meddle and dictate to them regarding their internal matters, and on 6 March 1932, they replied to Krüger that in future he was to be considered and dealt with as a private person, holding no recognised rank or office, and that all pending invitations or authorisations by him were to be ignored.⁶⁰ Upon the suggestion of the *Verhandlungsausschuss*, Hilgenstock, Welte, Kraak and Gierlichs decided to resign their posts within the *DSt*, since if they were to continue, it would necessitate close contact with Krüger, with whom co-operation would be rendered next to impossible following the events of the previous three months.

Their resignations were to be tendered on 19 March, but before they were announced, Krüger launched a new attack, this time against Gierlichs, accusing him of breaching protocol and misrepresentation. On 9 March there had been a private function which *Reichspräsident* von Hindenburg and also five corps students had attended; one *corpsier* gave a short address on the politicisation of German universities. Krüger seized upon the theme of the address and the fact that the *corpsiers* wore their corps colours at the function, as a gross misrepresentation of German students to the *Reichspräsident*. He contended in a letter to *KSCV* representatives that it was incongruous to speak of the hard economic straits of students while attending a lavishly catered function.⁶¹ The burden of these charges, as with most of Krüger's invectives against members of the *ADW*, was unsubstantiated. None the less, he announced that he refused to work further with Gierlichs and appointed Schickert the representative for the *Vertreterkonvent der Turnerschaften an deutschen Hochschulen (VC)* in his place. In light of Krüger's hostile attitude towards them, the four men resigned their posts with the *DSt* and disseminated their adventures with the *NSDStB* to all the student federations through the *ADW* on 5 April 1932.⁶² Not surprisingly, Krüger also used the resignations of the former *DSt* officers. He adopted the tactic of not immediately announcing their resignations and filled the interim period with demands for their withdrawals, charging them with untrustworthiness, misrepresentation and factionalism. He later of course took credit for having purged them from the *DSt* after their resignations were finally announced.⁶³

This then effectively gave the *NSDStB* a free hand within the *DSt*, with no executive resistance from other organisations to question *NSDStB* policy or tactics. The fight had been won within less than a year, from Lienau's election as president of the *DSt* in July 1931 to the purge of the last dissenters in March 1932. Schulz had taken the brunt of the attack against the *KSCV*. The tactics adopted by Krüger had not been unlike those employed by Schirach in Munich when negotiating with the Munich *SC*, and the *KSCV* began to accept that German universities had indeed been politicised with *völkischer* ideology, no matter how much they might deplore the fact. It had also become apparent to them that the Nazis were willing to abide only by their own rules of self-interest, regardless of what traditions and proper practices might demand.

THE *DEUTSCHE STUDENTSCHAFT* CONFERENCE, KÖNIGSBERG, JULY 1932

By the conclusion of the Goslar *Waffenstudententag* in January 1932, very definite lines were being drawn within the student population in general and particularly within the *DSt*, with the result that factions formed among the various federations of fraternities regarding relationships with the *NSDStB*. By March 1932 the *NSDStB* managed to gain possession of all *DSt* executive posts. The *ADW* federations found that, between February and December of that year, they were each forced to take a stance in relation to the *NSDStB*. Was the Erfurt Agreement being honoured by the *NSDStB*, and was it being adhered to? More to the point, were the constitutions of the various federations suffering infractions through continued dealings with the *NSDStB*? The alternatives open to the federations were quite simply only three. First, to hope that things would work themselves out for the benefit of all federations within the *ADW*, thereby taking no definite action to resolve the tension which had grown up. Secondly, to co-operate with and encourage the *NSDStB* by joining the *völkische* national movement as the *Deutsche Wehrschaft* had chosen to do. Thirdly, to leave the *ADW*. This last path was the one eventually taken by the *KSCV*. Most of the other federations chose the immediately more comfortable option of a coalescence, which eventually led to their being swallowed up with the *Gleichschaltung* of 1933.[64]

The Königsberg conference of the *DSt* in July 1932 prefigured within the student context, much as the conference of the previous year at Graz had done, the course of events which was in store for the German populace as a whole following January 1933. In order to set the stage for the next act, the *NSDStB* leaders planned thoroughly and established a reconnaissance network to provide information to its strategists. The scheme attempted to plant a *NSDStB* member within each local organisation of the various federations, such as every *SC* in the case of the corps, and where possible in every individual fraternity. These *Vertrauensleute* were to report on all pertinent matters to a *NSDStB Reichsleitung* appointee who in turn served as an adviser to the leadership of the *NSDStB* on all matters concerning the specific federation for which he was responsible.⁶⁵ Whether or not this spy network was effective with regard to the outcome of the Königsberg conference, it is difficult to determine, but from the viewpoint of the *NSDStB* and the Nazi Party it certainly does not seem to have hindered their cause.

The ceremonial aspects of the conference differed considerably from previous years, reflecting the predominant ideology of the *DSt*'s *NSDStB* executive. Representatives from the military and industry attended, and an honour guard was provided by a contingent of the *Stahlhelm*. When a delegate protested at the omission of the traditional church service at the commencement of the conference, he was heckled into silence; echoing the Nazi battlecry incapsulated in Krüger's ex officio address.⁶⁶ However, Krüger's address encompassed a great deal more than a mere call to arms. In accordance with Nazi doctrine, he called for the immediate replacement of the democratic parliamentary system within the *DSt* by the *Führerprinzip* and charged the incoming executive of the *DSt* to make the necessary administrative preparations in order to implement the new structure.⁶⁷

Krüger's restructuring of the *DSt* also brought about other more fundamental changes in its organisation. Upon leaving office, the *DSt Führer* was to install his own successor, who was to be a candidate whom he selected and the national executive had approved. Regional *DSt* leaders likewise were to recommend their own successors to the national *DSt Führer* for approval before installing them. In a similar fashion local *Studentenschaft* leaders were required to select and induct their successors after approval from their regional *DSt* leaders.⁶⁸ According to reports, a well timed telegram from the newly elected Nazi government of Mecklenburg-Schwerin added greatly to the status of Krüger, and with very little debate the Königsberg conference passed the resolution with 155 voters to 3, with 25 abstentions, thereby adopting through democratic methods the implementation of the *Führerprinzip*.⁶⁹

With the bitterness of the *NSDStB*'s attacks against Schulz which had been led by Krüger and the incidents of the previous year involving Lienau and Schirach still fresh in their memories, the corps of the *KSCV* federation chose to maintain their traditional neutrality regarding the Königsberg resolution.⁷⁰ In his account of the Königsberg conference, the *KSCV* chairman, Gunther Kraaz, makes the observation that student politics as defined by the *DSt*'s *NSDStB* leadership had in actuality changed to party politics, dealing not with matters pertaining to students within the realm of higher education, but rather with issues of political ideology.⁷¹ He later wrote in the *KSCV* journal:

For all these reasons we do not claim to be able to create a political group or even a political pressure group out of a student federation. History is our law and guide. In recognition of our own limitations we perceive it as sufficient when we impress upon our young members their duty to meet their obligations to society and the state and indicate to them such large political organisations which are able to do so.[72]

The neutral middle path of the *KSCV* became continually more difficult to follow. Rather than filling their historical position as arbiters of conduct within the realm of the student fraternities and university community in general, the corps came more and more to be seen as uncooperative, outmoded and anti-modern: the decline from being emulated to being spurned had been effectively set in motion.

THE BAD KÖSEN CONGRESS, 1932

The bank closures of July 1931 and the unemployment figures approaching six million in 1932 reflected economic problems which were felt within the *KSCV* as well. The number of students in pursuit of higher education dropped during the same period and with it the number of active members in the corps. As a result, several corps found themselves either directly or indirectly compelled through economic pressures to close or fuse with other corps.[73] In an effort to economise, the date of the annual congress which was usually held in the spring of each year at Bad Kösen, was set back until October of 1932, and the venue was altered to Göttingen in order to save the expense of transporting the presiding *SC* officers and related materials to the Rudelsburg.

The additional several months, along with the intense interaction with the *DSt* and the *ADW* as already mentioned above, and incidents precipitated by the *NSDStB*, furnished the 1932 Bad Kösen congress with a rather weighty agenda, one of the most profound since the formation of the federation in 1848. It was noted by the congress that the *KSCV*, as the oldest and most unified of the federations, had continued to co-operate in the promotion of intra-federation agreements, often at the expense of its own interests. The Erlangen Agreement, which had brought the fencing fraternities together and had made the formation of the *ADW* possible, had been due predominantly to the efforts on the part of the *KSCV*. The *ADW* was originally formed to deal with technical questions within the sphere of *Waffenstudententum*. Its growth through the enlisting of a large number of the smaller federations meant that the newer and equally enfranchised federations had caused the *ADW* to drift away from the original ideas of the Marburg Agreement.[74] As noted in the section dealing with the formation of the *ADW*, the *KSCV* had been adamant that any organisation to which it belonged was not in any way empowered to enact any legislation which would in any way bind either the *KSCV*, the various *SC* s of the *Verband*, or an individual corps.[75] The *ADW*, through the adoption of the Erfurt Agreement with the *NSDStB* by the majority of its member federations in the spring and summer of 1931, left the *KSCV* in a position where a major decision had to be taken. Either the statutes of the *KSCV* which clearly stated that the federation was not to engage in party political relationships had to be contravened, or the *ADW* s adoption of the Erfurt Agreement would have to be ignored, thereby placing the *KSCV* in an isolated position regarding the other federations. Indeed, both the *KSCV* and *WSC* corps had asked at the Goslar *Waffentag* in January 1932 for the removal of the recently established *Schiedsgericht* stating that questions of honour had become rhetorical dodging and more a clashing of paragraphs than the engaging of sabres. The tendency should be towards a court of honour and the establishing of grounds rather than evasive advocacy.[76]

The *Waffentag* did not accept the proposal as viable. However, the idea did not die out then and there. Quite the contrary. The feeling remained very much alive within the *KSCV*. The federation increasingly resented being drawn continually into issued by such organisations as the *DSt*, and *ADW*, which had appreciably altered their *raison d'être* since their inception. Quite naturally the sentiment only grew stronger with the passing of months and the occurrence of events. The result was that the Bad Kösen congress of 1932 unanimously adopted a motion for withdrawal of the *KSCV* from the *ADW*.[77] The *DSt* had been shattered because of the behaviour exhibited by *NSDStB* members, and, as the *NSDStB* was officially recognised by the *ADW* through the Erfurt Agreement, past performance strongly indicated that contention would soon recurr; this time within the *ADW*, and the *KSCV* wanted no part of it. In the same spirit, the congress indicated its unanimous support of the resolution adopted by the *Deutsche Hochschullehrer* at their seventh *Deutsche Hochschultag*, which requested the depoliticisation of the higher educational institutes and the end of party political feuds, in order that all German students might have the benefit of returning to a neutral position regarding party politics.[78]

Withdrawal from the *ADW* meant the adoption of an isolationist policy on the part of the *KSCV*. The other federations of corps, the

WSC, RSC, and NSC, initially had all ratified the Erfurt Agreement, thereby leaving the KSCV on its own. In an attempt to gain back some of the ground lost during its affiliation with the ADW, it was suggested at the congress that a general *Ehrenordnung* be established for all the KSCV corps, and the matter, true to form, was referred until the extraordinary congress scheduled for January 1933, in order that it could be discussed by the individual corps.[79] The ADW system of *Waffenringe* cartels had worked by the adoption of the extant local *Ehrenordnungen* rather than through the implementation of a uniform codex for all the *Waffenringe*. The new proposal called for the introduction of a general code which would be adopted by all SC's, whereas previously certain technical aspects regarding affairs of honour and their carrying out could differ from one SC to the next, depending upon local eccentricities. In the end, traditional practices were continued, with the only real change being that KSCV corps would henceforth fence *Mensuren* solely among themselves.

ISOLATIONISM

In accordance with the decision taken at the Kösener congress to withdraw from the ADW, the Kösener executive (*Vorort*) made a detailed statement on 5 November 1932.[80] The central reasons given in the KSCV memorandum were that recent resolutions passed by the ADW contravened the Marburg Agreement and ran counter to the statutes of the KSCV. The new ADW legislation empowered it to make decisions arrived at by the confederation as a whole binding on the individual member federations and their fraternities, whether or not they were in agreement with the decisions and even if those decisions violated their constitutions. As pointed out previously, the KSCV was, from the date of its constitution and its foundation in the period of 1848 to 1850, self-determined as neutral, and it purposely absented itself from party politics. The Erfurt Agreement of 1931, between the ADW and the NSDStB, was party-political inasmuch as the NSDStB was a political organisation. By entering into negotiations and an accord with the NSDStB and by adhering to the Erfurt Agreement, the ADW and the KSCV, as an ADW member federation, effectively became involved in party-political affairs. The ADW had been founded in order to provide a forum for the discussion of questions and technical problems pertaining to *Waffenstudententum*, not for the pursuit of political goals at institutions of higher education.[81] The memorandum went on to mention the attempt, through the *ADW* resolutions, to force all fraternities of the *ADW* federations to belong to the *Waffenring* of their local academic community. This would establish the *ADW* as a supra-federational body and allow the *ADW* to dictate policy both to the federations and to their fraternities regarding the relationships and agreements which they might enter into, regardless of their own wishes. The *KSCV* had stated from the outset that the *ADW* was in no way to have the powers of a supra-federational body, and therefore it could not condone the legislation or the spirit which it indicated. The communique closed by drawing attention to several errors made in the interpretation of the *ADW* by-laws by the *ADW* executive. Suggestions as to how the problems might be rectified included the implementation of several structural changes, such as proportional representation for *ADW* federations at its conferences based upon one vote per thousand members.[82] The memorandum was forwarded to the *ADW* executive, thereby giving notice of the *KSCV* withdrawing from membership and also affording time for discussion of the recommendations before the *Waffenstudententag* of the following month.

The *Waffenstudententag* at Goslar on 16–18 December 1932, was the second conference of the *ADW* in 1932 and the second held at Goslar, thereby departing from the traditional practice of holding an annual conference in different localities. it was faced with a smaller but no less poignant agenda than on previous occasions. Again the *Deutsche Wehrschaft (DW)* featured prominently in the proceedings by petitioning for readmission to the *ADW*, having complied with the previous *Waffentag* ruling that it retract the insults which it had published in reference to the *ADW*. The application was not endorsed with any great enthusiasm on the part of the conference, and a decision was deferred. The eventual decision found against immediate readmission of the *DW* to the *ADW*.[83]

The conference noted the *KSCV* notice of withdrawal from the confederation issued by the *Kösener Vorort*. The communique affirmed the *KSCV* acceptance of the concept of satisfaction and its approval of the *ADW* court of honour. However, the *KSCV* requested that serious attention be paid to its memorandum of 5 November 1932 which outlined reforms necessary for the *ADW* if it were to remain true to its original *raison d'être*.[84] Despite the *KSCV* criticism of the *Schiedsgericht*, the *ADW* strongly defended it in both principle and practice as an effective method of dealing with matters of honour which were not serious enough to warrant the actual crossing of blades.[85] This argument only served to reinforce the decision taken by the *KSCV* to withdraw from its affiliation with the *ADW* and to continue the principles of the Marburg Agreement to which it had originally subscribed.[86]

THE EXTRAORDINARY BAD KÖSEN CONGRESS OF 1933

As a result of the change in political climate, and with the objective of the *KSCV* withdrawing from any further groups or affiliations which might compromise its traditions and tenets, the *KSCV Vorort* of Greifswald, under the leadership of Dr Karl Friedrich Mohr of Corps Guestphalia zu Greifswald, called an extraordinary congress of the *KSCV* to enable the corps to regroup in preparation for the apparently independent stand which appeared to lie ahead.[87] As Mohr later stated in his memoirs regarding the congress:

> To make it even clearer one has to say that the corps did not want to be bothered by political questions, or by questions regarding university politics. But on the other hand they insisted that an all encompassing independent students' association would, and could, be created.[88]

It was decided at the congress to dissolve the special committee which had served as the department of external affairs with other federations and organisations, thereby giving the *KSCV* an official isolationist stance. Furthermore, the individual *SC*'s were to handle their own affairs with other local fraternities as they saw fit, thereby giving them much the same role as they had held prior to the formation of the *KSCV* in 1848. The hope was expressed that each *corpsier* would conduct himself in accordance with the guidelines and decisions of *KSCV* tradition. This followed expression by the majority of *SC*'s against the adoption of a general code of honour for the *KSCV*, on the grounds that subjective judgement on the part of the individual *corpsier* should determine whether or not his honour had been damaged and if satisfaction should be demanded. The feeling was voiced that *corpsstudentische Anschauungen* were contradicted when an injured party did not have the right, as in a case subject to the *ADW Schiedsgericht* to immediately demand satisfaction for the injury suffered. This course of action was denied by the implementation of the *ADW Schiedsgericht* and was a central factor in the decision of the *KSCV* to withdraw from the *ADW*.[89] No final or far-reaching decisions were taken as any substantive changes would also have to be discussed by the corps' alumni association (*VAC*) of the *KSCV*; since the congress adopted the motion of the Heidelberg *SC*, which recommended that the *KSCV* go into isolation, there appeared to be no great urgency in consolidating internal federation matters.[90]

1933 AND THE *GLEICHSCHALTUNG*

On the same day as the *KSCV* concluded its extraordinary congress, 15 January 1933, the Nazi Party won the election in Lippe, shortly to be followed on 30 January by Adolf Hitler's taking office as *Reichskanzler*. On 5 February, that is to say three months after the *KSCV* giving notice, the withdrawal of the *KSCV* from the *ADW* took effect, and any relationships which the *KSCV* corps were to have with fraternities of other federations came under the jurisdiction of the local *SC*'s for both negotiation and maintenance. But there soon appeared a brightening on *Waffenstudententum*'s previously rather gloomy horizon, for in April 1933, the government of Bavaria lifted the *Mensurverbot* and the Prussian legal profession was instructed to ignore cases involving *Mensur* fencing as long as normal safety precautions and equipment were employed by the combatants.[91] Furthermore, Oskar Stäbel succeeded Gerd Rühle in the post of national leader, *Bundesführer*, of the *NSDStB* in February 1933. As a *Landsmannschaft* member, it became apparent that Stäbel wished not only to bring about the adoption of the principles of satisfaction in the *NSDStB*, but also to make those principles and membership in a recognised student fraternity, mandatory for all students.[92] This was given approval by Gerhard Krüger of the *DSt* who stated in March 1933 that 'the executive of the *DSt* acknowledged, without question, the great value of the German fraternity federations.'[93] The virtual legalisation of the *Mensur* in April appeared to indicate government support for Stäbel's ideas and also that the new regime was interested in restoring the student fraternities to at least a portion of the privileged status which they had once enjoyed. But the *Mensur* was a very small part of the legal attention which German students were to receive prior to the summer of 1933. On 7 April, the *Gesetz zur Wiederherstellung des Berufsbeamtentums* (Restoration of Tenured Civil Servants) was adopted by the government and called for expulsion from the public service, including colleges and universities, of all persons having Jewish ancestry. The line of demarcation was one Jewish grandparent. On 12 April, Bernhard Rust, in his position in the Ministry of Culture, helped to enact the Prussian Student Ordinance, which was soon adopted, in many cases verbatim, by the other *Länder* of the *Reich*: Bavaria two weeks later and Baden in the following month. The net result was the abolition of representative democracy within student governments and the giving of authority to the local student leaders.[94] This was followed by a law which called for the enforcing of a *numerus clausus*, allowing only 1.5 per cent non-Aryan freshmen and requiring that the total of non-Aryan students not exceed 5 per cent of the total student population.[95] As an example, under the stipulations enacted in Baden, 20 and 24 May 1933, the student body was defined as comprising all fully registered students of German descent and mother tongue regardless of the citizenship they held. At immatriculation each student was required to give a declaration that to the best of his knowledge both his paternal and maternal grandparents were of pure German descent. The decision of whether or not to accept the statement (and the applicant as a member of the student body) was left to the discretion of each *Studentenschaft Führer* or his representative. Appeals might be heard by a special committee. The structure of each *Studentenschaft* followed very closely the form which Krüger implemented for the *DSt*. Each *Studentenschaft* leader was appointed for one year by his predecessor, subject to the approval of the *DSt* national leadership. During his term in office, each *Studentenschaft Führer (StFu)* was assisted by two elders, who served in an advisory capacity, and the officers of the local *Studentenschaft* whom he appointed.[96] He made the decisions and was responsible for all policies and actions entered into by the student body during his term. One elder was required to be from the *Bündische Kammer* and the other a past leader of the student body. The *Bündische Kammer* was comprised of representatives, each elected from one of the student fraternities, who were required to be fully registered students as well as *NSDStB* members.[97] This meant that, if the fraternities wished to be represented within local student affairs, at least one of their members would of necessity be forced to belong to the *NSDStB* in order for them to qualify for a seat in the chamber. Although for certain federations such as the *Deutsche Wehrschaft* this aspect of the new edict made little if any difference, the apolitical traditions of the *KSCV* were again placed in jeopardy.

The last organ of the new student legislative structure mentioned in the decree was that of the student assembly to which representatives of the student body were to be admitted. The function of the assembly was the instruction of students in the work and goals of the student body.[98] In theory, this implementation of the *Führer* Principle gave the student fraternities both representation and a voice in the *Bündische Kammer*, but their function in fact was limited to that of 'advising and supporting'[99] rather than holding any legislative power. The result was that each *Studentenschaft* was to be run very much according to the whims of its *Studentenschaft Führer*.

However, the *Gleichschaltung* did not stop after reorganising only the *DSt* and student governments in line with the *Führer* Principle and Nazi doctrine. On 21 April, Stäbel and Krüger ordered that all student organisations allow their members to seek membership in either the Nazi Party, the *NSDStB*, or the *SA*. Any dissenting group which refused to comply with or, to encourage new and open support of, Nazi sponsored activities was threatened with exclusion from all academic celebrations.[100] Additional edicts in line with Nazi tenets served to tighten the *NSDStB* hold of the fraternities and gradually removed the possibility of the fraternities not falling in line with party wishes unless they chose to disband. In the midst of this reorganisation and realignment of the fraternities, the *ADW* held an extraordinary conference, again at Goslar, the resolutions of which greatly affected all student fraternities, regardless of whether or not they were members of the *ADW* confederation.[101]

THE EXTRAORDINARY *WAFFENSTUDENTENTAG*, GOSLAR, 20 MAY 1933

Prior to *Gleichschaltung* the student federations were not greatly affected by the change in government which occurred in January 1933. However, with the general implication of Nazi doctrine at all levels of German society, the combination of political pressure and the momentum of rapid social conformity swept many of the federations into alignment with the precepts of the ruling party. The *ADW* was no exception, and when eighteen of its previous twenty federations met in May 1933, it was for the sole purpose of adopting and enacting a new constitution and code of honour for its member federations, which was to take effect on 1 July of that year. The new *Ehrengesetz* was to be binding for the fraternities of all *ADW* federations and thereby give them all one uniform code of honour. According to the new code, each individual *Waffenstudent* was to decide if and when his honour had been sullied and be prepared to give or demand satisfaction as the situation might dictate. As seen earlier, this point was essentially one of the major recommendations made by the *KSCV* only a few months earlier at the time of its withdrawal from the *ADW*. However, the context within which honour was to be interpreted under the new code was considerably altered. The rubric of the code stated that the concept of honour for a *Waffenstudent* was grounded in the living consciousness of his duty to the German nation and all members of the German community.[102] This extended the concept of an individual's honour to *völkisch* honour whereby the *Waffenstudent* was obliged to defend what he interpreted as the honour of his *Volk*. There was little doubt as to who qualified as a *Waffenstudent* for the code went on to state:

> Recognition as a federation of *Waffenstudenten* will be granted when it can be verified that the constitution of the federation in question agrees with the *ADW* code of honour, that is to say that there are neither persons with Jewish ancestry nor Jewish relatives through inter-marriage nor Freemasons among its members and that the *ADW* constitution inclusive of the code of honour is recognised as binding for all its chapters.[103]

These last two points of the new code of *völkische* honour and the exclusions of Jews, 'non-Aryans', and Freemasons brought into force the precepts of the Waidhofen Principle which the *Deutsche Wehrschaft* had demanded that the *ADW* adopt and enforce in 1931. The Waidhofen Principle as introduced in Austria denied Jews the right of satisfaction at arms or membership in a fencing fraternity. The new *ADW* regulations, while not stipulating this directly, did circuitously accomplish the same thing by refusing Jews membership within any *satisfaktionsfähige* fraternity, and thereby denying Jews the means by which to demand or give satisfaction to other students. The individual federations were left to determine for themselves the method and terms for expelling any of their members cited as unacceptable under a new code. In this, as with several other issues we have seen earlier, certain of the federations were more zealous than others in their enforcement of the new measures. At the conclusion of the discussions, the motion was put and unanimously adopted by the conference. Federations which belonged to the *ADW* as of 20 May 1933 would automatically have their membership continued without further approval being necessary provided they submitted a declaration by 30 June, which had been ratified by their respective conferences, acknowledging acceptance of the amended *ADW* constitution.[104] Both Krüger and Stäbel attended the conference, and, following the adoption of the above motion, Stäbel made a speech full of praise for the concepts of honour and the strong front provided by both the *Stahlhelm* and his own organisation, the *NSDStB*. He ended his address by stating that as the Führer's representative he took great joy in the fact the National Socialist Revolution had found a gateway to the circles of *Waffenstudententum* and that he would report back to Hitler on what he had seen and the new constitution which had been adopted.[105] The rift between the *KSCV* and *ADW* had widened yet again and an attitude of neutral isolation continued to appeal to *corpsier* both young and old.

THE BAD KÖSEN CONGRESS OF MAY 1933

Having withdrawn from membership, the *KSCV* naturally was not represented at the *ADW* conference. As a whole, the *KSCV* and its member corps, in accordance with their statutes, could not adopt or enforce any of the party-political tenets encompassed within the new *ADW Bundesgesetz*. Following the Tolerance Principle upon which the *KSCV* had founded its constitution, individual corps members were not restricted from holding any personal political or religious doctrine outside the fellowship of their fraternity. With the momentum which swept the Nazis into power, a number of very active and dedicated corps members became involved with the Nazi movement as members of the *NSDStB*, the *SA*, or the *NSDAP* proper. As with most sections of German society following January 1933, the number continued to grow and would be impossible to determine, given the information presently available. This minority, enthusiastic over the advent of the new Reich and encouraged by the legal reforms regarding the universities and the *Gleichschaltung* of the *DSt*, hoped to move the *KSCV* into closer proximity to the tenets of Nazi ideology. In mid-April of 1933, Mohr, the *KSCV Vorort* chairman, was advised, by a number of what he refers to in his memoirs as the more reactionary of Nazi corps members, that if he did not join the party, at least *pro forma*, they would engineer a number of calamities at the forthcoming *KSCV* congress. According to them, he alone would be responsible for bringing to an end his own previously irreproachable leadership of the *KSCV*.[106] Mohr eventually joined the Nazi Party in late April, but he mentions elswhere in his memoirs that he began to regret his actions even later the same day, for when he attended a meeting of party members of long-standing and listened to their comments he was moved to write: 'I found them basically repulsive, their pathos hollow, their ideas unrealistic and confused.'[107] He also mentions that not long before the congress he and Kraaz, the previous year's *KSCV Vorort* chairman, met Krüger and Hederich. Hederich was a member of the *Deutsche Burschenschaft* and the *NSDStB* representative for dealing with student fraternities. In that same month Hess had established a commission to deal with the federations and any related questions. Krüger, Hederich and Stäbel had been charged with the task of assisting the student corporations to realise the Nazi tenets associated with *Gleichschaltung*. At the subsequent meeting with Krüger and Hederich, according to Mohr there was little discussion and the two *KSCV* representatives were informed that their federation would be required to make certain changes in order to come into line with party wishes. This entailed the *KSCV* returning to the membership of the *ADW*, with the adoption of the guidelines incorporated in the Tenured Civil Servants legislation as set down in the *ADW Bundesgesetz*, thereby excluding all students having Jewish descent or relatives.[108] Mohr noted that while exceptions could be made for the descendants of former servicemen and civil servants who might otherwise have been categorised as Jewish, there was no such loophole available to those with Jewish relatives or spouses. He made the observation that much of the attack levelled by Hederich was based solely upon the old animosity of the *Deutsche Burschenschaft* towards the *KSCV* and that Hederich used his new position to continue *DB* prejudices inherited from the previous century. As Mohr later reflected, 'It had nothing to do with National Socialism or the like as was illustrated later on. Such perceptions existed only on paper and not uniformly anywhere else. As Göring later said, "I will decide who is Jewish!" '[109] This gives quite an insight into the manipulation and implementation of Nazi tenets. Idealism was used time and time again as a stalking horse for settling personal scores and the enforcement of individual prejudices. A uniform doctrine existed only in theory. Mohr relates that, following the meeting, he was fairly optimistic that nothing would come of the incident, as he felt that anything as ridiculous as the *Versipptenfrage* introduced by Hederich regarding the exclusion of persons having Jewish spouses or relatives could not be taken seriously.[110]

Mohr was not to have much rest, for only a few days later he was called to Frankfurt, where he was informed that certain of the Nazi faction within the *KSCV* were planning to seize control of the approaching congress. He was assured, however, by certain of the corps alumni, who were well connected within the Nazi movement, that they would obtain an authorisation from the party leadership which would thwart any such disruption of the congress.[111] As if this did not give Mohr enough to keep himself occupied until the congress, he was, only a few days later, informed of a notice which had been published in the

Völkischer Beobachter calling for all National Socialist corps members to meet at the Landswehr Casino in Berlin. The recently published agenda for the *KSCV* congress had sparked this rather fiery and heated meeting. A *corpsier* had apparently given notice to the *Kösener Vorort* that he wished to put a motion to the congress for the sharpening of regulations regarding corps membership and more particularly the membership of Jews. The instigators of the meeting at the Landswehr Casino were incensed that the *Vorort* had relegated the proposed motion to come under 'any other business'. To the organisers of the meeting, the fact that it was a private motion and therefore did not qualify for consideration under any other heading according to *KSCV* statutes, was totally irrelevant. To them the motion concerned an issue of such importance that it should be given precedence over all others. Mohr noted that at the meeting nothing was said about the obligations of corps members towards the *Volksgemeinschaft*, but it was clearly expressed that most of the Nazi members present felt that the corps had shown negligence in not moving to embrace the Nazi movement. One alumnus present demanded that the *Führer* Principle be adopted and implemented at the approaching congress and that the whole of *Corpsstudententum* should come under a single leader. Several possible candidates of long standing, both with the *KSCV* and the *NSDAP*, were put forwards for the non-existent new leadership position.[112] After these brief and exaggerated proceedings, the meeting digressed into the hurling of invectives and slogans rather than a useful discussion.

While in Berlin, Mohr took the opportunity to seek the counsel of Secretary of State Landfried and Dr Pfundtner, Secretary of State to the Minister of the Interior, Frick. Both Landfried and Pfundtner were corps alumni and gave Mohr immediate consultation and assured him that, to the best of their knowledge, the attitude of the government towards the *KSCV* was not hostile. Furthermore, reorganisation of the *KSCV* would not be required unless it became obvious that open opposition to the regime was prevalent; but he could rest assured that no disruption of the Bad Kösen congress had government approval.[113] Fortified with the assurances of two Secretaries of State, Mohr felt relatively secure and continued with the preparations for the forthcoming congress. A special train was made available for the nearly 1000 participants who travelled from Bad Kösen to the cathedral in nearby Naumburg to celebrate the beginning of the congress on 31 May 1933. This was to symbolise the transition of the *KSCV* into the new Reich. In the church service, emphasis was placed on the great role played by corps members of the *KSCV* in recent German history, and the address given by Mohr indicated a conscious attempt to blend the old and the new.[114]

On the day preceding the congress the Nazi faction of corps members met and discussed what changes would be possible and necessary in order to bring the *KSCV* into line with the Nazi state. It was proposed that an amendment to remove the apolitical nature of the *KSCV* as set down in Paragraph 43 of its statutes should be of primary importance. However, the discussion broke down over an acceptable alternative wording and whether or not Hitler's name or merely the Nazi Party should be incorporated into the new text.[115] Other issues deemed worthy of immediate attention were the exclusion of Jews from the membership, implementation of the *Führer* Principle, close co-operation and work with the *NSDStB* and *DSt*, and the enrolment of all *Kösener* corps students in the *SA*, the return of the *KSCV* to the *ADW*, and the installation of *Oberpräsident* Brückner, who had been selected by a majority of the Nazi members present, as the *Führer* of the *KSCV*.[116] But this last proposal was to prove more easily suggested that enacted, for shortly before the scheduled meeting of the congress it became apparent that several persons had been empowered by various offices within the leadership of the *NSDAP* to preside over the proceedings, thus casting doubt on the candidacy of Brückner. It was soon established that the same authority had been given to Dr Heringhaus by Rainer of the *NSDAP Verbindungsstab*, and to *SS-Sturmführer* Biermann through the joint efforts of Krüger, Stäbel, Hederich and Secretary of State Lammers. The *KSCV Vorort* hurriedly attempted to establish which of the three candidates was actually empowered to preside. The meeting was delayed in order that telegrams could be sent to the *Reichskanzler*, the *Reichspräsident*, the Minister of the Interior and the *NSDStB*.

During the wait for replies, an *SS* member in full uniform threatened those in the assembly hall and the surrounding area with the ultimatum that should the appropriate reorganisation of the *KSCV* not take place, those gathered there would be dealt with by a column of the *SA* which was already on its way from Berlin. Biermann attempted to establish order by calling a meeting of all Nazi and *Stahlhelm* members, so that he could present his authorisation to assume control. However, his efforts to take charge were not overly successful, and Dr Blunck, also a party member of long standing, was called upon to moderate the proceedings and took charge. It was decided that representatives should go to Berlin in order to present the situation in person. The following day they met Krüger, Hederich and Secretaries of State Lammers, Keppler and Korner, with the result that Lammers empowered *Landeshauptmann* and party member Otto to carry out the changes necessary to reorganise the *KSCV*.[117]

On 1 June Mohr also corresponded with several government ministers outlining the dilemma and requesting a clarification regarding the three approved party candidates.[118] He also published a statement that he would continue to act in his role as *Vorort* chairman until a clarification of the situation could take place and it was possible for him to recall the congress. Copies in telegraph form were forwarded to von Hindenburg, Hitler, Frick and the *Reichsleitung* of both the *NSDAP* and the *NSDStB*.[119]

After receiving a directive and verbal indication of official support for Brückner as the future *Führer* of the *KSCV*, Otto entered into liaison with Mohr, but the following telegram arrived from Berlin to put a very different light on the matter:

Am appointed *Führer* of *Kösener Corpsstudenten* by Secretary of State Lammers, Körner and Krüger of the *Deutsche Studentenschaft*. Await unquestioned following in light of mutual high goals. Dissolve *Vorort* office immediately.

Blunck[120]

Otto and Blunck then met in Hamburg on 20 June to discuss the transformation of the *KSCV*. Otto was accompanied by Krüger and Hederich to represent *NSDAP* interests, and Blunck was attended by Kraaz and Heringhaus, whom he had, in accordance with the *Führer* Principle, appointed as his assistants. Otto made several strong suggestions, verging upon the imperative, regarding the personnel and procedure which he felt Blunck should employ in the new hierarchy; notably the replacing of Blunck's newly appointed assistants Kraaz and Herringhaus by persons of Otto's acquaintance. The result was that Blunck managed to cut the ground from under Otto by drawing to the attention of the *Reichsleitung* that there was some question as to the regularity of Otto's corps membership in the past and thereby calling into question Otto's credibility for the tasks that lay ahead.[121] Blunck was thereby approved as uncontested leader, and a new era began for the *KSCV*.

The relationship between the *KSCV* and the Nazi Party had reversed. Instead of contesting for political neutrality, which was their traditional position, the corps found themselves with a Nazi executive bent upon implementing the *Gleichschaltung* and adhering to National Socialist tenets rather than promoting corps traditions and attitudes. But would Blunck be able to keep the corps in check? It is this relationship and the interaction of the various federations within the new regime which will be examined next.

4 Blunck as *Führer* of the *KSCV*

At their meeting of 20 June 1933, Otto demanded that Blunck conduct a thorough investigation into the events which had taken place behind the scenes in Bad Kösen the previous month. The enlightening details were then to be circulated to all *KSCV* corps and *SC*'s.[1] Blunck agreed in principle to Otto's requests but asked for time to sort out certain details; in particular Otto's demand that he replace his newly appointed assistants, Werner Heringhaus and Günther Kraaz. On 29 June Otto was instructed by official letter that any criticism on his part of Blunck's method of carrying out his new office as *KSCV Führer* would be considered by the *Reichsleitung* as mutinous and contrary to party interests. In addition, the letter informed Otto that he was relieved of any further power to act in the matter. It appears that the meeting with Otto was actually superfluous, for records show that Blunck and his aides met with Mohr and his assistant, Ulrich Wetzel, on the day previous to their discussions with Otto, in order to establish what business remained to be completed by the *KSCV Vorort* and to draught the constitutional changes required to satisfy Nazi doctrine.[2] The subsequent amendments and organisational changes which the *KSCV* corps were expected to adopt, were made known to the *SC*'s and *CC*'s through circulars written predominantly by Blunck, although his assistants did from time to time also author portions of the directives. These circulars were released as Blunck felt necessary, averaging a fortnightly distribution and reached nearly fifty in number by the time that Blunck left his position as leader of the *KSCV*. The first two of Blunck's circulars were published in the *KSCV* periodical, the *Deutsche Corpszeitung*, of June 1933. They outlined, with some rather judicious pruning of the facts, the details of Blunck's appointment as leader of the *KSCV* and the *Reichsleitung*'s endorsement of his taking office.

Perhaps more interesting though, is the reproduction of a letter dated 3 June 1933, from Hitler's Secretary of State in the Chancellery, Hans Heinrich Lammers, who on behalf of the *Reichskanzler* acknowledged receipt of a telegram from the *KSCV* on 1 June. The telegram indicated the offer of a monetary contribution towards the government's efforts in alleviating the distress of *deutsche Volksgenossen*.³ This appears to have been the trump card which Blunck played to assure his certification by Hitler and the *Reichsleitung*. It is corroborated by a short article written by Kraaz which appeared in the same group of circulars reproduced for the *KSCV*. Kraaz recounted that on 7 June 1933, Blunck had been received by Lammers at the Reich Chancellery.⁴ While seated on the terrace, Lammers informed Blunck that the *KSCV* was to renew its former membership in the *Allgemeine Deutsche Waffenring (ADW)* and to implement the *ADW* Aryan membership regulations. Hitler eventually joined them on the terrace, at which point Blunck presented Hitler with a gift of 5000 Marks on behalf of the *KSCV*, which the *Reichskanzler* turned over to the Minister of Culture, Berhard Rust, for the aid of needy students.⁵ Hitler apparently spoke to Blunck for an hour and a half, the essence of which is quoted by Gerhard Neuenhoff. 'We could promise the world ten years of peace if it were possible for today's generation to overcome the history with which it is encumbered. The situation is like that of Moses, who, after having led his people to the promised land, found they had to wait before entering.'⁶ The audience with Hitler gave Blunck a virtually uncontestable seal of approval and thereby consolidated his position as *Führer* of the *KSCV*. In light of this it is not at all surprising that he later was able to have Otto's authorisation terminated following their disagreeable meeting on 20 June.

One of the primary criteria in the selection of new persons for leadership positions of the fraternity federations was that of Nazi *alte Kämpfer*; that is to say, holders of a party membership number which was issued prior to 30 Jaunary 1933. This went some way to ensure that persons appointed to positions of authority within the student federations were not merely opportunists but conscientious party members. Indeed, the majority were more interested in promoting party interests and ideology, and thereby their own careers in the new regime, than they were in fostering the heritage of their own particular federation. Mohr, who served as chairman of the *KSCV Vorort* prior to Blunck's verified appointment as its *Führer*, was relieved of his duties, presumably on the technicality of his membership number.⁷ He had never been enthusiastic or terribly sympathetic to the Nazi cause, and as mentioned previously, he had joined the party only after being threatened with the disruption of the annual congress over which he was to preside. But Mohr apparently was called before the *USCHLA* or Nazi court for party discipline, which would seem to indicate more than his merely being discredited. In the spring of 1933 the Nazi Party had moved against Freemasons as well as Jews. The *Völkischer Beobachter* of 26 May 1933, carried an article entitled 'No Freemasons in the NSDAP' and the *Reichs-USCHLA* cautioned party organisations that Freemasons were to be excluded and removed from party membership.[8] In his memoirs, Mohr mentioned that his father was a Freemason and this, coupled with the alterations to the *KSCV* statutes brought into force by Blunck and Mohr's less than zealous attitude toward the party, could well have been what completed the case against him.

In his Circular Number 2 of 7 June, Blunck indicated that amendments would be needed to bring the *KSCV* statutes into line with party doctrine – in particular Paragraph 43 which dealt with the traditional apolitical disposition of the federation. The edict issued in Circular Number 3 left little doubt as to Blunck's political denomination. It ran as follows:

> Paragraph 43 of the Kösener Statutes shall henceforth read: A corps is an association of students enrolled at the same university, which unites its members in the true friendship of the spirit of National Socialist *Weltanschauung*, and educates them to be representatives of an honourable studentdom comprised of incorruptible, highly motivated, loyal German men.[9]

In addition it stated that no fraternity could be recognised as a *Waffenbund* as long as it retained members who did not comply with the directives of the *ADW Bundesgesetz* regarding the exclusion of Jews, those with Jewish relatives and Freemasons. This was to incorporate the spirit of Paragraph 3 of the Law for Restoration of Tenured Civil Servants (7 April 1933) which outlined the allowable exceptions from the strict interpretation for racial discrimination:

> Paragraph One is not applicable to civil servants who have served since 1 August, 1914 or those who have fought on the front in the world war for the Reich or its allies or whose fathers or sons fell in the world war. Other exemptions may be allowed by the Reich Minister of the Interior in concert with the responsible department minister.[10]

At their meeting in the Reich Chancellery, Lammers had advised Blunck that it was necessary for the *KSCV* to renew its former membership in the *ADW* if its corps wished to survive. In accordance with that directive

Blunck conferred and corresponded with the *ADW Führer*, Dr Sauermann, on 21 and 22 June in order to ascertain the alterations necessary for the *KSCV* to qualify for membership under the new *ADW* regulations.[11] On 24 June, Blunck guaranteed that the *KSCV* would comply with the *ADW* regulations, which he then conveyed to the corps in Circular 4, giving them until 31 July to confirm with him that they had implemented his directive.[12]

Each corps *Führer* received a copy of Form Two, which he was to complete, thereby verifying the racial purity of his corps. In turn each corps member was required to complete Form Three, which testified that his grandparents and his wife's grandparents were pure Aryans, that he did not belong to a lodge of Freemasons and that he would adhere to the regulations of the *ADW*. The *KSCV* was not alone in this regard, for the leader of each federation was required to complete Form One, in which he declared that he accepted responsibility for the exclusion of Jews and Freemasons, and for strict adherence to the *ADW Bundesgesetz* within his federation.[13] But due to the *KSCV*'s withdrawal from the *ADW* earlier in the year, the other federations completed the above procedure well before the *KSCV* made overtures to be readmitted to the *ADW*. This presented certain technical difficulties since the *ADW Bundesgesetz* took effect as of 1 July. Therefore, Blunck's declaration to Sauermann on 24 June was meant to act as a stop-gap until such time as the readmission of the *KSCV* to the *ADW* could be formalised.

The technical aspects for the *KSCV*'s acceptance back into the *ADW* were in hand, but by late June, Blunck began to receive reports of corps members being harassed and/or denied the right of satisfaction at arms by other fraternities. In Marburg for example, the *SC* was compelled to send out 15 challenges for matches with heavy sabres, the weapon reserved for settling the gravest matters of satisfaction, to the executives of the other fencing fraternities of the Marburg *Waffenring*. This had been provoked by the abuse which many *corpsiers* received, because the *KSCV* had been less than enthusiastic in taking up the racial tenets of Nazi doctrine. Furthermore, when Marburg *SC* representatives carried their corps colours, and did not conform with the other fraternities by forming up behind the *SA* standard in a local ceremony associated with the midsummer festival, the corps members had been pelted with stones and verbally abused.[14]

By early July such incidents became more frequent. The *Senior* of the Corps Paliomarchia, the presiding corps in Halle, reported to Blunck that it appeared the members of other federations, in particular those of the *Deutsche Burschenschaft*, were seeking out opportunities to provoke corps members. As the *KSCV* was no longer a member federation of the *ADW*, its corps were in most cases excluded from their local *Waffenring*. This meant that until such time as the *KSCV* was readmitted to the *ADW*, corps members could only fence or demand satisfaction of *ADW* fraternities through the practice of *Waffen belegen* or sponsorship of a second *ADW* fraternity. The report goes on to mention that on the day upon which the report was written, a *corpsier* had met a member of the *DB* with heavy sabres, with the result that the umpire had found against the *corpsier*, even though his ruling was in direct contradiction with the local *comment*.[15]

It was very clear that the *KSCV* had fallen from its previous prestigious position among the student fraternities and its corps were easy targets, without any protection from the new political environment in which they found themselves. In an attempt to protect the *KSCV* corps from continued attacks, such as those in Halle and Marburg, and to give himself credibility as leader of his federation, Blunck wrote to both Sauermann, the *Führer* of the *ADW*, and to Stäbel of the *NSDStB* on 12 July, requesting that something be done to defuse the situation. He reminded Sauermann of their recent correspondence and the directives which had been given to the *KSCV* in order to assure its readmission to the *ADW*, pointing out that the incorporation of the *ADW Bundesgesetz* principles into all corps and *SC* statutes was already well underway. He requested that Sauermann take direct action and intercede in what he too must find an unacceptable situation.[16] To Stäbel, Blunck made the suggestion that members of a fraternity which had time to be quarrelsome and search for ways to create incidents with corps members, were obviously neglecting their obligations in the *SA* and their duty to fulfil Nazi goals.[17] Neither letter had great effect.

The manner and intensity with which *Gleichschaltung* was enforced varied considerably from one university community to the next and was left, at least initially, very much to each individual local student *Führer*. In Würzburg for instance, the local presiding corps, Moenania, reported in late July, that representatives of the Würzburg *SC* were attending meetings of the local student assembly (*Bündische Kammer*), despite their previous exclusion.[18] In Kiel, on the other hand, the local student *Führer* attempted to establish himself as somewhat of a potentate and issued decrees for the disbanding of all student fencing fraternities for a period of at least two semesters. During that period, student fraternity members would be allowed to meet only once a week, no fraternity insignia other than chest bands were to be displayed and the fraternities were to accept no new members. Their fraternity houses were to be placed at the disposal of the Kiel *Studentenschaft* for the quartering of students returning from student work camps, and fraternities which did not comply with these orders, would face extinction. Not surprisingly there was great protest on the part of the fraternities in Kiel. They appealed for moderation in this translation of Nazi doctrine from theoretical to practical, but found that in general, the new regime was beginning, if anything to tighten its fist, rather than loosen it, regarding student fraternities.[19]

By late July, Blunck had informed the *KSCV*, through Circulars 5 and 6, that the *Führer* Principle was to be implanted within the constitutions of each corps, making each corps leader responsible for all members of his fraternity. Corps members, who had attended four or less semesters of university, or who were not already members of the *SA* or *Stahlhelm* for at least six months prior to 1 January 1933, would be required to complete a work period of three months. The Aryan Principle was to be enforced in all corps by 31 July 1933, and the final deadline for the return of Forms One and Two was November, as the *ADW* would have to vote as a whole, at its autumn meeting, regarding the readmission of the *KSCV*.[20]

However, possibly the most worrying aspect for the existence and fibre of the fraternities, was the rumour regarding mandatory establishment of *Kameradschaftshäuser* (comradeship houses). There appears to have been little clear, or at least uniform, indication of what such establishments would entail or incorporate into their structure. It was no secret that the party's student association had long been envious of the houses and other resources in the possession of the student fraternities. Therefore, a fear foremost among the fraternities was that their houses might be expropriated and put at the disposal of the local *Studentenschaft*. It was not until the sixteenth national students' conference held at Aachen in mid-summer 1933, that the first indication of an official outline was given. It was later transmitted by Blunck to the corps, that any corps which wished to co-operate with this *DSt* programme, should renovate their houses in such a way that they would contain living quarters to accommodate all the fraternity's active student members and executive. Notification of such alterations, along with a *Dienstplan* which outlined the programme of proposed activities for the winter semester of 1933–4, were to be submitted by the individual corps or Blunck for approval. In future all students would be required to spend six months on work projects approved by the *DSt* prior to commencing their studies. Upon arriving at university, new students would be obliged to join either a fraternity, or one of the new *Kameradschaften*, which were to be set up under the sponsorship and supervision of the local *Studentenschaft* to accommodate between 100 to 200 first and second semester students. The first of these facilities were to be set up in Breslau, Kiel, Königsberg and Rostock.[21] This programme was to eliminate the existence of independent and free students by placing all students either directly under the cognisance of the local student leader or indirectly under his control in a fraternity. The new programme was taken up by several federations in order to demonstrate their zeal for the Nazi cause. Wishing to be in the vanguard of change, the *Deutsche Burschenschaft* for example, ordered that all its chapters make and comply with the arrangements necessary to implement the plan in time for the next semester.[22]

Blunck's take-over had occurred towards the end of the summer semester, 1933, and following traditional practice, all correspondence, etc., of each corps was seen to by an appointed member who acted as an interim functionary during the recess. This of course did little but add confusion to the process of transmitting information to corps members during the holiday period, and only served to make murkier still an already unclear situation. To help clarify matters, Blunck called a gathering of all corps leaders for the end of the summer recess, to meet at Leubsdorf in Thuringia.[23] The four main points of discussion were the establishment of *Kameradschaft* houses, the position of the *KSCV* in the *Studentenschaft*, the jurisdiction of each corps leader and the position of the corps alumni.[24]

In his Circular 9, Blunck indicated that there was some confusion with respect to the *Kameradschaft* houses as the *NSDStB*, the *Reichsleitung* and the *DSt* had all issued statements in that regard.[25] At Leubsdorf Blunck was finally able to relate to corps representatives that fraternity-sponsored *Kameradschaften* were to come under the jurisdiction of the *DSt* and that Stäbel, as *Führer* of the *DSt*, wished the corps to co-operate. He, however, was not pressing for *KSCV* acceptance of the programme.[26] Starting in early September, students would be expected to completely devote three weekdays, in addition to Sundays, to activities arranged by the *Studentenschaft* and to work related to the military.[27] All students would be obliged during their first eight semesters of higher education, to enroll with the *SS*, *SA* or student *Stahlhelm Langemarck*, in order to fulfil the military training requirements for scholars. The student division of the *Stahlhelm* actually had been absorbed by the *NSDStB* and *SA* in July 1933 and Blunck decreed that as of 15 September corps members would henceforth receive their military training with the *SA*.[28]

Regarding the role previously held by each corps *Senior*, Blunck emphasised at the Leubsdorf meeting that, while a *Senior* previously had been *primus inter pares*, in accordance with Nazi administrative practices, the appointed corps *Führer* was not required to listen to opinions or advice offered by his corps brothers, unless he so chose – since parliamentarianism was no longer condoned. Corps *Alte Herren* were to be represented by a plenipotentiary who, as a party member, functioned as *Führer* of his corps' alumni office. However, in order to reflect leadership by the young, he was required to act in accordance with the wishes and policies of his corps *Führer*. The *Senioren-Convente* were to function as before, as local organisations of corps, with the difference that they were to be known as *Führer-Ringe (FUR)*.[29]

In regard to fencing and matters of honour, Blunck's adjutant Dr Hermann Druckery, was able to announce that as of 25 August 1933 he had established readmissions of the *KSCV* corps to the *ADW* and therefore all *Senioren-Convente* were again members of their local *Waffenring* and were instructed to abide by the new *ADW* codex of 1 July 1933. He also indicated that plans existed to establish an agreement for the reciprocal recognition of a code of honour between the *SS, SA, ST* and the *ADW*. However, until such time as it was made binding, all incidents which involved questions of honour, were to be reported immediately in detail to Blunck, in order that the proper steps for settlement could be taken.[30]

These above points could be seen as merely the tidying up of loose ends, but there was more. The most interesting and sweeping matter, which Blunck presented at Leubsdorf, was very much an item of new business. He announced the formation of a new association to be known as the *Nationalsozialistische Gemeinschaft corpsstudentischer Verbände (NSGCV)*. This new organisation had been formed in Berlin on 29 September for the purpose of bringing *Corpsstudententum* in line with the conventions of the National Socialist state. In addition to the *KSCV* and *WSC*, the organisation included the *RSC, NSC* and the *Miltenberger Ring* as well. The *DL* apparently was closely affiliated, but not a member federation of the organisation. Each federation was to be represented either by its own *Führer* or his appointed delegate who was expected to attend meetings of the society's task-force in Berlin. The first task-force leader of the organisation was Dr Hermann Druckery of the *KSCV*.[31] The rather brief agreement sought to facilitate mutual assistance among the various federations of corps, through the adoption of the principles of *Führertum, Gleichschaltung* and other Nazi tenets. Local chapters of the association were to be established in centres such as Munich, Berlin and Dresden where corps of more than one federation existed. In general, every effort was to be made so that all external corps activities such as fencing, political education, and festivities could be co-ordinated, organised and participated in jointly.[32]

These, however, were only the practical aspects of the new association. The actual credo was later published in the *Deutsche Corpszeitung* of October 1933 declaring a belief in the importance of the work entrusted to those pursuing academic goals and in the educating of German youth for the new age. This was to be undertaken in a healthy, open and comradely atmosphere of co-operation in conjunction with all students of the *DSt* and the *NSDStB*.[33] Druckery, whom Blunck had appointed as one of his assistants on the *KSCV* executive, was placed in charge of liaison for the new association, and as noted above, was appointed head of its executive council (*Führerkreis*). Druckery's letter of early October to the leader of the *DSt* stating the intentions of the *NSGCV*, received a favourable response from the *DSt* which acknowledged with great joy the willingness of the *NSGCV* to work with the leadership of the *Studentenschaft* in carrying through political education within its framework. The *DSt* letter also welcomed the fact that all *NSGCV* student members were to hold mandatory membership in the *SA*.[34] The establishment of the *NSGCV* received notice in the public, as well as student press. The *Dresdener Anzeiger* of 1 October 1933, announced the formation of the new association, followed by a verbatim publication of the acknowledgement (*Bekenntnis*), which later also appeared in the *Deutsche Corpszeitung*. Blunck's address to the forty-fifth general gathering of *corpsiers* in northern Germany was carried in summary by the *Lübecker-Generalanzeiger*. In his speech, he briefly indicated the difference in development of the corps when compared to other fraternity federations. He then went on to emphasise the ability and preparedness of the *KSCV*, and its new affiliate, the *NSGCV*, to accept and to fulfil their duty and obligations to the nation.[35] An account of the speech in the *Deutsche Allgemeine Zeitung* stated that *Corpsstudententum* had a meaningful and demanding educational task for young students of the National Socialist state. Through service and devotion to the community, students would develop personalities of solid character and honour.[36] Blunck's speech, reported verbatim in the *Deutsche Corpszeitung*, ended with the panegyric 'Long live our beloved German Fatherland, Long live the German People, Long live he who has reborn Germany, Our honoured and most beloved Führer!'[37] When compared with the *KSCV Vorort* which Mohr led only a year previously, or to the efforts on the part of the *KSCV* in 1931–2 to resist taking up the

Nazi cause – actions which brought about the *KSCV*'s withdrawal from both the *DSt* and the *ADW* because of clashes with *NSDStB* and *NSDAP* functionaries – Blunck's stance was an alteration in course for the *KSCV* executive of close to 180 decrees. In four months Blunck had managed, albeit with *NSDAP* support, to bludgeon a federation which had previously opposed any party politics within the university community, into becoming at least a theoretical supporter of the Nazi regime's ideological student wing.

The trend towards amalgamation did not stop with the formation of the *NSGCV*. A report from the *NSGCV Führerkreis* meeting of 4 November mentions the work which lay ahead of each local chapter of the *NSGCV*. It also makes reference to remarks made by the leader of the *Deutsche Burschenschaft* who suggested that the *NSGCV* was formed merely to compete with the *DB*. A short rebuttal to the *DB* simply stated that the members of the *NSGCV* were of one mind; agreeing that its founding was a great step for understanding and camaraderie among the fencing federations, and that the *NSGCV* would abstain from any involvement in petty disputes between student federations.[38] To this end the report also advocated the preening of relations with the *Deutsche Landsmannschaft* and the possibility of an accord for joint ventures with the *Deutsche Wehrschaft*. In order to better facilitate co-operation between the federations it suggests a review and standardising of the methods employed by the different federations to implement the exclusion of non-Aryans and Freemasons.[39]

In line with this trend Blunck mentioned in his Circular 15 that the *Deutsche Wehrschaft*, of which Hermann Göring was the honorary leader, had approached the *NSGCV* with a request for entering into a working agreement with that organisation.[40] In light of their opposed views within the *ADW* only two years previously, this goes a long way to explain the sudden goodwill between the *KSCV* and the *DW*. More significantly, it helps again to illustrate the great shift in direction imposed upon the *KSCV* following Blunck's appointment as its *Führer*. As mentioned above, federation leaders were almost without exception Nazi *Alte Kämpfer* and functioned for the proliferation of party achievements rather than the continuance of fraternity aims and traditions. The *DW* was led by Göring and the *Miltenburger Ring (MR)* by Secretary of State Lammers, ensuring that both federations' sponsors were very highly placed within the *Reichsleitung*. The *MR*, Lammers' association, was a very small organisation of only some seven or less fraternities in September 1933,[41] and its *raison d'être* was almost identical with that of the corps. Therefore it was not surprising that following the establishment of the *NSGCV*, the *MR* adopted the same nominal prefix as those federations in order to fit in with the other corps.[42]

At the meeting of the *NSGCV Führerkreis* on 18 November 1933, the *DW Führer*, Dr Schmidtkampf, announced that his federation wished to become a partner with the *NSGCV* in forming a new organisation to be known as the *Kameradschaft waffenstudentischer Verbände (KWV)*. An agreement was signed between the two associations at that meeting to support and co-operate with each other for 'the uniformly implemented education of young *Waffenstudenten* in the spirit of National Socialism'.[43] The *DW* agreed to abide by the *Bekenntnis* which had been adopted by all corps at the founding of the *NWGCV* in September.[44] Druckery wasted little time in communicating news of the new organisation to Stäbel,[45] who, as of 22 September, had become leader of both the *DSt* and the *NSDStB*. Not surprisingly, the national press made much of the new student organisation, reporting that the new accord brought 70 000 students together in the task of National Socialist work.[46]

BLUNCK AND THE *KSCV* VERSUS SCHWAB'S *DB*

As seen at several points above, relationships between the corps and the *Deutsche Burschenschaft*, other than in isolated incidents prior to 1933, were at best less than cordial and more often than not almost hostile. The advent of the Nazi state allowed the *DB* to further animate its traditional advocacy of active nationalism and adopt programmes such as the voluntary *Kameradschafthaus* scheme, which had been muted by the *Reichsstundenten Führung* in 1933 and which provided an excellent opportunity for the *DB* to illustrate its submission to the purposes of the Third Reich. In contrast to the zealotry of the *DB*, the *KSCV* was less than co-operative with the new state's *völkisches raison d'être*. Dr Otto Schwab, leader of the *DB*, took great exception to the formation of the *NSGCV* and accused the new association of having been formed for the sole purpose of attacking the *DB*.[47] The same attitude was reflected in the October edition of the *DB*'s periodical, *Burschenschaftliche Blätter*, which stated that the *KSCV* had always been an organisation of words rather than deeds and had ignored its duty to the German *Volksgemeinschaft*. The article was purported to be based upon an interview with a prominent *corpsier*, but it later evolved that the evidence cited, as well as the interview, were completely spurious. Unfortunately Blunck's speech of October, in which he outlined the differing developments of the two federations, did not help to quell the volatile situation; especially as his address was reported in the national press at approximately the same date as the article in the *DB* periodical. The agreement between the *DW* and the *NSGCV* in mid-November isolated the *DB* even further. The *DW* was known for its extreme racialist activism and, if the corps and the *DW* were able to reach an agreement, the *DB* would either have to join them or attempt to go solo in a political climate where amalgamation was not only approved of, but actively touted, by the state.

On 11 December, Schwab made a speech at Erlangen in which he further castigated the corps.[48] Several newspapers attempted to carry a balanced view of the one-sided attack but drew the conclusion that it was only bickering within a rarified section of society which could better turn its energies to the tasks that lay ahead of the new state.[49]

The interpretation placed upon events by Schwab had the potential for rupturing the fabric of collaboration which Stäbel as *Reichsstudenten Führer* sought to promote. A great deal of fence-mending would appear to have gone on behind the scenes, for an agreement was announced during the first week of January 1934, which previously had been signed by Schwab, Blunck and Druckery. It stated that all misunderstanding had been resolved and implored all members of the *DB*, *KSCV* and the *NSGCV* to unite in the work ahead in a manner 'compliant with the spirit of *Waffenstudenten* camaraderie'.[50] The point which appears to have united Schwab and Druckery was provided by a Roman Catholic students' federation, the *Cartell Verband (CV)*, which had made the foolhardy suggestion that the *ADW* be dissolved; a glib comment, as neither Jews nor Freemasons were likely to be found in Roman Catholic fraternities. The intimation incensed both Schwab and Druckery, who then agreed that the *CV* must be brought to heel.[51] This did occur, but the *CV* was not alone.

On 20 January, Stäbel ordered that with immediate effect all student fraternities were to be placed under his control and that all political questions were to be viewed in accordance with the *DSt*.[52] On 7 February, Stäbel was appointed the national leader for all students at Germany's post-secondary educational institutions which gave him jurisdiction over the *DSt* and all the federations as well. Shortly afterwards, Lammers was appointed to a newly created position within the *DSt*, which was *Obmann der Verbände*. The duties of the new office were to arbitrate in disputes between the federations and thereby decrease the possibility of another conflict such as the one started by Schwab. As has been mentioned, Lammers' own federation, the

Miltenberger Ring, which had joined the *NSGCV* in the previous autumn, was a very small organisation both in terms of the number of fraternities and individual members. A study giving 1929 fraternity statistics shows the *MR* as having six fraternities, 374 student members and 1251 alumni.[53] This smallness in conjunction with Lammers' position as a Secretary of State to Hitler in the Chancellery, gave him the advantages usually enjoyed by an objective third party. However, this did not stop conflicts between the federations: indeed, the very fact that the office was created indicates that a need for mediation existed. The disputes continued to result largely from actions on the part of federations while vying with each other for approval by the regime – as party sanction became ever more important in order to survive within the new state.

Another area which continued to be volatile was the interaction between party associations such as the *SA* and *SS* on the one hand and the student federations on the other. Reports such as the following one from the *SC* of Frankfurt am Main to the *KSCV* leader in January 1934, were not uncommon. The *ADW* fraternities in Frankfurt had come under heavy criticism by the local press for not appearing in large numbers at the municipal celebration marking the first anniversary of the new regime. It later came to light that the reason for the small attendance on the part of the fraternities was that they were neither given tickets for the function, nor were their officers permitted to participate wearing their traditional ceremonial uniforms and colours. Apparently the *ADW* managed at the eleventh hour to arrange for five tickets per fraternity, but even those were not given with any goodwill or gesture of largess on the part of the organisers.

In further incidents at Frankfurt the local *DSt Führer, SS Sturmführer* Müller, attempted to remove the leader of the Frankfurt *Waffenring* and replace him with a former *Burschenschaft* member. However, the appointee had been expelled from his *Burschenschaft*, thereby making him no longer a *Waffenstudent* and hence ineligible to hold a *Waffenring* post. Furthermore, through a personal whim, rather than acting in line with a directive from the *Reichsleitung*, Müller issued orders that local fraternities in the future were not to display insignia or to take any formal or ceremonial role.[54] Such incidents were not uncommon and although widespread, they were difficult to combat for the simple reason that there was no uniform policy being enforced by the party.

Lammers' appointment as *Obmann* was to deal with problems between the federations, or problems between the federations and the *NSDStB*. On 27 January, Stäbel declared that all incidents involving matters of honour between students of the *SA* and fraternity members were to be dealt with immediately and if irreconcilable at the local level, were to be referred to Langhoff, in his capacity as leader of the *ADW*.⁵⁵ The *ADW* continued to expand its membership and student federations which had previously had no tradition along the lines of fencing, changed their statutes and orientation in order to become viable under the jurisdiction of the *ADW*. An example of such a change was the *Wartburg-Kartell akademische-evangelischer Verbindungen*, a Protestant students' federation which had neither the practice of adopting specific colours nor that of adhering to the principle of unquestioned satisfaction. In January 1934 this federation announced that henceforth it would adopt both practices and was admitted to the *ADW*.⁵⁶

Schwab's polemical invective, along with the general attacks of the *DB* against the corps, were laid to rest by the agreement signed by Schwab, Blunck and Druckery. But Schwab's efforts against the *NSGCV* were impressively energetic. In early 1934 a number of small independent fraternities such as the Königsgesellschaft and the Normannia of Tübingen, both founded prior to 1843, and the fraternity Gaudeamus of Stuttgart were absorbed into the *DB*.⁵⁷ Schwab had great ambitions for his federation and is recorded as stating in a confidential circular to his operatives in February 1934, that in future the *DB* should adopt the same type of position within academe as the Nazi party within the state as a whole. In the next six months the *DB* grew, so that its 175 fraternities of 1929 reached 205, 145 of which were situated within the *reichsdeutsche Gebiet* and Danzig.⁵⁸ The newly affiliated fraternities were accepted immediately without any probationary period which caused a certain amount of resentment among long-standing members at the waiving of the regulations. In addition, there was generally strong resistance to Schwab's attempts to introduce certain early *Burschenschaft (Urburschenschaft)* ideas, among which was the adoption of a standard dark red cap and a red, black, red chest band for all *DB* members, regardless of their particular fraternity. Eventually a compromise was reached on this point, whereby only the officers of the individual fraternities wore the prescribed colours. A further and undesirable result of the momentum which Schwab managed to generate was open dissension within his own federation, despite the federation's apparently swelling ranks. The Burschenschaft Bubenruthia of Erlangen, as well as Alemannia and Franconia of Bonn were all expelled from the *DB* for not complying with the federation's rulings on racial purity, and the *DB* itself left the *ADW* on 27 October on the grounds that the *ADW* had not truly embraced the *völkischer* spirit of the National Socialist Revolution.⁵⁹

In February 1934 the *NSGCV* was dissolved. Factionalism had been abundant. However, the reason given for termination was that the objectives of the league and its member federations had not changed, but the strictures of organisation has retarded the attainment of those goals. The league therefore dissolved so that those common objectives might better be reached independently.[60] As an example of the fissuring, shortly before this date the corps of the agrarian students' *NSC* had renamed their federation the *Deutsche Bauernschaft* in order to emphasise their advocacy of the *völkische* movement.[61] The same organisation later changed its name again, this time to the *Naumburger Thing*, harking back to the great meeting places of their Teutonic ethnicity and emphasising the connection between blood, soil and their study of agrarian sciences.[62] Such tendencies towards non-alignment with *NSGCV* policy and striving for independent identity within the new state which appeared bent upon favouritism, broke the bond of the *NSGCV* and aided Schwab in his fight for predominance among the federations.

With the growth of this reverse trend towards decentralisation, Blunck found himself very much the meat in the sandwich, for in his circular to *ADW* federation leaders of March 1934 Langhoff amended the racial criteria governing membership within the *ADW* and Blunck was therefore responsible for the enforcement of the new rulings. The *ADW* regulations which had previously given exemption from its Aryan Paragraph to members who qualified under the Tenured Civil Servants Act, no longer gave that dispensation. Without exception, no person with Jewish grandparents, or in-laws, was eligible for membership in an *ADW* fraternity, either as a student member or as an alumnus. This new directive, which had been given by Rudolf Hess as acting *Führer*, stated that both the *SA* and Nazi Party were to be free of any Jewish tincture and that the previous *ADW* restrictions had been far too broad. Langhoff's subsequent circular stated that he was neither willing, nor in a position, to allow a single instance of Jewish membership within the *ADW* and gave until 20 March for the federations to take appropriate action.[63]

A TIME OF DECISION

In late January Blunck gave notification that the exemption previously given to Freemasons who held membership in certain of the oldest Prussian lodges was now withdrawn and that those corps members affected were to come under the general rulings of the Aryan Paragraph.[64] There are no records to indicate how this new edict affected the corps but the later removal of tenured civil servants' exemptions definitely made a profound impact on the *KSCV* as a whole.

A good example of this is what happened to the Munich *SC*. Blunck had attended a function in January 1934 where in a private discussion with local corps functionaries, he indicated that the racial exemptions under *ADW* statutes would stand. However, Blunck's credibility came into serious question when only two days later Fritz Langhoff, leader of the *ADW*, announced the new regulations to *ADW* representatives. On 26 March, at the Landswehr Casino in Berlin, Blunck was obliged to transmit these regulations to representatives of all the *KSCV* corps.

At a meeting of the *ADW* on 24 March, Lammers had stated that it was his hope that *Waffenstudententum* could survive to serve within the new state and that the new measures introduced by the *ADW* would assist greatly in attaining that goal.[65] Langhoff's original directive called for the achievement of racial purity within *ADW* federations by 20 March, but as the order was not clarified until the conference on 24 March, Blunck gave the *KSCV* corps until 10 April to certify their memberships' purity. A hurdle to swift implementation of the new regulations was the simple fact that the universities were in recess for the period between first and second semesters. Furthermore, the directive was not received by many of the corps from Blunck until after 1 April; a point which was appealed by almost every corps. Blunck's response to their entreaties was in most cases well after the term for the enforcement of the regulations. None the less, he declared that by his authority as *KSCV Führer*, those persons affected under the new directive were, as of 25 April, no longer members of a corps. Such a decree contravened accepted *KSCV* practices whereby regulation of membership lay solely within the jurisdiction of the individual corps. Blunck's high-handed tactics were not well received.

In Munich the twelve local corps of the *Kösener SC* met to discuss the situation and the following position was adopted. Two of the corps managed to circumvent the new problem, three corps bade time and thereby left their answer open, four corps were not affected as they had no racially ineligible members and two other corps were relieved of having to decide through the resignation of their members in question. The remaining corps, Suevia, blatantly refused to expel any of its members. Within days the five corps which had declined to comply or not specified their position (the sixth in the meantime had suffered an internal split between its student and alumni sections), were required to appear before Blunck's representative in Munich in order to explain their actions. They based their defence on the fact that under the *KSCV* statutes Blunck was not empowered to take decisions which had such wide and dire ramifications for individual corps.[66] This point had little potency, for according to Blunck the matter already had been brought to Hitler's attention by Hess and Lammers, resulting in strong hints of reprisal by the *Reichsleitung* and threats to dissolve the corps altogether for their insubordination.[67] This coercion brought four of the remaining Munich corps to heel by 12 May. Corps Suevia, however, stood fast with the result that it was expelled from the *KSCV* for its principled obstinance.[68]

But Munich was not an isolated incident and on 22 May four other corps, Vandalia of Heidelberg, Suevia of Tübingen, Borussia of Halle and Rhenania Strassburg of Marburg, were also expelled from the *KSCV* by Blunck on the same grounds. They were henceforth to be excluded from all corps relationships and functions and were also deemed to be outside the community of fencing fraternities. An additional pronouncement came two days later from Heinz Zaeringer, the new leader of the *DSt*, which excluded the new outcasts from representation in their local *Bündische Kammer* and *Studentenschaft* as well. Not surprisingly, a subsequent and similar expulsion barred them from their respective local *ADW Waffenring* as well.[69]

The five expelled corps launched an appeal on the grounds that Blunck had acted well outside his jurisdiction as *KSCV* leader. They put the case that under the *KSCV* statutes a vote of 2/3 majority by all corps of the federation was required in order to expel a corps from the *KSCV*. Not surprisingly, the appeal was not successful and the five corps voluntarily suspended their activities as of 1 October, in the hope that at some date in the future they might be able to reactivate their membership in the *KSCV*.[70]

Another incident occurred in Leipzig where a portion of an article from the internal publication of Corps Lusatia was quoted in the *Leipziger Tageszeitung* on 8 March. The original article, which lamented the recent loss of the close camaraderie at universities which previously had existed among fraternity students, was further dissected to serve Nazi purposes and appeared in the *Völkischer Beobachter* of 25 April 1934, under the rubric:

Still haven't understood!
Gambling and stag parties more important than *SA* duty?
The unique 'cry of distress' of a Leipzig corps journal.[71]

As a result, charges were laid with the Rector of Leipzig University against Corps Lusatia, calling for a full suspension of the corps. The case was referred to the High Court of Honour of the *DSt* for its decision but with the unexpected result that Stäbel, who had led the attack against Corps Lusatia, gave up his post as leader of the *DSt* in May and later submitted his resignation from the leadership of the *NSDStB* in July. The result for Corps Lusatia was favourable in that the new *NSDStB* leader, Derichsweiler, did not follow through with the charges against the corps, and Lusatia found that the case had been dropped and the threat of imposed suspension removed.[72] Corps Lusatia in Leipzig and the *SC* in Munich were not isolated cases, but as a result of widespread disregard for *DSt* and *ADW* proclamations, the majority of federation leaders came under increasing pressure to bring their member fraternities into line.

ATTACKS AGAINST THE FRATERNITIES

By mid-1934 Blunck and the other federation leaders found themselves having to moderate an ever increasing number of incidents on several fronts simultaneously: interfederation disputes and rivalry, disagreements and unco-operativeness within the federations themselves, maintenance of good relations with all levels of government, and lastly the improvement of what was fast becoming a shabby, if not derogatory, public image.

In early June 1934 a film *Bei der blonden Kathrein*, which romantically depicted student life much like Sigmund Romberg's *The Student Prince*, was released in Berlin. The new film, even though not warmly received, did cause a reaction within the student community. A number of newspapers reported that as many as 300 protesters had gathered outside the cinema and considered the film an antiquated representation of an outmoded lifestyle which was inapplicable and unpalatable to students who were true National Socialists. The protesters were eventually placated with assurances that the film would be brought to Hitler's attention and the attack was nipped in the bud.[73] In contrast, later commentary by non-Nazi related sources referred to the reaction of the protesters as over-sensitive[74] and a review of the film by the industry itself, defended the film as making an interesting and useful contrast between fantasy and the world of real events.[75] These were the most immediate and direct results of the film. But more importantly the reactions to the film reflected a growing enmity towards the traditional student organisations and their members who increasingly were seen as stultified dwellers in a storybook world, reticent to move with the progress of the new regime. The wearing of fraternity colours came under even heavier attack, to the point where the leader of the *ADW*,

Langhoff, decreed that by 16 July, the display of fraternity colours, whether in the form of caps, chest bands or flags, was to cease. Blunck answered in a special circular of 13 July, that *Kösener* corps students would not give up their colours; they would wear them as before: not more, not less![76] Blunck followed this statement only a few days later by a very impassioned defence of the fencing fraternities drawing attention to the proud student tradition of fighting for and wearing colours which by far predated a united German state. Indeed, he argued, it should be a requisite for the National Socialist creed to protect rather than to attack the practice of wearing colours.[77] The *ADW* edict was not complied with, but neither was it withdrawn.

By August 1934 the *KSCV* numbered 119 fraternities with a total membership of approximately 27 000 including its alumni. The *DB* could count 210 fraternities with 37 000 members, which as a single federation gave it considerable superiority in terms of numbers. In March the ranks of the *WSC* swelled by 18 000 members in 111 fraternities after it absorbed most of the *RSC* corps.[78] The *RSC* dissolved into the *WSC* on 25 March, in the hope that a larger organisation would carry more weight and thereby stand a better chance of survival within the new political system.[79] One can understand to a certain extent the apprehension on the part of Schwab as leader of the *DB*, for the *KSCV* and the *WSC* combined well outweighed his federation had they wished to band together at that time. But the federations all adopted an egocentric approach to survival and it was that division which eventually allowed Nazi tactics to defeat the federations.

THE FEICKERT PLAN

The next, and potentially by far the most crippling attack on the corps, was launched by Andreas Feickert shortly after he took office as *Reichsführer* of the *DSt* in the autumn of 1934. Backed by ideas from his book *Studenten Greifen An*, which had been published that August, but apparently acting without consultation with Lammers, or Derichsweiler who had succeeded Stäbel as head of the *NSDStB*, Feickert announced a plan on 20 September which was to take effect as of the coming winter semester.[80] Points One and Two of his plan stated that every student beginning studies after 1 October 1934 would be required to register and participate in the student work service programme. In addition he would be required to live in a *Kameradschaftshaus* which was recognised by the

DSt. Senior students could have lodgings in such houses only if they were members of the *NSDStB, NSDAP, SS, SA* or Hitler Youth prior to 31 January 1933. This was not a great departure from previous directives by the *DSt* except that under his plan the housing could not merely be in a fraternity house but was required to be in a fraternity which met with the approval of the *DSt.* The housing provided by each local *Studentenschaft* was classified as the *Kameradschaft* for that specific student community and those provided by approved fraternities were referred to as *Wohnkameradschaften.* The houses had been renovated, many at great expense to the fraternity involved, in order to comply with previous directives from the *DSt* which stipulated that all fraternity houses and *Kameradschaften* were to be placed at the disposal of each local student leader.[81] This meant that without his approval specific fraternities would not be sanctioned and would therefore receive no new members; eventually forcing them to suspend their activities, as a student organisation. Initially the only fraternities which endorsed and implemented the suggestions regarding *Wohnkameradschaften* were those such as the *DB* which were searching for a means by which to express their loyalty and co-operation with the new government. But other fraternities were encouraged as well through promises of tax relief. On 28 February 1934 the Prussian Finance Minister issued a decree in which it was declared that the property of national organisations was to be freed from real estate and property rental taxes.[82] However, the various regional governments of Germany varied as to when and how they implemented the tax relief. A proposal of 31 July to incorporate the idea into national law underwent several revisions, but by early 1935 Blunck stated that although it was not yet law, assent was expected soon and student *Wohnkameradschaften* would be eligible for the special tax concessions.[83] Initially as a prerequisite for a fraternity to qualify for tax exemption, the leader of the fraternity was required to spend one semester in a *DSt* sponsored *Kameradschaft*,[84] but the ruling seems to have been applied with varying regularity.

On the strength of promised reduction in property taxes, very few fraternities did not renovate, or in some cases even buy new houses, in order to qualify under the new scheme. But Feickert's plan went even further in that under his programme the property of all fraternities would be placed at the disposal of the *DSt* and its local leaders. The local *DSt* leaders were to be given additional control over the fraternities through their power to appoint or approve whom they saw fit to serve as leader of the various *Kameradschaften* within their local jurisdiction.

Another stipulation of Feikert's plan was that fraternity colours were not to be worn by new members during their first two semesters and *Kameradschaft* houses were to have no instruction or leadership of a religious nature. Feickert also stated that he reserved the right to remove and replace any university student leader, any fraternity leader or the leader of any student society, as he saw fit. However, his most presumptuous announcement was that a new code of honour and discipline was to be drawn up by the *DSt* and that all pertinent cases were to be handled within the new framework.[85] This of course would have usurped the position of the *ADW*, called into question its code of honour and undermined its statutes. Needless to say there was considerable disagreement regarding Feickert's plan, both from the other Nazi functionaries whom he had not consulted and from the federation at all levels.

An emergency meeting of *KSCV* representatives was called in order to consolidate opposition to the plan which had the potential of imposing both crippling and annihilating restrictions on the corps. This extraordinary congress authorised Blunck to co-operate with *NSDStB* and *DSt* leaders, as well as to work with the leaders of the other federations in order to protect *Waffenstudententum* through blocking the enactment of Feickert's plan.[86] With this endorsement in hand, Blunck took the initiative in calling a meeting of the federation leaders on 8 October which was also attended by Feickert, Derichsweiler and Lammers. Feickert assured those in attendance that his plan had been discarded and that no scheme existed for its enforcement.[87] Blunck's Circular Number 33 to the *KSCV* later that same month indicated that Minister of Education Rust had been empowered by Hitler to deal with the matter and the enforcement of Feickert's plan did not have any official party approval.[88] Several national newspapers picked up the story and emphasised that Rust had cleverly only acquiesced and had not stopped any fraternity or federation which wished to adopt Feickert's guidelines. The point was well taken. Rust had stopped only the mandatory implementation of the programme and thereby allowed the fraternities the opportunity to voluntarily make any adjustments which they saw fit in order to align themselves with the National Socialist state.[89] Again intimidation was the weapon used in yet another ruse to bring the federations under the party banner.

Rust was still supporting this same stance a few weeks later when he appeared with Alfred Rosenberg to address a meeting with foreign press representatives. Rust spoke on the foundations of National Socialist education and emphasised that a consciousness of being German rather than Roman Catholic or Protestant must henceforth be the basis upon which education was to be based.⁹⁰ Pervasive nationalism had become a religion and the atmosphere for potential skulduggery became still riper.

On 15 October, Feickert, again without consulting Lammers or Derichsweiler, gave a radio address on the topic of his plan and strongly intimated that it would be enforced in the near future. On the same day the *Deutsche Burschenschaft (DB)* and the *Deutsche Wehrschaft (DW)* hosted a meeting of representatives from the six federations which were most favourably disposed to Feickert's plan. The other five federations present on that occasion were the *Verband der Turnerschaften (VD)*, the *Deutsche Sängerschaft (DS)*, the *Sonderhäuser Verband (SV)*, the *Schwarzburgbund (SB)* and the *Akademische Turnbund (ATB)*. When the *ADW* leader Langhoff asked why his federation, the *WSC*, had not been invited, he was informed that corps had purposely not been invited to attend. The discussion centred around the voluntary adoption and implementation of the Feickert Plan of 20 September, regardless of the fact that Hitler had disapproved of its effectuation.⁹¹ The *DW* and *Turnerschaften* both voted in favour of implementing Feickert's plan at a meeting on 8 October. Less than a fortnight later the *DB* announced its withdrawal from the *ADW*. The rationale given was that the local *Waffenring* no longer offered an acceptable setting for active politics, and that in accordance with *DB* interpretation, the seriousness and importance of *Kameradschaft* house education demanded uncompromising adherence to Nazi ideology and methods. Therefore, *DB* members, as members of the new student generation of National Socialist fighters, could not be expected to tolerate the company of other fraternity students who exchanged oaths of loyalty during their *Landesvater* (Founder's Feast), with fraternity brothers of Jewish ancestry.⁹² A short time later Blunck responded to this in a *KSCV* internal memo stating that previously he could have considered working with the *DB*, but its disposition and attitude had changed so radically that any co-operation had become unthinkable. Blunck went on to describe Schwab's attempts to gain special recognition for the *DB* as pitiful and the most stupid and unsophisticated he had seen anywhere to date.⁹³ The next move was even more astounding.

THE *VÖLKISCHE WAFFENRING (VWR)*

On 15 December, the *DB* and *DW* were joined by the other five federations which favoured Feickert's plan. Together they formed their own fencing association known as the *Völkische Waffenring (VWR)*, an exhibition which the *ADW* federations deemed 'National Socialist Phariseeism': claiming to be truly more Nazi than any of the other federations. The *ADW* concept of honour was considered to be too narrow for the secessionists and their new *VWR* extended the interpretation of honour to the *völkische* plain whereby an insult to the German people could not go unanswered by any true German.[94] In giving obedience to this interpretation the honourable student served not only the scholastic community but more particularly the establishment of a truly German collective honour. This development was a very simple step after the refusal to give satisfaction to non-Aryans purely on racial grounds, as seen above in the adoption of the Waidhofen Principle and *völkische* honour became the accepted norm for the federations of the *VWR*.

But interfederation criticism was not confined to matters of honour alone. The *DW* wasted few words when voicing its indignation with the *KSCV* in the autumn issue of its periodical, the *Der Wehrschafter*. The article contended that the corps had never served anything other than self-interest and had made their contribution to the German nation only inadvertently. To this, and other allegations, Blunck sought advice and assistance from Lammers,[95] but he also used his own *KSCV* press in order to outline some of the significant erosion of the *DB* under Schwab's leadership. Between October and December 1934 the *DB* had lost some 22 of its fraternities, among them some of its oldest and their exodus was attributable to Schwab's imperious behaviour.[96] Blunck also emphasised the basic differences between the corps and the *DB*, but also stressed Schwab's misinterpretation and departure from traditional *Burschenschaft* tenets.[97] Throughout 1934 the *KSCV* had tried to find an acceptable middle ground between the renunciation of its apolitical traditions and the total adoption of Nazi ideology. The booklet *Die corpsstudentische Idee*, authored by the *corpsier* Christian Meissner in 1934, outlined the precepts of corps philosophy and structure, with a special section to delineate the relationship of the corps to National Socialism. Significantly Meissner did not describe the role of the corps within the Nazi state but rather the relationship of the corps to the *NSDSAP* regime, an orientation supported by heavy quoting from Hitler to substantiate the *KSCV* position of autonomy: 'I do not wish to regularise people and ideas. What is important are certain concepts and principles of the movement which must remain unaltered and to which everyone must adhere. But on the foundation of these concepts the wealth and uniqueness of the German people can freely develop.'[98] Meissner quite naturally closed by bringing attention to the great contributions made by distinguished corps alumni. He posited that the exemplary record of fine statesmen produced by the corps spoke well for itself and in light of such contributions, it hardly seemed necessary for the corps to modify themselves in order to continue their predisposition of service to Germany in the new chapter of its history.[99] But incidents viewed by the regime as blatant disrespect, such as the one already cited concerning the article from Corps Lusatia which appeared in the *Völkischer Beobachter* in the abridged form, were used to substantiate claims that the corps were a bastion of the conservative and reactionary resistance to the new regime.[100]

The statistics which placed the 104 *reichsdeutsche* corps at variance with the *VWR* and its interpretation of the Aryan Principle were very simple. In 1934, of the approximately 28 000 *corpsier*, that being the aggregate of both student and alumni members, 239 could be classified as non-Aryan and a further 125 members designated as related to non-Aryans.[101] As the new regime gained momentum in the reification of its ideology, it grew further away from the promotion of the fencing fraternities as a suitable medium and method for the education of students in their duties to *Volk* and *Vaterland*. Voluntary service was replaced by mandatory duty and organic growth with organisation. Blunck became convinced that the National Socialist Revolution was to be accepted and joined at any price. The rigours of organising became at best an objective and at worse the goal in itself. It demanded that the *KSCV* and with it all fraternity students, were to offer no less than their lives to the services of the *Führer* and to the Nazi interpretation of obligations and duties.[102] Those who would not co-operate were pruned from the vine and cast aside by the movement.

THE *GEMEINSCHAFT STUDENTISCHER VERBÄNDE (GStV)*

It was in this atmosphere of compliance for the sake of favourable recognition that the *ADW* met for its annual meeting in Berlin on 10–12 January 1935. The previous autumn had seen the controversy regarding Feikert's plan followed by a splintering within the *ADW* and the forming of the *VWR*. With these events in the recent past the *ADW* federations approached the conference with caution. The one point more significant even than Hitler's telegram of good wishes for the conference was the fact that he had indicated the honour codex of the *ADW* was to be the only valid and acceptable code for student fraternities.[103] This gave the *ADW* legitimacy and cut the ground from under the *VWR*. Any hopes of the *VWR* receiving official recognition were dashed regardless of its energetic and extreme nationalistic stance. Following the conclusion of the *ADW* conference there was another meeting of the same representatives. The second meeting was to have an even greater bearing on the events of the student fraternities during the next nine months, for it was the founding of a new league known as the *Gemeinschaft Studentischer Verbände (GStV)* under the leadership of Secretary of State Lammers.[104]

The vehement attacks of the *Deutsche Wehrschaft* against the *KSCV* reached such a point that in late January Blunck's assistant Heringhaus wrote to Lammers. He requested that Lammers, in his capacity as *Obmann* of the federations, force the *DW* to dissolve its federation and cease publication of its periodical, *Der Wehrschafter*, because of the *DW*'s seemingly tireless 'actions detrimental to the community of the nation'.[105] The *DW* received only a slight reprimand but its credibility as one of the central federations within the *VWR* came into question not long afterwards, due to a spurious claim for distinction in the Nazi state. It apparently came to the attention of the *Reichsleitung* that the *DW* claimed Hitler as the honorary leader of its federation. Both Martin Borman and Hans Lammers investigated the matter and informed the *DW* leader, Dr Schmidtkampf, that Hitler had neither been offered, nor accepted, the distinction of *DW Führer*.[106] By the time an appeal was sent to Hitler officially extending an invitation, the *VWR* ceased to exist, the *DW* was in disarray, and the question of Hitler accepting the position was unthinkable.[107]

To return to the founding of the *GStV* on 12 January, Wagner sent Lammers a telegram of congratulations at the formation of the new league, accompanied by his good wishes for every success in leading the student federations into a closer relationship with the party and its work.[108] The new league consisted of the 13 member federations which then composed the *ADW*. However, the *GStV* also made membership available to the non-fencing fraternities in the same way that the earlier Erlangen Agreement had done.[109] Lammer's first circular which announced the formation of the league, stated that the federations had agreed that all questions dealing with matters related to fencing and duelling were solely within the jurisdiction of the *ADW*. Similarly, all matters related to university politics and political situations were to be dealt with by the *GStV*.[110] The first sitting of the new league's eight man executive committee occurred in Berlin on 30 January. As well as formalising the organisational aspects of the *GStV*, the committee stated that the energies of the league were to be directed to support for the

NSDStB in the political training and education of students, voluntary co-operation with the *NSDStB* in the establishing of the *Kameradschaft* programme and participation in ethnically German, rather than foreign, work schemes for students during university recesses.[111]

Indeed, the co-operation of the *GStV* with Nazi organisations flourished so much so that on 12 March 1935, an accord was signed by Lammers, Derichsweiler and Wagner whereby the *NSDStB* and the *NSDAP* refused to recognise any federation of student fraternities unless it held membership in the *GStV*. Both the party and its student association stated a further benign disinterest in fraternity matters with the understanding that all student members of *GStV* federations would adopt the regulations which governed members of the *NSDStB*.[112] When the *GStV* held its first general meeting in Braunschweig at the end of the same month, the assembly was greeted with a telegram of good wishes addressed to Lammers from Hitler, giving both Lammers and the league the regime's seal of approval and thereby a virtual monopoly as the representative of the fraternities.[113] In his speech to the gathering, Lammers reiterated that adoption of the already well known precepts of the *Führer* and the expulsion of Jews and Freemasons were required of all *GStV* federations. However, the confessional fraternities, in other words the federations with religious regulations regarding membership, would also be welcomed under the *GStV* banner, but with the stipulation that they released their members from confessional requirements. He emphasised that all student members were required to come into line with Nazi Party regulations and all federations were to give Lammers an affidavit empowering him to act on their behalf. His address to the general meeting went as far as to include the battlecry enshrined within the lines of a time-honoured student song *Burschen Heraus* which had seen great service among the nationalistic fraternities during the nineteenth century:

'When it's for the Fatherland,
Loyally take your blades in hand!'[114]

Lammer's approach and the condonement by Hitler of his actions brought about the desired result for by late March the ranks of the *GStV*, which had numbered 170 000, were swollen yet again when Glauning, as leader of the *DB*, at strong protest from the *DW* and *VTD*, shattered the delicate cohesion of the *VWR* and brought his federation into the *GStV*.[115] As a result the *VWR* dissolved, giving the *GStV* a clear sweep in an already uncontestable field.

All appeared to be going well for Lammers and the *GStV*. Indeed, for a short time it was relatively peaceful among the federations, and the *KSCV*, which had been a founding member of the *GStV*, enjoyed a type of quiet ignominity. But this proved to be only the eye of the hurricane and the subsequent, apparently unavoidable upheaval, swept the *KSCV* into a position of being censured by both Lammers and the party. When observed only a little more closely it becomes clear that the lull really only corresponded to the university semester recess, for reports again started to appear on Blunck's desk in mid-May. Of the three cases which will be cited below, the first occurred in Munich where a number of young members left Corps Bavaria. Two of the departing members were *NSDStB* officers for the district of *Oberbayern* and all of them apparently found in Corps Bavaria an unsuitable atmosphere for conscientious and discriminating Nazi students. Their exit occurred on 3 May and on 14 May one of their number, Seipel, informed *NSDAP* authorities that derogatory remarks had been made regarding the party at a recent meeting of the Munich *SC*. When Seipel's actions became known, Corps Hercynia brought a case for ban against him on the grounds of his transgressing the confidentiality of a *SC Convent*. Blunck had the charges against Corps Bavaria investigated by his representative in Munich. The findings concluded that political work such as that carried out by the *NSDAP* and the *NSDStB* would not yet be possible with Corps Bavaria as its attitudes and perceptions of the future were not suitable.[116] The end result was that Blunck expelled Corps Bavaria from the *KSCV*.

The second incident actually caused such a reaction on the part of Nazi authorities that it reached national attention and the story was carried in its later stages by the *London Times*. On 21 May members of Corps Saxo-Borussia of Heidelberg were celebrating the reception of several new members and in a rather less than sober order, entered a local inn to the tune of their leader blowing into an empty *sekt* bottle. This might have gone relatively unnoticed except that their entrance into the inn occurred during Hitler's address to the nation which was being listened to both by the publican and his guests. Only a few days later a further incident of disrespect concerning Hitler took place as members of Corps Saxo-Borussia sampled the new asparagus crop in another Heidelberg inn. Their table conversations grew louder, possibly in anticipation of the meal ahead, so that other guests in the inn heard one *corpsier* ask how one currently was expected to eat asparagus and more especially how would Hitler eat his asparagus? For a few moments of mirth at the *Reichkanzler*'s expense the academic disciplinary committee of the University of Heidelberg, comprised of the Rector, the leader of the *Dozentenschaft* and the leader of the *Studentenschaft*, unanimously agreed upon a two-year suspension of Corps Saxo-Borussia from the university – effective from the autumn of 1935. The ringleader was rusticated and lost accreditation for the semester's study, while the other offenders were given written reprimands – 'Because of gross violations of duty to the nation, the government and the university.'[117]

But the ramifications of what became known as the *Spargelessen* (asparagus eating) were felt by more than just the members of Corps Saxo-Borussia. The incident, when combined with the next case, served as lethal ammunition which was used by the *NSDStB* against the *KSCV* as a whole. Corps Palaiomarchia of Halle achieved its notoriety through disrespect to Nazi regulations in general, rather than insolence to Hitler. The incident arose from the facts as summarised by the headlines carried in the *Mitteldeutsche National-Zeitung* of Halle on 29 August 1935. 'Jewish corps brothers in Palaiomarchia – National Socialists leave the corps under protest.'[118] In short, the story went as follows. In accordance with the *ADW* and *GStV* regulations all new fraternity members were required to comply with the same regulations governing membership as the *NSDAP* and the *NSDStB*. Six of the newer student members of Corps Palaiomarchia, who were ardent National Socialists, discovered that two corps alumni were Jewish and therefore did not fall within the bounds for Nazi membership. The young Nazis demanded that the two alumni be expelled from the corps without delay. In actual fact both of the *Alte Herren* in question came under the exemptions of the Tenured Civil Servants' ruling of 1933. One of the men had been born in 1878 and had emigrated to North America long before the regulations regarding Jewish fraternity membership. Furthermore, he had been most generous in helping to refinance and resuscitate his corps following the First World War.

The credentials of the second alumnus were more impressive still. As a young *corpsier* he had given distinguished service to his fraternity and had been decorated as an officer in the First World War. Later as a captain of German industry he had worked with both Mercedes and Zeppelin. His brother, also a member of Corps Palaiomarchia, had fallen in the First World War and his father had served with distinction in the 1866–70 campaign, followed by service as an officer in a guards regiment. In addition to the distinctions already noted, genealogically speaking, neither alumnus was more than one quarter Jewish.[119] However, these facts were not sufficient to satisfy the young Nazis in Corps Palaiomarchia who presented the ultimatum that either the two

'Jewish' alumni were to be expelled or they themselves would leave the corps. In order to save the corps any further embarrassment and disruption, the two *Alte Herren* both offered to surrender their colours and leave the corps. But the response of the corps leader, Hoffmann, himself well known for his very active role in the *Stahlhelm*, affirmed there was more than enough true German spirit among the corps' 250 members to shield two alumni from the inquisitional arrows directed at them. 'Whosoever wears the colours of my corps is my corps brother.... I do not sacrifice my brother for my own sake or for that of my race.'[120] The resignations of the two *Alte Herren* were refused by the corps and the exit of the six Nazis requested. They quickly complied but with much noise, protest and provocation. It was this very point around which the incident in Corps Palaiomarchia revolved that proved the undoing of the *KSCV* within the Third Reich: the difference being between Nazi interpretation and the technically acceptable measures which were enforced. This gap between mandatory and voluntary limits of co-operation became of increasing importance and groups which contributed only the minimum required by the state were classified as indolent by party functionaries.

LAMMERS' WITHDRAWAL

On 6 September 1935, Lammers announced to a meeting of the *GStV Führerkreis* that due to a lack of co-operation, mostly on the part of the *KSCV* and the *DB*, he was resigning as leader of the *GStV*. The organisation which had initially moved from strength to strength had reached a point in May where it began to reverse its trend and started to fragment. The federation had managed to co-operate during the university recess but the *KSCV* soon found itself again attacked by its enemy of long standing, the *DB*. Adolf Wagner, an alumnus of the *DB*, addressed his federation's annual conference at Eisenach, claiming for the *DB* the role of arbiter for all fraternity federations and attacking the *KSCV* on its policy of retaining Jewish members.[121] Blunck protested to Lammers regarding the *DB*'s attitude and actions on the grounds that the *DB* was neither the prototype upon which student fraternities had, nor necessarily should, fashion themselves. Furthermore, Blunck had spoken to Wagner's assistant at Nazi Party headquarters in Munich and had been assured that the party was not interested in the purging of one or two non-Aryan alumni from a fraternity: it was really the confessional fraternities which came into question.[122] This greatly reassured

Blunck regarding official party policy on the racial questons for the student federations. Confident that he had the racial question answered, Blunck turned his attention to the next issue raised by the party directives – this time initiated by Albert Derichsweiler of the *DSt*.

Shortly after he assumed office as leader of the *GStV*, Lammers' position and authority as the sole arbitrator for all student fraternities was authorised by Hitler. In addition, an agreement was reached whereby the *NSDStB* and the *DSt* also recognised the *GStV* as the exclusive representative of fraternity interests. However, a serious problem arose, when in late June, Derichsweiler, then the leader of the *DSt*, announced a new party-approved political education programme which would be mandatory for all fraternity students. The programme called for each fraternity to send three of its members to special training camps which would be held during the university summer recess. At the conclusion of the sessions, the members were to return to their fraternities and assume the leadership of its political education, in co-operation with the local chapter of the *NSDStB*.

Blunck was quick to point out to Lammers that the implementation of Derichsweiler's plan would meet with considerable opposition and its imposition would bring about merely a technical observance of its regulations.[123] The point was taken by Lammers, who quite reasonably, saw Derichsweiler's surprise programme as an affront. Wagner of the *NSDStB* and Lammers met with Derichsweiler for an explanation of his plan and he quickly qualified its dimensions, insisting that it would not contravene the previous agreement between the *GStV*, the *NSDStB* and the *DSt*. Derichsweiler was willing to have the *DSt* assist with the organisation of the training camps, but as the goal of the *NSDStB* was to gradually acquire control of all fraternity activities, their political training and the camps, naturally the new programme should come under the jurisdiction of the *NSDStB*, rather than the *DSt*. Derichsweiler also drew attention to the fact that he had no funds to mount such a programme, since the *DSt* received only 5 RM per student each semester, while the *NSDStB* would be able to draw moneys from the party for such a programme.[124]

Following their meeting Lammers wrote a letter of admonition to Derichsweiler pointing out that the approval for his scheme had come only from other party members and not from Hitler himself. He reminded Derichsweiler that the federation leaders, all of whom were also party members, had not been advised on the matter and, more to the point, he, Lammers, as head of the *GStV*, had been neither consulted nor confided in regarding the proposal. He went on to say that it was not proper *NSDAP* practice to set groups within the state against each other as Derichsweiler had done through his dredging up past differences; especially when others worked ceaselessly to accomplish co-operation within a united new Germany.[125]

However, Derichsweiler was not alone in making decrees regarding party organisations and the fraternities. On 6 July Baldur von Schirach seized the opportunity to renew old animosities by citing the incident concerning Corps Saxo-Borussia as indicative and typical of the attitudes held and exhibited by the fraternities towards the party and the new state.[126] There is little doubt that as Saxo-Borussia was a corps of the *KSCV*, Schirach took a certain amount of vengeful pleasure in making the allegations, remembering the heated exchanges he and Walter Lienau had had in Munich with other corps of the *KSCV* only a few years before. His new edict was very straightforward. No member of the Hitler Youth was allowed to hold membership in a student fraternity as well. Anyone holding such dual membership was required to put the situation in order immediately.[127]

When the *GStV Führerkreis* met at Berchtesgaden on 14 July it was the implications and incidents leading to Derichsweiler's and Schirach's proclamations which were discussed. Blunck apologised for the problems caused to all the federations and fraternities by the behaviour of Corps Saxo-Borussia. He hastened to point out that within hours of the verdict given in Heidelberg against Corps Saxo-Borussia, the corps also had been expelled from the *KSCV*. Other members at the meeting felt that Blunck had not acted quickly enough against the corps, but it was fairly obvious that the other federations were searching for a scapegoat on which to blame the new edicts. That aside, it was felt that Schirach's edict, which could affect some 250 000 academics, had to be rescinded and a modified version of the decree shown to Hitler for his comments. Blunck also mentioned that the policy regarding non-Aryan members within the *KSCV* was well known to the party and had been given verbal sanction by Wagner's assistant at party headquarters. He also noted that, while Corps Saxo-Borussia had received publicity adverse to the fraternities in general, there were examples of insubordination in other federations as well; Burschenschaft Holzminda of Göttingen being only one.[128] As summarised in a regional newspaper, several members of Holzminda removed a maypole from opposite their fraternity house, garnished it with swastikas and dragged it through the dust of the Göttingen streets.[129] This case mentioned by Blunck, only gave emphasis to what was already apparent; the federations were not uniformly integrating themselves into the Nazi state.

On 15 July, the day following the meeting, Hitler met Lammers as well as other party functionaries responsible for various aspects of student affairs. The results of the audience at Berchtesgaden were transmitted to another meeting of the federation leaders in Berlin on 24 July 1935 and were to be treated as highly confidential. Hitler apparently indicated that dissolution of neither the federations nor the fraternities was desired. Furthermore, Derichsweiler's programme was surprisingly altered. Fraternities need not be *NSDStB* organisations nor would the *GStV* fraternities and federations come under the jurisdiction of their local *NSDStB* leader. Political education of students was to be the task of local *NSDStB* groups, but the *NSDStB* was not empowered to appoint the education officer for the fraternities nor would the leaders of individual fraternities need their approval. Derichsweiler's further suggestion, that fraternity alumni had a stultifying effect on the political development of their younger fraternity brothers and should therefore be prevented from any interchange with the junior members, was considered by Hitler as unreasonable. Hitler expressed the opinion that such exchanges provided an excellent opportunity for elder and more experienced party followers to teach the young. However, the education camps were strongly endorsed and three members of each fraternity were to enrol for mandatory instruction courses by 25 July.[130]

Under 'other business' Lammers stated that if the combined goals of the *GStV* were to be achieved, he required, in writing, power to act on behalf of all the *GStV* federations. All the federations signed the requisite document that same day except the *DB* which requested until 1 August. The document gave Lammers complete power to act unilaterally in all matters regarding the *GStV* and thereby remove the atmosphere which had caused something similar to sibling bickering among the federations.[131]

Not surprisingly, the *KSCV* received special mention and attention at the 24 July meeting in Berlin. The *KSCV* asked that any further disciplinary measures to be taken regarding Corps Saxo-Borussia and Corps Palaiomarchia be administered internally within the *KSCV*.

Regarding the universal enactment of Nazi Party regulations against non-Aryans within the fraternities, the few federations which had not already done so agreed to expel their unsuitable members by 1 November. Blunck, however, requested that the *KSCV* be given until 1 August in order to give the matter further study and Lammers consented.[132] But in retrospect it can be seen that Lammers' patience had been tried almost to the full and that the end had begun.

Blunck informed Lammers' assistant, Nordmann, on 16 July that the

KSCV, contrary to the allegations levelled against it, also had a *volksdeutsche* focus. This had arisen through the years and was borne witness to by the many fraternities outside of Germany which turned to the *KSCV* for affiliation and guidance: twenty-four in Austria, six in the Baltic, two in Romania and one in Budapest. Furthermore, he stated, the federation had undertaken projects such as the construction of the handwork training school at Windhoeck in the former German colony of South West Africa and had a financial aid programme for the town of Clarenthal in the Saar. Blunck closed his letter to Nordmann by stating that the *KSCV* had a National Socialist heart, not merely one of *Corpstudententum*.[133] Blunck's profession of obedience to Nazi precepts and direction of policy met with a cold and indifferent reply by Nordmann on behalf of Lammers.[134] The fact that Nordmann answered Blunck, rather than Lammers, is in itself significant, as previously Blunck and Lammers had dealt directly with one another. Nordmann's taking charge of dealings with Blunck indicated a drop in standing for Blunck and the relegation of his business with the *GStV* to that of only secondary importance.

In his speech of 8 September 1935, which summarised his work and formally announced his resignation from the position of leader of the *GStV*, Lammers left little doubt about his actions toward both the *DB* and the *KSCV*. Lammers expelled the *DB* from the *GStV* on 21 August for several reasons, but the most poignant was that Hans Glauning had misrepresented the position and readiness of his federation to co-operate with Lammers when they talked at the Berchtesgaden meeting of 14 July. Lammers felt it was impossible to further represent the *DB* with Glauning as its leader after his gross misrepresentation. In addition, Glauning had balked at giving Lammers power to act for the *DB* and had shown no readiness to comply with Lammers' directives. Instead Glauning had claimed special privileges and consideration for the *DB*.[135]

In his proclamation published on 6 September, Lammers had stated that he found it necessary to expel two federations, the *DB* and *KSCV*, from the *GStV*; the *DB*, because its leader would not co-operate in achieving *GStV* objectives and the *KSCV* because its executive refused to enforce voluntarily the unconditional implementation of the Aryan regulations which all the other federations had unequivocally pledged to enact by 1 November. He stated that his task and goal of forging a unified student association had been made impossible by such uncooperative behaviour throughout his term as leader of the *GStV* and he therefore announced his intention to resign the position. His reasons would be given in detail to a meeting of the *GStV Führerkreis* called for 8 September.[136]

In his address Lammers outlined the problem which the *KSCV* had presented to him and why he felt compelled to expel it from the *GStV*. Regarding the question of the Aryan regulations, which had been raised at the 24 July meeting, only the *KSCV* out of nineteen *GStV* federations had hesitated in its implementation and had asked until 1 August to comply. Lammers stated that even then no clear indication had been forthcoming from the *KSCV* until a written reminder was sent to Blunck by Lammers' office. On 13 August Blunck sent to Lammers what Lammers described in his resignation speech as a long-winded memorandum of well-worn historical descriptions and arguments regarding the develoment of the Aryan question, supported by quotations from Hitler and other *Reichsleitung* members. Blunck cited Minister of Culture Rust as having stated he found nothing objectionable in the corps not complying totally with the other *GStV* federations. Blunck also mentioned that Dr Wagner's assistant at party headquarters had assured him that the party was not interested in purging the few non-Aryans or those with Jewish relatives from the almni of the *KSCV*.[137]

As Blunck had been one of the signatories to the document which had given Lammers power to act for the *GStV* federations, the delay and unclarity of action appears to have greatly annoyed Lammers. Not surprisingly, a later statement in Blunck's same letter had infuriated Lammers, or at least he so indicated in his speech of 8 September. Blunck had written that the *KSCV* would, if given an assurance by Lammers that their non-Aryan members would not have to be expelled, consider unlimited co-operation with the *GStV*.[138] Lammers responded on 28 August by telegram, stating that he awaited a definite, distinct, clarified answer as to whether or not the *KSCV* was prepared to implement Aryan regulations without exception by 1 November 1935.[139] Blunck's return telegram, supported by letters on 28 and 30 August,[140] stated that Nazi Party regulations for admittance and membership had already been practised for some time by the *KSCV*.[141] Blunck continued to differentiate between the active or student members of the corps, who were all in line with party membership requirements and the corps alumni with their very few non-Aryan members who came under the exemptions of the Tenured Civil Servants ruling. Lammers wanted the more stringent regulations imposed and was not willing to allow any exceptions. He wanted the harsher rulings voluntarily accepted by the *KSCV*.

In his resignation speech, Lammers went on to say that there had been a meeting of the *GStV Arbeitskreis* on 23 August and during the aeroplane flight to Berchtesgaden he had clarified through strong intimations to Blunck's assistant Kraaz, what in fact would be the ramifications should any of the federations not voluntarily comply with his directives. Lammers purposely did not make any specific suggestions as the voluntary nature of the exercise would have been destroyed. He went on to question what Kraaz had absorbed from their conversations, if in fact he had gleaned anything at all, judging from the final results. He claimed to have specifically stated to Kraaz that a non-Aryan was not to be granted the right of satisfaction. Such an incident had already happened, and would no doubt occur again, as the *KSCV* still had members who were *unsatisfaktionsfähig* under *ADW* regulations. In the case of Corps Palaiomarchia of Halle, Lammers related that because of two non-Aryan alumni he had been forced to send his assistant Dr Michaelson to investigate the situation with the result that Lammers had to expel Corps Palaiomarchia from both the *GStV* and the *KSCV*. This disciplinary action against a *KSCV* corps by Lammers without consultation with Blunck, evoked considerable protest from both Blunck and the corps, which Lammers then interpreted as insubordination on the part of the *KSCV*.[142] In the late afternoon of Thursday, 5 September 1935, Blunck received the following telegram:

> I hereby expel the *KSCV* from the *GStV* as its executive refused to voluntarily carry out my wishes for the complete implementation of the Aryan regulations.
>
> Lammers[143]

Blunck apparently was thunderstruck by the message; so much so that Kraaz was asked to contact Lammers on his behalf. After much effort Kraaz managed to contact Lammers by telephone and asked him to reconsider and to withdraw his decision to ostracise the *KSCV*. Kraaz was instructed to phone again later that same evening, which he did only to be told that Lammers did not wish to speak to him any further on the matter. Kraaz phoned again shortly before midnight to leave the message that the *KSCV* had imposed Lammers' wishes. It later came to light that Kraaz was actually playing for time and that the corps had been instructed that they had until 1 November to apply the Aryan regulations to their total membership without exception. The following day the *GStV* Circular 23/35 appeared in which Lammers announced the expulsion of both the *DB* and *KSCV* and also called the meeting for 8 September indicating that he would resign at that time.[144] Needless to say, Blunck had Kraaz appealed and protested to Lammers as to the unfairness of the expulsion, particularly as no indication of Lammers' displeasure with the *KSCV* had been evident prior to the notice of excommunication. Blunck again tried to point out that, technically speaking, Lammers had expelled the *SC*'s, in other words the student members, which were in fact in line with Nazi membership regulation procedures. Lammers had not moved against the *Verband Alter Corpsstudenten*; the alumni of the federation. Secretary of State Pfundtner, as a corps alumnus, was asked to intercede with Lammers on behalf of the *KSCV* and Blunck, and complied with the request. Lammers in turn asked Pfundtner to speak to Blunck, in order that a solution might be found for the situation. But the events which ensued between 6 and 8 September hardly made the efforts worthwhile.[145]

At the meeting on 8 September, Lammers explained that in his conversation with Hitler regarding the *GStV* on 16 July and again on 6 August, Lammers had indicated to Hitler that he wished to withdraw from his position as leader of the *GStV*. But in both instances he had been encouraged by Hitler to continue and had been given assurances by the *Führer* that he did not wish the federations disbanded, nor the fraternities dissolved.[146] However, Lammers received a letter from Wagner stating that in accordance with the wishes of the *Führer*, made known on 15 July at Berchtesgaden, the boundaries between the *NSDStB* and the student fraternities had finally been clearly drawn. The *NSDStB* therefore gave notice of its withdrawal from the 12 March agreement with the *GStV*. *NSDStB* training programmes were hence forth not open to the federations, but should vacancies become available, fraternities and individual students could seek information and apply through their local *NSDStB* office.

Wagner's letter, although dated 16 August, was not received by Lammers until 20 August, illustrating again a lack of co-operation with Lammers from yet another quarter; in this case the *NSDStB*. The *NSDStB* did not come under Lammers' jurisdiction as head of the *GStV* but at that point both the *DB* and the *KSCV* did. Lammers indicated that, had the *KSCV* been ready to expel Corps Palaiomarchia, then perhaps the *KSCV* federation under a new leader, could have remained within the *GStV*. But, had the *KSCV* remained in the *GStV* without such alterations, Lammers stood a very real possibility of censure for allowing the *KSCV*, with the non-Aryan members, to remain and skirt the issue while all the other 18 federations were ready to implement the regulations. By expelling both the *KSCV* and the *DB* from the *GStV* because of their unco-operative behaviour, Lammers voided the *GStV* of its two largest federations and he apparently was not prepared to work with a rump organisation.¹⁴⁷ Following Lammers' formal resignation on 8 September, his appointed successor and previous assistant Dr Michaelson, in consultation with the federation representatives to the *GStV*, decided to dissolve the *GStV* as of 1 October 1935. They saw no point in attempting to continue without Lammers as their leader. It was felt that if Lammers, with his position in close proximity to Hitler, could not facilitate co-operation between the federations and Nazi organisations, any further attempts by others were also likely to fail.¹⁴⁸

The *KSCV* was left without allies and had been marked by the *NSDAP* as unco-operative and unacceptable within the National Socialist state. Because of the conflict which had arisen between himself and Lammers, Blunck met with representatives of as many *KSCV* corps as could attend on such short notice, in Hamburg on 8 September. The result was Blunck's resignation from the position of leader both of the student and the alumni sections of the *KSCV*. Also effective as of the following day, Blunck's former assistant, Heringhaus, succeeded him as leader of the *KSCV*. Blunck's parting words to the federation appeared soon after in the *KSCV* periodical. He stated that he had been proud to serve as leader of the *KSCV* and that all his dealings had emanated from his love for *Corpsstudententum* combined with a deep desire to serve the German *Volk* and *Führer*.¹⁴⁹ But Blunck was not to get off quite that lightly. On 15 September a court of honour, composed of five *corpsiers* who were *NSDAP* members, met in Berlin to examine charges against Blunck which alleged that his mishandling of *KSCV* affairs had caused Lammers' censure of the federation. Blunck was cleared of all charges except one minor allegation, that of withholding information from the *SC*'s and the alumni. However, it was conceded that disclosure of the facts in question would not have made any appreciable difference to the eventual outcome and Blunck was exonerated.¹⁵⁰

THE NUREMBERG BLOOD LAWS AND THE LUTZE DECREE

On the same day that Blunck resigned, the Nuremberg Laws dealing with 'Blood Protection and *Reich* Citizenship' came into existence. Under Section Two, Clause Four the exemptions from the Aryan regulations previously granted to tenured civil servants and ex-servicemen were revoked. Any persons given exemption under the earlier legislation were to be superannuated as of 31 December 1935. No one having Jewish blood was eligible for the new citizenship of the *Reich*.

Only persons of German and related blood were qualified to hold *Reich* citizenship and marriage or extra-marital relations with those who were ineligible, was strictly prohibited under the new law. Allegedly the new law was not widely advertised, because Hitler, in order to host the 1936 Olympic Games, had assured the International Olympics Committee on 7 June, that no differences existed between Aryans and Jews in Germany.[151] Because of Lammers' close contact with Hitler as his *Chef der Reichskanzlei*, it is very possible that this accounted for the great emphasis which Lammers had placed upon a voluntary, quiet acceptance and implementation of *NSDAP* membership regulations for the federations. It is fairly certain that something as important as the Blood Protection Act would have been known to Lammers in advance of its introduction and having all *GStV* federations purged of any unacceptable members prior to the introduction of the law would have gone a considerable way to strengthen the position of the *GStV* in the eyes of the state.

The Blood Protection Act was a definite body blow for the corps, but they also received further particular attention. On 19 September, *SA* Chief of Staff, Lutze, published an edict whereby no *SA* leader or member was allowed to hold membership in the *KSCV*, for the simple reason that the federation had declined to implement the general Aryan regulations as practised by the party. *SA* personnel who were also members of a *KSCV* corps, were allowed until 15 October to give notice that they had terminated their corps membership. If not, they would face automatic expulsion from the *SA*.[152]

On 28 September 1935, the decision was taken to dissolve the *KSCV* federation in order that each corps might have the opportunity to align itself directly with the *NSDStB*[153] and thereby find its own path to survival within the new regime. In the *KSCV* Circular Number 46, published on 9 October, Heringhaus stated that the disbanding was not as a result of the Aryan regulations issue, nor a result of Lutze's decree regarding the *SA* ban on corps members. Heringhaus claimed that the dissolution of the *KSCV* had been found necessary in order to give the corps a free hand to facilitate their co-operation, and in particular their integration, into the *NSDStB*.[154] Each of the many factors alone was perhaps not sufficient to bring about the disbanding of the *KSCV*, but with the history of animosity between the *NSDStB* and the *KSCV*, the Lutze Decree appears to have been the final straw regarding its dissolution. Heringhaus' argument is not terribly convincing, for newpaper articles with headlines such as 'Jews, Freemasons and Kösener *SC*' *(Juden, Freimaurer und Cösener SC)* were still being published in mid-October. The article above appeared in the *Deutsche Wollen* and described the battle of National Socialism against the archaic fraternities and in particular the *KSCV* which designated itself as apolitical. Indeed, more than half of the lengthy article is given to describing the transgressions and lack of co-operation exhibited on the part of the *KSCV* towards the National Socialist state.[155] Interestingly, a number of very pro-Nazi newspapers insisted upon using a 'C' in spelling Kösen. This is clearly in opposition to the practice at the time of Germanising words. It would appear that this anomaly was the product of certain newspapers wishing to attack the *KSCV* by emphasising its *unvölkisch* attitude through associating it with foreign letter 'C' rather than the German 'K'.

On 25 October, Lutze issued a further proclamation; namely that as the dissolution of the *KSCV* was to take effect, members of any individual corps which did not enforce his edict of 19 September, stood under threat of the same censure regardless of whether or not they were still a corps of the *KSCV* federation.[156] The rout was almost complete as far as restraints on the non-Aryan members were concerned. Through dissolution, the *KSCV* reverted to what it had been 90 years previously, a grouping of loosely affiliated and similar student fraternities. However, there was now one great difference. The corps were required to take an interest in ideological politics and their members forced to enrol in the *NSDStB*, both of which violated *KSCV* traditional practices and statutes.

In sharp contrast, the *Deutsche Burschenschaft (DB)* and the *NSDStB* concluded a special agreement on 5 October 1935, known as the Plauen Agreement, whereby the *DB* was to join the *NSDStB en bloc*. The agreement was signed by Glauning and Derichsweiler and called for all *DB* fraternities to convert themselves into *Kameradscahften* in accordance with *NSDStB* regulations and to be placed under the auspices and direction of the *NSDStB*. No fraternity colours or flags were to exist for the new *Kameradschaften* and their identity were to be solely that of an entity within their local *NSDStB* organisation.[157]

On 18 October 1935 a special ceremony was held at the *DB*'s traditional meeting place; the Wartburg in Eisenach. The occasion was to join both formally and symbolically, the historic and nationalistic traditions of the *DB*, with the vital and ongoing student movement of the new state, embodied in the *NSDStB*. The *DB* flag from 1818 was handed over ceremoniously to *NSDStB* leaders, indicating that the *DB* had completed its chapter in German history and through transfer of its colours gave recognition to the new leadership offered by the *NSDStB*.

Blunck as Führer of the KSCV

This was followed by each fraternity of the *DB* parading past a large bonfire, into which all members threw their fraternity caps and bands – thereby symbolising the fusing together of the *DB* and the *NSDStB*.[158]

As so often before, the paths taken by the *KSCV* and the *DB* were very different, and both consistent with their individual histories. Following its nationalistic bent the *DB* joined the *NSDStB*, marked by the ceremonious proceedings outlined above. The *KSCV*, on the other hand, equally true to its traditions, dissolved its federation rather than comply with further Nazi directives.

5 The *Verbotzeit*, 1936-45

THE *KAMERADSCHAFTEN*

By mid-November 1935 the majority of federations formed by student fencing fraternities had submitted to Nazi pressure and disbanded; the most prominent of these being the corps and the *Deutsche Burschenschaft*. The latter, as stated above, had given their traditional banners from the 1818 Wartburgfest into the custody of the *NSDStB*, thereby symbolically acknowledging their joining the marchstep of the 'Brown Column' and ceding to newer, stronger hands, their historic, self-appointed role as leaders in the struggle of German student nationalism. The corps of the *WSC* co-ordinated the dissolution of their federation on 20 October 1935, with the conversion of their houses into *Kameradschaften* in the hope that as independent entities, rather than as an amalgamation, their corps could survive within the *Reich*. The corps of the *KSCV* refused to expel their non-Aryan and Freemason members, and dissolved their federation of fraternities rather than compromise their traditional apolitical policy of tolerance.

The defeat of the fencing fraternities' federations was not enough for national student Führer, Derichsweiler, or the Nazi Party, and apparently nothing short of a complete rout would suffice. Many student fraternities had hoped, as had the *WSC*, to ingratiate themselves with the *NSDAP* through complying with the *Kameradschaften* programme. These new fraternity-like hybrid societies were set up by those fraternities which opted to co-operate with the *NSDStB* scheme for reforming post-secondary educational institutions, through the introduction of this Nazi approved alternative to the old student fraternities. The very significant difference was that the *Kameradschaften* were established primarily for the political education of academe. With their federations techically disbanded, many of the fraternities, and particularly those with a strong nationalistic bent such as the *Deutsche Burschenschaften*, lost little time in complying with Nazi Party wishes to create *Kameradschaften*. The renovations were undertaken in the belief that the fraternities involved would be given a special place in the academic community of the Third Reich.

The Verbotzeit, 1936–45   143

A less grandiose position was adopted by other fraternities which cooperated merely in the hope that if they continued to give enough ground, it would be interpreted by the party as a token of good faith and that they would eventually be left in peace. These fraternities felt that a compromised existence was preferable to the complete extinction of their organisations and traditions. Apparently a considerable number of the fraternities which renovated their houses as required by the *NSDStB*, used the conversion period to stall and in fact they were found to have not become *Kameradschaften* in anything more than the alterations to their houses.

This was perplexing enough for Derichsweiler, but the corps of the *KSCV* repeatedly posed an enigmatic problem for him. Initially they had declined *en bloc* to become *Kameradschaften* and following the dissolution of their federation, each individual fraternity had to be dealt with as an autonomous entity rather than through a federal executive which could be held responsible for the actions of its members. In an attempt to bring the corps and other dissenting fraternities into line, Derichsweiler issued a directive in November 1935 declaring that members of the *NSDStB* were not allowed to hold additional membership in an existing or suspended fraternity as well. Those members affected by this ruling were given until 1 January 1936 to verify their termination of any fraternity membership. Exemption was given to the members of such fraternities as had already become *NSDStB Kameradschaften*.[1] The *Kameradschaften* of the *NSDStB* naturally housed only *NSDStB* members and Derichsweiler also stated that no first semester student would be allowed membership in any fraternity which had not become a *Kameradschaft* in accordance with the directives and under the auspices of the *NSDStB*. But it was Rudolf Hess speaking at the tenth anniversary celebration of the *NSDStB* at Munich in January 1936, who illustrated the definite animosity which the *NSDStB* and the Nazi Party felt towards the student fraternities. From that date onward, the *Kameradschaften* were to have no alumni associations (*Altherrenschaften*).[2] In that way the party sought to eliminate what was thought to be the conservative and reactionary influence of the *Alte Herren* on the younger fraternity members.

Hess's further comments, which were carried by *Die Bewegung* of January 1936, made it very clear that the party leadership felt the traditional student fraternities had outlived their usefulness.

> Just as they once helped to overcome irrelevant conventions, so must they today in turn be voided that the new can grow! . . . In the long run they must yield if anyone tries to adapt them to the new times,

especially at this time when the nation is still too strongly steeped in the memories of the past.³

The fraternities which had not moved eagerly into step with the 'Brown Column', apparently were also to be eliminated from the Nazi student movement.

In describing the animosity of the *NSDStB* for the corps in Freiburg during the winter semester of 1935–6, Leo Richter relates that members of the *NSDStB* and Hitler Youth adopted the habit of grabbing and tearing-off fraternity members' tricolour bands whenever they saw one worn. It then became a symbol of protest on the part of corps members to wear their bands in public and they eventually dampened the enthusiasm of the young Nazis by lining razor blades to the inside of their bands which soon made the Nazis think seriously before attempting to seize bands as souvenirs.⁴

Reicharztführer Dr Wagner, himself a *Burschenschaft* alumnus, was the party representative who delivered one of the final blows to his own federation on 27 January 1936. It was he who announced that the Plauen Agreement, which had been reached between the *NSDStB* and the *Deutsche Burschenschaft* on 5 October 1935, and promised to give the *Deutsche Burschenschaft* special status as the only federation of student fraternities allowed to continue their traditions within the Third Reich, was henceforth annulled because he, Wagner, did not agree with it in principle. *Die Bewegung*, as official organ of the *NSDStB*, had made much of the agreement, but apparently that bore little weight in favour of the case for the *Deutsche Burschenschaft*, which following Wagner's proclamation, found itself in much the same situation as the other federations.⁵ But that was not all. The *DB* chapters, which had co-operated with the *Kameradschaften* programme were also to lose their alumni associations. Apparently the whole system of *Kameradschaften* was to be reorganised along completely new lines and would ignore even the efforts made by the more compliant fraternities. In fact, this left only those fraternities which had not complied with the party's programme of *Kameradschaften*, more specifically the *KSCV* corps, to be brought into line.⁶

The corps were not optimistic about the treatment to which they would be subjected. If the *DB* fraternities, which had co-operated so faithfully with the wishes of the *NSDStB*, were subjected to broken agreements, what awaited the corps which had formed no *Kameradschaften* whatever during the same period?⁷

Press coverage reflected the Nazi attitude towards the corps. An

The Verbotzeit, 1936–45   145

article in the *Bremer Zeitung* on 27 January 1936, exhibited the headline 'Against Corps Students and Communism' and its author made claims that only the *NSDStB* was fighting against the subversive activities of the corps and communists at the universities.[8] As seen above, the traditional apolitical stance of the corps had been maintained, which meant that such statements and allegations were in actual fact untrue. But the corps had no means by which to defend themselves other than through their own internally circulated publications. This, then, left the party and the *NSDStB* free to make whatever accusations they wished without being challenged.

Sensing that immediate action was necessary if the corps of the *KSCV* were to continue their existence in any form whatsoever, Dr Ernst Schlange, leader of the *KSCV*, called an extraordinary general meeting of *Kösener* corps in Berlin for 2 February 1936. Following Blunck's resignation as *KSCV* leader, his successor Heringhaus, in conjunction with the new *KSCV Vorort* of Hamburg and the *VAC* (*KSCV* alumni association) had appointed Schlange leader of both sections of the *KSCV*. The observation was made at the meeting of 2 February, that the attacks of the *NSDStB* against corps were based upon university politics and primarily against the 'active' or student section of the corps. Therefore, if the corps no longer existed as active student organisations, the main target for criticism would disappear and it could be assumed that the attacks by the *NSDStB* would subside. With that in mind, Schlange advised, and it was adopted, that the corps would cease to be 'active' associations. Party edicts already forbade the corps to recruit new students and without new members there was little point in expending the efforts necessary to continue activities within the university community. The solution suggested to deal with the situation was for each corps to place its student members within its alumni association, thereby removing them from the roll of 'active' fraternity students and out of the *NSDStB*'s direct line of attack.[9] This then, would relieve the immediate pressure on the corps, as they could not be accused further of reactionary behaviour within the university community if they no longer existed as a student group.

As a second precaution, Schlange advised all corps students to join the *NSDStB* in order to remove possible further grounds for Nazi criticism of the corps; either individually or collectively.[10] In this way the corps were to become merely groups of student alumni who previously had studied together and who wished to meet occasionally for the purpose of reminiscing. These alumni groups, with no active student membership, would die out with their last members. In his *Besondere Mitteilungen* dated Potsdam, 2 February 1936, Schlange made the point that a corps, by the very nature of its constitution, could not be dissolved, only suspended, since its members had life tenure and a corps was its membership, not the property which it might possess. However, within the context of the university a suspension could be seen as a dissolution of the corps, as no more activities would take place centred within the university community by its members. Such suspensions, described as dissolution, were to be communicated by each corps in writing, to the Rector of its respective university as soon as possible, in order to protect the *alumni* from possible attacks by the party.[11] Schlange further requested that the decision of 2 February 1936, regarding the placing of student members among the *alumni* be completed by 1 April 1936 so that they could be officially entered upon the composite corps roll as such. The *KSCV* periodical, *Die Deutsche Corpszeitung*, was to be terminated in April, following a decision taken on 2 February 1936, and all notices for regional or social meetings were to be received by the editor prior to 1 April 1936, so that they could be conveyed in the last issue of the monthly magazine. Any correspondence regarding the corps was to be addressed to Schlange personally so as not to draw attention within the post office. This, it was hoped, would allow the corps of the former *KSCV* to slip quietly into a rather less obvious and innocuous existence.[12]

In brief, there was no official federation of *KSCV* corps because it had been dissolved on 29 October 1935, and no active corps would exist at any *Reich* university as the new Nazi students were forbidden by party edicts to join any fraternity. Furthermore, no active corps would exist as a notice of dissolution would have been submitted by each corps to the authorities at their respective university. To non-members the corps would appear to exist only for the purpose of occasional gatherings such as a *Stammtisch* or a ladies' evening. They would be small associations of academic alumni, growing ever smaller through the attrition of the years and ceasing to exist with the death of their last members. It was hoped that the appearance never would become reality.

This manoeuvre was employed none too soon, for *Die Bewegung* of 20 May 1936 stated that at which the *NSDAP* previously only had hinted: Rufolf Hess, as spokesman for the party, made the declaration that any member of the party, or member of a party associated group, was forbidden membership in any extant student fraternity.[13] The corps technically had successfully managed to side-step a direct confrontation with the party.

However, Hess made a further statement in the form of an appeal which outlined the party's new plan regarding the reformation of the *Kameradschaften*. The defunct Nazi student movement assistance fund, the *NS-Studentenkampfhilfe*, which had been founded in 1933 on the strength of a mere statement by Hitler that the *NSDStB* should be assisted, was to be re-established along new lines to aid the work of the *Kameradschaften*. Hess called upon all those who had post-secondary school training to support the youth as true comrades by joining and contributing to the *Studentenkampfhilfe*.[14] Under the new scheme the participating alumni, known as *Altakademiker*, were to be organised into a system of *Ort*, *Kreis* and *Gau* organisations. These groups were to support the new system of *Kameradschaften* in general but were to have no direct connection with a particular university or *Kameradschaft*.[15] This meant that the *NS-Studentenkampfhilfe* would be an organisation of alumni who were willing to support the party's political education programme at the universities, but who, after giving their financial support to the programme would not be allowed any affiliation with either the students or the *Kameradschaften*. The programme, needless to say, was not a great success.

On 15 April 1936, the *SA* and *NSDStB* finally reached an agreement on the form which the new student organisation would take. As of the summer semester 1936, each institution of higher education would have a *Stamm-Mannschaft* comprised of up to sixty members. The students chosen for membership would be either party members or those considered to be of a compatible mentality and the tenure of membership within a *Stamm-Mannschaft* would be at least three semesters. In addition, there were to be *Stamm-Kameradschaften* composed of up to thirty members, who were to possess the qualities of 'ideologically reliable comrades'. These new *Kameradschaften* of the *Stamm-Mannschaften* were to serve as training units for student leaders of the fraternity initiated and funded *Kameradschaften*. Under Point Six of the agreement the *NSDStB* accepted responsibility to ensure that all German students would become members of at least one of the *NSDAP*, *SA*, *SS*, or *NSKK*. Following these *NSDStB* guidelines all students were to be organised into *Kameradschaften* of not more than thirty members, in line with the type of association which they had with the *SA*, *SS*, *NSKK*, etc.[16] This effectively made party affiliated groups the only legitimate student associations at the universities.

Derichsweiler's speech at the *NSDAP* national party conference at Nuremberg in 1935 had foreshadowed the dissolution of the student fraternities and disclosed the party's displeasure at their harbouring what were considered to be 'outmoded corporative ideals'. As national

NSDStB leader Derichsweiler freely stated, 'anyone who still wears fraternity colours is considered by the *NSDStB* to be a reactionary and an enemy of its *Weltanschauung*'.[17]

The *Kameradschaften* which had been set up by many of the fraternities between 1934 and 1936, in an attempt to adapt themselves to the Third Reich, apparently had not been radical enough in their attempts to participate in the *NSDStB*'s 'march' and were to be eradicated for their timid efforts. Even the corps, which had always followed a policy of non-involvement in party politics and had struggled not to implicate themselves in the daily and ideological politics of the Third Reich, were forced to suspend their activities at the universities. The field had been cleared of the *NSDStB*'s opponents and *Die Bewegung* smugly wrote that the traditional symbols of the student fraternities finally had gone to the grave. 'And the rising rumble from the marchsteps of the brown columns of our National Socialist students fills the fresh air with ringing songs. And the hazy fumes are blown out of smoke-filled student taverns.'[18] Theoretically the rout was complete.

However, no great success was forthcoming for the new system of *Kameradschaften*. There was little impetus for students to form *Kameradschaften*[19] and few of the potential *Altakademiker* were sufficiently enthused with the idea of the new party training units to pay out a minimum of two *Reichsmark* a month to an organisation with whom they were to have no contact.[20] Most fraternity alumni had little interest in supporting an organisation which had been responsible for the demise of their fraternities and which after carrying through its measures of enmity, seemed interested only in the acquisition of fraternity houses and other property for the further promotion of the *NSDAP*. For this reason many fraternities sold or rented out their houses and held their meetings secretly in rooms hired solely for that purpose so as not to expose their communal property to the danger of confiscation by the party.

By July 1936, the future looked rather gloomy for the *Kameradschaften* and Adolf Wagner, who was by this point, leader of the *NS-Studentenkampfhilfe*, *Gauleiter* and *Staatsminister*, attempted with little success, to inspire membership in the programme. 'The community of German academics marches in unison under my leadership; the veteran beside the young guard at the institutes of higher education, in loyalty and for the good of the German nation.'[21] The new system had proved not to be a success and could quite easily have dwindled away into oblivion had the leadership of the Nazi student organisation not changed. On 5 November 1936, Derichsweiler was replaced by Dr

Gustav Adolf Scheel, who combined his new leadership of the *NSDStB* and his existing position as *Führer* of the *Deutsche Studentschaft (DSt)* under the title of *Reichsstudentenführer*. Scheel had himself been a member of a *satisfaktionsfähig* student fraternity while studying at the University of Tübingen, which goes a great way in accounting for the radical change of approach and attitudes adopted by the *NSDStB* leadership towards the fraternities; a stance which previously had exhibited little other than open hostility.²² However, the change of course was not adopted without protest on the part of a good many *NSDStB* members.

This change of attitude went so far that by 23 February 1937, *Die Bewegung* actually praised the fraternities for their work in the years before the founding of the Third Reich. Apparently, in that era nobody had bothered with the proper political education and the well-being of students, and the fraternities had served the important function of nurturing their student members to become men of strong body and character. Scheel's new approach almost reached the proportions of a public relations campaign. He further supported plans by the city of Würzburg to establish an archive for materials associated with university and student history; particularly that of student fraternities and federations.²³ But even such open courting of the fraternities in his attempt to induce them to form *Kameradschaften* could not be successful if the students were unwilling to form the units.

In order to induce the old fraternities to adopt the new system of student associations, Scheel, shortly after his appointment, announced the introduction of a new code of honour which would require all *NSDStB* members to give satisfaction at arms, if the situation arose.²⁴ Scheel's own fraternity had been one of the type which demanded that its members gave satisfaction at arms but had not practised the *Bestimmungsmensur*. It is therefore quite easy to see an attempt on the part of Scheel to promote the traditions of his own fraternity and to synthesis them with the ideology of the *NSDAP*, in order form a new type of student association in the *Kameradschaften*. The penal code of 26 April 1933, legalised the *Bestimmungsmensur* in contrast to its illegality during the Weimar Republic, yet under its own disciplinary code the *NSDStB* did not allow its members to fence *Mensuren*. Scheel's amendment to the *NSDStB* code of honour did not change the association's position disallowing its members to fence *Mensuren*. The code as originally published in *Die Bewegung* of 8 July 1930 and presented to the *ADW* by the *NSDStB* at Erfurt, called for all *NSDStB* members to give satisfaction – either *Verbriefte* or at arms – whenever called upon.

Scheel's amendment did prompt some of the fraternities to apply to the *NSDStB* for permission to found *Kameradschaften*, but the response was still not in the proportions needed to form the type of organisation which Scheel had in mind and it soon became clear that further measures would be necessary if the idea was to reach fruition.

German students traditionally had enjoyed a certain amount of academic mobility which allowed them to transfer from one university to another in order to pursue certain courses of study. It became the practice of many students during the early years of the Third Reich to use this convention as a means of avoiding the regulations requiring mandatory membership in an *NSDAP* affiliated organisation.[25] In order to facilitate the *NSDStB* education programme during the first three semesters of study, Scheel issued an edict, the *Stammhochschulerlass*, which required all students to spend, at least their initial three semesters of study at the same university. This was ensured by a new regulation which refused students registration at any other than their initial university until at least their fourth semester, unless an applicant for transferred immatriculation was able to present documentation from the Rector of his previous university which cited appropriate reasons for the change.[26] *Die Bewegung* of 2 March 1937 boasted of 14 000 members in the new *Kameradschaften* which had been founded at the universities and other institutions of higher education. The accuracy of the number is open to some doubt, but the article went on to state:

> The goal of this new way of life, based upon National Socialist *Weltanschauung*, is to create men who, because of their deportment, abilities and determination, will be able to master the tasks produced in the reorganisation of higher education and in their later professional life.[27]

But Scheel's statement of November 1936, regarding the giving of satisfaction at arms by members of the *NSDStB* had not yet been fully implemented. This was finally accomplished through an article in *Die Bewegung* on 17 April 1937 by *SS-Hauptsturmführer* Dr Sandberger. He stated that the duties of every *NSDStB* member were not easy, but the task given to the organisation by the *Führer* was to create a distinguished and ideologically sound leader class for the nation and state. Therefore, anyone wishing to be taken seriously while studying and also wishing to prepare themselves for a life of leadership, must himself adopt and live the laws of the German student community.[28] The article further stated that all matters of questioned honour must be brought before the national *NSDStB* executive for a ruling as to whether sufficient grounds existed for the demanding of satisfaction. Instruction in fencing with a modified lightweight sabre, which was the weapon adopted by the *NSDStB* for its members, was to be given by the instructors of the local institute of physical education and two periods of instruction per week would be mandatory for all *NSDStB* members. The point was driven further home by the fact that the *Wehrmacht*, the *SA* and the *SS* had recently also adopted the practice of their members giving satisfaction at arms. The *NSDStB* was not to prove an exception and Scheel stated: 'I proclaim for all members of the *NSDStB* and its *Kameradschaften*, the axiom that offended honour can only be redressed by force of arms. Any other concept of honour will no longer have any currency among German students.'[29] Through the above measures, all German students were required to give satisfaction at arms. This development re-established a practice which roughly corresponded with the traditional *comment* of the *Senioren-Conventen*. However, the great difference in this case was the strange mixture of traditional honourable deportment with the *völkische* ideology of the Third Reich. This strange combination of Nazi concoction declared all and only German students *satisfaktionsfähig*.

Another traditional strong point of the fraternities had been the relationship of the alumni to the younger members. With that in mind, Hess announced on 14 May 1937 that the *Studentenkampfhilfe* was to be incorporated into the forthcoming Nazi association for fraternity alumni, the *NS-Altherrenbund*. The *Studentenkampfhilfe* was to be structurally modified so that members of the new *NS-Altherrenbund* would be allowed to choose the academic community which they wished to support and a specific *Kameradschaft* within that group, if they so desired.[30]

But any hopes of re-establishing themselves through the new programme which the suspended fraternities might have fostered upon learning of the scheme, were soon dashed, for only the new Nazi sponsored *Altherrenschaft* would be given official recognition. Although not explicitly stated, this meant that all other alumni associations, even if associated with a dissolved fraternity such as the corps, would be considered illegal if they refused the invitation offered through Hess to affiliate with the *NS-Altherrenschaft*.

Within a month of the above declaration, there appeared an appeal entitled 'Proclamation to old *Waffenstudenten*!' which bore the signatures of the federation leaders of all the major fencing fraternities. This publication followed a meeting of the signatories in Berlin on 25

May 1937 and stated that all those who were members of one of the represented federations were to stand aside no longer and should join the new party sponsored alumni association, the *Altherrenbund deutscher Studenten der NS-Studentenkampfhilfe*. It further asserted that no one who considered himself to be honourable could ignore this great obligation to establish one large organisation which united students and alumni.[31] This was followed by the formal introduction of the amended *NSDStB* code of honour on 23 June 1937 which called for unquestioned satisfaction to be given by members of *NSDStB Kameradschaften* when called upon; albeit only with the lightest of sabres. Following this policy change, many of the fencing fraternities were moved to take a more favourable attitude towards forming *Kameradschaften* under the new system. However, the corps, with very few exceptions, were still not sufficiently enthralled to move into an alliance with their former enemy. But Scheel apparently became impatient, and declared in a press announcement on 2 February 1938, that only a certain number of *Kameradschaften* would be allowed to form at any university and those fraternities which did not join the *NS-Altherrenschaft* by 15 May 1938, with at least the majority of their Alte Herren,[32] would be excluded from forming their own *Kameradschaft*.[33] However, the deciding factor in most cases was that fraternity alumni associations which co-operated with the new *Studentenkampfhilfe* programme and placed their houses at the disposal of a *NSDStB* approved *Kameradschaft*, were to remain the sole owners of the property. This appears to have been the motivating force for most of those corps which finally formed *Kameradschaften*. The greatest problem for the younger corps members, was to persuade the *Alte Herren* that they should in fact join an association which only a few months previously had denounced them as an arch-reactionary element, working in conjunction with communists to undermine the progress of National Socialism. But apparently the wish to preserve their common property outweighed the scepticism which the alumni felt regarding the *NSDStB*.

In some university communities, such as Würzburg and Freiburg, most of the local corps managed to organise a sufficient number of their *Alte Herren* in order to form their own individual *Kameradschaften*. In many other centres such as Göttingen and Heidelberg, the local *SC* banded together to form one *Kameradschaft*; usually under the leadership of the corps which provided the house used by the organisation for its activities. A hybrid version of the two former arrangements also existed at other universities such as at Erlangen, where the *SC* formed several *Kameradschaften*, each composed of members from two or more corps.

However, one of the questions plaguing the new *Kameradschaften* centred upon the lack of an adequate outline stating the requirements which the party and the *NSDStB* would demand from the organisations. This was finally answered by Scheel's publication *Die Reichsstudentenführung* in which he set down the duties and obligations not only of the *NSDStB* but of the *Kameradschaften* as well. The *Kameradschaften* were to be educational and residential communities which encompassed the whole life of the student. The duties of the student *Kameradschaft* were to be reflected in their names which would encapsulate their goals and obligations. Names of individual *Kameradschaften* were to be taken from those of German warriors and the battlefields upon which the fate of the nation had been decided. These names would illuminate the goals and provide symbols for the tasks ahead. The *Kameradschaften* were to fly flags of the *NSDStB* which would be entrusted to each *Kameradschaft* as it earned the honour.[34]

There were also regulations to be enforced regarding the rank and file of the *Kameradschaften*. After a waiting period of four weeks, a new student who was found to be suitable for membership by a *Kameradschaft* was allowed to join.[35] He was required to swear that during his mandatory three semesters at his *Stammhochschule* he would abide by the Ten Laws of the German Student as set down by the *Reichsstudentenführung*, to accomplish the tasks assigned to him by the *NSDStB*[36] and to give satisfaction at arms, by means of sharpened swords, in disputes of honour.[37] During his obligatory three semesters in the *Kameradschaft* a new member was known as *Jungkamerad*, then elevated to *Altkamerad* and after completion of his studies he was allowed to become an *Alter Herr* of his *Kameradschaft*. This further emphasised the difference in approach between Scheel and his predecessor. Derichsweiler had tried to eliminate the relationship between students and alumni, while Scheel in turn sought to promote and restore the connection.

Each *Kameradschaft* was led by a *Kameradschaftsführer* whose duty it was to administer the *Kameradschaft* in line with the *Führer* Principle of the *NSDAP*. As seen above, this method by its very definition, dispensed with the traditional corps *Convent* from which the corps *Senior* took a democratic mandate upon which to act. Further regulations called for a semester plan, broken down into daily and weekly activity periods, which was to include political education, communal meals, cultural events and even monthly meetings with the alumni.[38] But despite Scheel's reorganisation of the *Kameradschaften*, the most vital aspect, that of camaraderie, could not be enforced and was sorely missing in the case of most *Kameradschaften*. As membership in a party affiliated organisation was mandatory for all students, many students were not particularly enthusiastic and by the winter semester of 1938-9, the complaint of 'paper members', that is to say those in name only, became rather commonplace among the local *NSDStB* leaders.

At the local level of organisation, activities at less than 10 of the 22 universities have been chronicled, but interestingly, despite the lack of movement and liaison between the university communities after 1936, many similarities existed in the reactions of the *Kameradschaften* established by former corps, towards the edicts of Scheel's *Reichsstudentenführung* and the programme in general.

Between 1936, and Scheel's pronouncement of 1938, the corps remained basically private social groups. The houses, in most cases, were used to accommodate relatives and friends of corps members and corps members confined their group meetings to prearranged *Stammtische*, etc. in keeping with the decisions taken by *KSCV* leaders in 1936. But certain traditional corps practices continued regardless of official policy and direction.

The Nazi penal code of 1933 had exempted the *Mensur* from the category of armed assault. However, the *NSDStB* code of honour, by which all students were expected to conduct themselves, did not allow *Mensur* fencing. Furthermore, all students were required to belong to a party affiliated organisation, none of which sanctioned *Mensur* fencing. This then meant that in theory *Mensur* fencing was allowed, but under *NSDStB* regulations nobody was permitted to engage in it, with the result that *Mensur* fencing was viewed as illegal by the *NSDAP*. However, in several centres, such as Tübingen, corps members continued *Mensur* fencing in strict secrecy.[39] In Freiburg, as early as January 1936, a local *Waffenring* was formed by twelve of the local fencing fraternities. This organisation was not only protected, but unofficially promoted by the local *NSDStB Führer*, Andreas Rost and his successor, both of whom had been *Landsmannschaft* members. However, they in turn were followed in office by Pagels, who was a *SS* member and was described by acquaintances as being no less than a 100 per cent Nazi. When Pagels discovered that between 60 and 70 per cent of the *Kameradschaft* members under his jurisdiction had engaged in *Mensur* fencing, he immediately began proceedings against the offenders. Intercession on behalf of the offenders was made through personal connections at the national *NSDStB* headquarters in Munich, by Professor Wirth. His appeal for amnesty, in conjunction with the beginning of the Polish Campaign, broke the momentum of the case against the Freibrug fencers and in the end they only were barred from holding membership in the *NSDStB* and *NSDAP*.[40]

The new *Kameradschaften* formed in 1938, were required to undergo a probationary period, during which time they were known simply by a designated number such as *K5* or *K7*, etc. This was much the same as the nomenclature used for other Nazi groups such as the *SA Sturm* and the Hitler Youth *Bann*.[41] After the third month of the trial period a new *Kameradschaft* was allowed to fly the flag of the *NSDStB*[42] and to take the name of a personality of importance in the struggle and history of the German nation.[43] The *SC* corps *Kameradschaft* at the University of Göttingen for example, took the name Freiherr vom Stein and the *SC* of Leipzig, that of the Markgraf von Meissen. Each name was assigned to only one *Kameradschaft* and had first to be approved by the national *NSDStB* executive before the *Kameradschaft* was allowed to officially take the name. The most logical name for the *SC Kameradschaft* of Göttingen to adopt would have been that of Otto von Bismarck, as he had been a member of Corps Hannovera zu Göttingen. However, another *Kameradschaft* made an earlier application for the use of Bismark's name and was awarded the right over the application of the *SC Kameradschaft*.

With the beginning of the war in 1939, many of the universities temporarily closed their doors and when they reopened the composition of their respective student bodies was in many cases appreciably changed. Most of the *Kameradschaften* formed by corps tended to be composed predominantly of military personnel or relatives of corps alumni. In the Kameradschaft Freiherr vom Stein for example, of the 72 members received into the *Kameradschaft* during its six years of existence, 15 were officers in the cavalry. The proportion of university students composed from army personnel on study leave continued to grow throughout the war and was a very influential element within the *Kameradschaften* for several reasons. In the first instance, military personnel were neither eligible for membership in the *NDSDStB*, nor were they under the jurisdiction of the *NSDStB* which allowed them to act with a certain amount of impunity. Furthermore, they had little appetite for the propaganda sessions led by civilian members of the *NSDStB*, most of whom, although they had never seen military action, extolled at great lengths the virtues of fighting and dying for the *Vaterland*.[44] These soldiers having returned from the front well understood the meaning of camaraderie and wanted to experience the traditional *joie de vivre* of academe, not suffer through pompous ravings on 'Blood and Soil' by the party faithful.

In addition to the soldiers on study leave, there were other military groups, such as the Institute for Naval Medicine which moved from Kiel to Tübingen in 1941 and the Ambulance Medical Corps which relocated at Münster in 1942; both of which helped to enlarge the non-*NSDStB* population of those universities. In 1941, a group of army officers at the University of Bonn formed a society called the *Aktive Wehrstudenten-Korps* and approached the local *SC Kameradschaft*, Yorck von Wartenburg to sponsor them as a group interested in *Mensur* fencing. They were welcomed into the local fencing society and proved to be a great asset for they furnished eight opponents for the sixteen matches fenced during the Summer Semester of 1941. This paved the way for their eventual adoption into the *SC* as part of the former Corps Rhenania zu Bonn following to war.[45]

At least as far as appearances were concerned, the daily and weekly programmes submitted to the local *NSDStB* office for approval, were followed faithfully. In actual fact, there are numerous accounts of *Kameradschaften* which completed the semester summary reports of their political education lectures and other activities at the beginning rather than at the end of the semester. It was freely admitted that many members considered *NSDStB* programmes a great waste of time and felt they could spend their time better doing almost anything else.[46] Along with this indifference to *NSDStB* programmes, there developed a gradual readoption of certain fraternity insignia and an interest in traditional fraternity practices. The use of the traditional fraternity *Zipfel* to indicate personal membership in a specific *Kameradschaft* soon became a general, although secretive practice, within corps circles and before long incorporated the reappearance of both fraternity colours and *Zirkel*. In many cases, the weekly periods which were designated for political education, were actually used for the tuition of new members in the traditional identification of corps by their specific colours and insignia, as well as instruction in corps history and etiquette; much as novices would have been taught in any corps only a few years previously.

The encroachment of traditional fraternity practices soon became almost second nature within the *Kameradschaften* and by 1942 even the *NSDStB* was referring to its *Kamaradschaften* members not as *Kameraden*, but as *Jungbursch, Bursch* and *Alter Herr*. By the Summer Semester of 1942, the Kameradschaft Freiherr vom Stein had altered its constitution to such an extent that it resembled that of its forerunner, Corps Hannovera, almost verbatim. There were, however, two exceptional items to the document. The first was the introduction of a minimum age for members which was specifically designed to exclude a specific new party sponsored group of students, the *Langemarkstudenten*, whom the *NSDAP* placed in the universities at a relatively young age. The second item was a statement supporting *Mensur* fencing and declaring the hope that it would be practised again in the near future.⁴⁷ In addition, all written items such as internal bulletins had to be meticulously scrutinised for glib or careless wording, since all material for distribution was vetted by the local *NSDStB* leader and a lack of foresight could have provided written evidence against the *Kameradschaft*.

Another suprising example of protection occurred in Münster, where the Ambulance Medics, under the sponsorship of the alumni from the Corps Rheno-Guestphalia, formed a *Kameradschaft* named after the former Westphalian Centre politician Friedrich Harkort. They fenced in strict secrecy and were awarded the added advantage of the interest and protection of many local officials, not the least of whom was the police chief. The *Kameradschaft* leader was expelled from studies when the local *NSDStB* authorities began to suspect illicit activities, but the fencing continued under the patronage of older *Waffenstudenten*.⁴⁸

In Jena on the other hand, the *SC* Kameradschaft Saaleck did not fare nearly as well as the previous cases, for with the exception of five sons of *Alte Herren* there apparently was neither companionship, nor interest in traditional corps practices. One of the well-indoctrinated Nazis whom the *Kameradschaft* had asigned to it as its *Führer*, felt that parachute jumping would be an excellent pastime and group activity for the members.⁴⁹ In contrast with this, the indifference to Nazi propaganda on the part of most corps affiliated *Kameradschaften* is indicated by the Kameradschaft Freiherr vom Stein, where only minutes before a visit of inspection by regional *NSDStB* officials, the *Kameradschaft* members realised that they had no picture of Hitler anywhere on the premises. The resultant forced and frantic search eventually produced a picture which was borrowed from a neighbouring house for the occasion. A further indicator of their less than obedient attitude toward the *NSDStB* is illustrated by the fact that their *Kameradschaft* had two funds: the one used for *NSDStB* activities was almost invariably empty. The other, an unofficial, secret fund was used to support traditional 'corps' activities and was well topped up through voluntary contributions from the pay drawn by the group's military members.⁵⁰

When the University of Freiburg reopened in 1940, *Mensur* fencing was resumed with great zest in spite of previous party investigations. The Kameradschaft Schwabenland, which was formed by Corps Suevia zu Freiburg, is estimated to have fenced some five hundred *Mensuren* prior to 1944, when investigations by the regional *NSDStB Führer* in Stuttgart made it necessary for a precautionary halt be made to the activities. The organisation and secrecy of the *Waffenring* had even provided a hunting cabin in the Black Forest where those who received wounds during *Mensur* fencing were sent to recuperate.[51] This was in the interest of the *Waffenring* as a whole, for anyone caught with fresh wounds, which might have been received while fencing, would have been in contravention of *NSDStB* regulations and an investigation of the incident by party authorities undoubtedly would have ensued; as witnessed previously in Freiburg.

THE CORPS REVIVED

Although liaison between *Kameradschaften* at different universities was not allowed under national student regulations, by 1943, some students had managed to achieve a certain amount of mobility between universities and had renewed contact with other 'corps' *Kameradschaften* of their previous *Kartell* corps. The knowledge that, although isolated, *Kameradschaften* in other centres had reacted similarly in efforts to maintain their traditions, albeit under the 'Brown Shirt', served to strengthen and hearten the members of corps affiliated *Kameradschaften* and gave them further determination to continue their resistance to the national student authorities and Nazi policies. A type of zeal began to rise among the former corps and in Göttingen some students took to almost open display of their colours; showing considerable restraint on their enthusiasm by restricting themselves to wearing their chest bands only in local student pubs.[52]

Perhaps the most dramatic defiance was illustrated by Kameradschaft Markgraf von Meissen in Leipzig. Prior to 1939, its members dutifully participated in the activities assigned them by the *NSDStB*, such as the Borderland Labour Programme and training in *NSDStB* sabre techniques at the physical education institute. But members found the *Kameradschaft*, as seen elsewhere, sorely lacking in the most essential element, one which could not be legislated into existence – a sense of *esprit de corps*. However, this was to change. Klaus Rössler, a young alumnus of the Leipzig Corps Lusatia, decided that the inter-personal relationships within the *Kameradschaft* of his former corps, needed to be revitalised and implemented the adoption by the *Kameradschaft* of Corps Lusatia's pre-1933 constitution. The revived by-laws returned a number of traditional corps practices to the community such as the novice and mentor (*Leibfuchs-Leibbursch*) relationship for new members, which was denied under *NSDStB* regulations.[53] The corps *Convent* was also reintroduced to serve as a forum for democratic discussion and the previous *SC Comment* was adopted to regulate fencing and general behaviour. Realising that these innovations would need protection Rössler spoke with the bureau chief of the *NS-Alteherrenbund*, *Studentenführer* for Saxony, Osterhild, who was an alumnus of Leipzig's Corps Saxonia. According to Rössler's memoirs, Osterhild was most pleasantly surprised at the initiative shown in Leipzig and promised unofficially to do what he could through his position to shield Kameradschaft Markgraf von Meiseen from scrutinisation by *NSDStB* headquarters in Munich. Rössler's next problem was not, as one might expect, to inspire the young members, but rather to urge restraint in their zeal for readopting corps traditions. By 1942, due to the efforts of Rössler and his successors, Corps Misnia secretly was constituted as a subsection within the Kameradschaft Markgraf von Meissen. The name Misnia was taken as there were members of all the Leipzig *SC* corps in the Kameradschaft Markgraf von Meissen and the organisation was a joint effort which sought to re-establish corps institutions and traditions rather than to resuscitate one specific corps. A *Senior* soon was elected and a *Waffenring* formed with three other fencing fraternities. As a precautionary measure the *Waffenring* charter was backdated to 1934 in order to mislead the inquisitive, should it fall into the wrong hands.

A situation very similar to the one which developed with Corps Misnia also arose in Munich, where from 1941 onwards the Kameradschaft Graf Spee moved consciously towards the re-establishing of its forerunner, Corps Cisaria of the *WSC*. By January 1943 the *Kameradschaft* members had adopted traditional democratic corps tenets to replace the infrastructures of *Gleichschaltung* and the *Führer* Principle required by the *NSDStB* for the running of their *Kameradschaft*. In November 1944, a dramatic step was taken when Kameradschaft Graf Spee, under the name of Corps Cisaria, signed an agreement with *KSCV* Corps Suevia creating a new *Senioren Convent* for Munich; something which had not existed since the dissolution of the student federations in 1935 and a definite breach of law within the Nazi state.[54]

These two cases, Corps Misnia and Corps Cisaria, were perhaps the most dramatic, but as seen above, were not the only examples of *Kameradschaften* formed by previous corps which adhered to their traditions under the guise of *NSDStB* membership. Spurred on by their own local success, the members of Corps Misnia stretched out to neighbouring university centres in an effort to make contact with the *Kameradschaften* which had been established by other corps. Kameradschaft Saaleck in Jena, of the previous Corps Guestphalia and Kameradschaft Gustav Nachtigal, of Corps Palaiomarchia in Halle were the first to be approached.[55] Misnia was welcomed with cool scepticism in Halle, which was disappointing, but not surprising considering the treatment which Corps Palaiomarchia had received from both Lammers and Blunck in 1935. In Jena, apparently Corps Guestphalia had truly suspended activities and Kameradschaft Saaleck did not respond with any enthusiasm whatever to the overtures made by Corps Misnia. However, news gradually, and intermittently, came to Misnia of other *Kameradschaften* further afield which also had continued to uphold corps traditions. Based upon this information, the idea developed within Corps Misnia that such like-minded *Kameradschaften* should be formed into an association and invitations were sent out to the appropriate *Kameradschaften*; Yorck in Bonn, Schwabenland in Freiburg, Carl Almenröder in Marburg, Theodor Körner in Tübingen, Axel Scheffold in Heidelberg and Kameradschaft 10 in Würzburg. Two, those of Marburg and Freiburg, were forced to decline the invitation due to conflicting commitments by their members to the war effort. However, representatives of the other invited *Kameradschaften*, along with observers from favourably disposed *Kameradschaften* in Halle, Jena and Munich, met at Leipzig on 10 June 1944 for a *Kommers* to be followed the next day by a visit to the traditional site of *KSCV* congresses – the Rudelsburg castle at Bad Kösen.[56]

Upon arrival in Leipzig each of the guests was met by an opposite number from Corps Misnia who acted as his personal host for the initial reception prior to the *Kommers*. During the preliminary stages of the function each host was responsible to discern the attitude of his guest toward the establishment of an association of *Kameradschaften* which were willing to adhere to the principles of *Waffenstudententum*. The idea was presented as a *Waffenring* for like-minded *Kameradschaften*, rather than a restoration of traditional fraternities. However, that stalking-horse was soon discarded as redundant. The next day the group boarded a boat which took them up the river Saale to the haunts of the *KSCV* near Bad Kösen. The members of the party defiantly all wore full traditional corps colours, including caps; a practice which had long been forbidden by the Nazi regime. Upon reaching the Rudelsburg, the hosts from Corps Misnia made it clear to the other representatives that it was their intention to re-establish the *KSCV*. Several of the guests felt that they could not act for their own organisations without further consultation but Corps Misnia was joined in the venture by Corps Franconia of Tübingen, Corps Bavaria of Würzburg and Corps Rhenania of Bonn. All four parties signed an agreement whereby they mutually adopted the principle of:

absolute adherence to:
i. honour as the characteristic feature of academic deportment
ii. unquestioned satisfaction
iii. the *Bestimmungsmensur*
iv. strict adherence to and fostering of the traditions and *Comment* of *Waffenstudententum*.⁵⁷

Sections Two and Three of the agreement re-established the holding of regular meetings, the rotation of leadership for the new federation, as well as a regular monthly publication, formal social relationships between the four reactivated member corps and a reaffirmation of the traditional *KSCV* principle of tolerance which the *NSDAP* had forced the federation to delete from its statutes in 1933.⁵⁸

During the course of the following summer both Franconia and Rhenania found themselves placed in positions from which they were unable to fulfil their obligations to the new federation and withdrew their memberships. This left only Misnia and Bavaria to continue the re-established federation. In September, Misnia found itself charged by the *Gestapo* with attempting to form a new political party and high treason. Apparently a copy of the invitation to the Leipzig and Rudelsburg meeting had found its way into the hands of the regional *NSDStB* leader for Baden, who had in turn had forwarded the information to the *Gestapo* for investigation. The war effort slowed the legal procedures considerably and the whole action against Corps Misnia came to a sudden stop following the Allied Forces bombings of Berlin in early 1945, with the result that the case was eventually dropped.

As a Nazi organisation, the *NSDStB* and its *Kameradschaft* programme disappeared with the demise of the Third Reich. In general, the *Kameradschaften* were not significant in the revitalisation of the corps. With the relatively short duration of the Third Reich, the *Kameradschaften* were not a necessity in assuring the existence of the corps. The *Kameradschaften* were basically not a student-like type of community; they were an illogical compromise of the totalitarian politics of the *NSDAP* and traditional academic freedom. Whether this compromise did any good for either one of them only history will tell.⁵⁹

The degree to which the *NSDAP* was able to control the student *Kameradschaften* through the *NSDStB* served as an interesting study for gauging the degree to which the regime had control of the populace in general. As the party continued to strengthen its position within popular organisations through the use of state institutions, the *NSDStB* eventually was able to intimidate corps alumni into forming *Kamerads-chaften* rather than face the extinction of their fraternities. However, with the onset of the war the focus of the state's attention moved from the domination of domestic affairs to the subjugation of foreign territories, thereby inadvertently allowing the corps ethos, which had not been totally eradicated by the *Gleichschaltung*, once again to surface. The *Mensur* became an open act of defiance which symbolised a tie between the students and their national history which the Nazi *Weltanschauung* sought to forget. The growing fissure between Nazi doctrine and its implementation was sensed and exploited by youthful enthusiasts which revived other traditional corps practices not the least of which were the readoption of the prefix 'corps', in addition to the establishment of local fencing organisations and the temporary reconstitution of the *KSCV* – all illicit, and all carried out accordingly during the Nazi regime. Although not in the proportions of the plot against Hitler on 20 July 1944, the actions of the corps were none the less actions of resistance against the totalitarian regime with which they fundamentally disagreed.

6 Epilogue

The collapse of the Third Reich in May 1945, brought with the Allied Forces occupation a ban on most German organisations until such time as they could be vetted by the new military authorities. Associations such as student fraternities were, not surprisingly, among those temporarily discontinued. Within days of the German Forces' capitulation and the capture of Admiral Doenitz, the American Military Government of Germany issued a questionnaire which was to be completed by all German civilians. The form, printed both in German and English, was accompanied by instructions which stated that should any discrepancy exist between the two texts, the English version was to be considered authoritative. Such a discrepancy occurred in Question 25, which read: 'Welchen deutschen Universitäts-Studentenburschenschaften haben Sie je angehört?' and in the English version: 'List any German University Student Corps to which you have ever belonged.'[1] As has been noted before, a corps is a student *Korporation* but the reverse is in most cases not necessarily correct. It is difficult to assess to what extent this error affected the results of the questionnaire, but it undoubtedly left open a possibility for circumvention of the question and a misleading result in the poll.

The laws enacted by the Allied Forces included further obstacles to the fencing fraternities. Paragraph 210a of the Nazi penal code from 1933, which stated that the *Mensur* was not punishable as armed assault, and Paragraph 226a: 'Whoever commits bodily assault with the consent of the injured party is only in contravention of the law if the injury, in spite of the consent of the injured party, violates accepted modes of behaviour,' along with many other sections of the Nazi legal codex, were rescinded.[2] These revocations gave the *Mensur* the status under law of assault with a deadly weapon which was punishable by imprisonment – the Allied authorities having dispensed with mere confinement as a sentence. This then returned the possible sentence for *Mensur* fencing to that which had existed during the Weimar Republic. In addition to this, until 10 June 1950, the traditional corps fencing sword, the *Schläger*, was deemed by the occupying forces to be an offensive weapon and the mere possession of such a sword was also considered punishable.[3]

The above measures, together with the disruption suffered throughout German society following the nation's defeat, impeded and dampened any enthusiasm on the part of the corps for an immediate reconstitution of their federation. The Nazis had been outright hostile to the corps but the Allies initially were not well disposed to them either. However, by late 1949, the atmosphere had cleared sufficiently for several corps to again enter into correspondence with one another. In January 1950, representatives of eleven *SC*s met in Bonn for the purpose of: 'creating a working committee with the aim of re-establishing and fostering German *Corpsstudententum* incorporating as closely as possible its traditions.'[4] Subsequently a committee was established to study the best method by which to reconstitute the *KSCV* and the committee was asked to report its findings the following year, at Pentecost 1951; that feast-day being the traditional date for the *KSCV* annual congress. By March 1950 there were 48 former *KSCV* corps functioning in West Germany and the number continued to grow.[5]

The three most probable approaches by which the *KSCV* could be reconstituted were as follows. First, the federation could start from a completely new footing with a new constitution. Second, it could reconstruct itself on the old statutes or last, it could annul the 1935 decision of voluntary dissolution and amend or modify the old statutes as necessary.[6] It was a combination of the second and third approaches which was eventually chosen by the congress in 1951. The voluntary dissolution of the *KSCV* from the autumn of 1935 was rescinded and the statutes of 1927, that is to say the last pre-1933 *KSCV* statutes, were adopted until such time as the newly appointed statutes committee could make the necessary revisions to fit the contemporary socio-political setting.

But what of *Mensur* fencing? Under the 1927 statutes no *corpsier* was to receive corps colours without first fencing at least one adequate *Mensur*. It was decided at the 1950 congress that since 59 of the 63 reconstituted corps were already practising *Mensur* fencing, the ruling of 1927 would be continued. The following congress in turn, ruled that as of 19 May 1951, any *corpsier* who was not already an *Alter Herr* would be required to fence at least one *Mensur* or be released from his corps membership.

The *KSCV* managed to reconstitute its federation in a form almost identical to that which it had held prior to 1933. By 1957, the *KSCV* congress was able to welcome representatives from 92 of its previous 106 corps, which left only 14 corps without a reactivated student section.[7]

Just as during the Weimar Republic, *Mensur* fencing was officially forbidden in post-war Germany. An important landmark in legal precedent was set when on 19 January 1953, the federal court of justice acquitted several students who had been charged with lethal assault following an investigation involving *Mensur* fencing. The grounds for the acquittal stated that in the light of the protective equipment worn and the strict procedural regulations involved, the *Mensur* could not be ruled as assault with a deadly weapon as cited under Paragraphs 201 and 210 of the penal code. Additional similar judgements in 1960 and 1962, subsequently removed the *Mensur* from any further censure and it has remained so until the present.[8]

Reconstruction of the *WSC* corps occurred along lines very similar to those of the *KSCV*. Particular recognition is given to one alumnus, Dipl. Ing. Weizsaecker, who was very much the driving force and instigator for the reforming of the *WSC* alumni association, *Weinheimer Verband Alter Corpsstudenten*, in October 1949. The goal and purpose of the association was to strengthen and unify the alumni of *WSC* corps and then upon that foundation to move towards the reopening of the former *WSC* corps for the reception of new student members. At a meeting of *WSC* representatives at Bad Wimpfen in early 1950, a resolution was put forward that the new *WSC* statutes which were to be drafted, should not endorse mandatory *Mensur* fencing as a prerequisite for full membership in a *WSC* corps. Furthermore, the practice of wearing corps colours in public was also to be discontinued in future. This Wimpfen Resolution as it came to be known, seemed particularly expedient for the political atmosphere of post-war Germany and was taken into consideration by the *WSC* task-force which was established in May 1950 to study the possible method of re-establishing the *WSC*. But, as mentioned above, the political climate began to change and with the ever more lenient attitude of the courts towards the *Mensur*, the Wimpfen Resolution was defeated by the conference which re-established the *WSC* in May 1952.[9]

The corps of the *Rudolstädter Senioren-Convent (RSC)* joined the *WSC* in 1934, an amalgamation entered into for collective security in the early months of the Third Reich. Following the Second World War there was no attempt to re-establish the *RSC* and almost without exception, the previous *RSC* corps joined the reconstituted *WSC*.[10]

The fraternities of the previous *Naumburger Senioren-Convent (NSC)* dissolved their federation, then known as the *Naumburger Thing*, on 19 October 1935 and made no attempt to reconstitute their federation after the war. Of the ten *Kameradschaften* which evolved from the *NSC* corps, their post-war successors formed six fraternities which followed no standardised course of affiliation – three joined the *Coburger Convent* of *Landsmannschaften*, two the *WSC*, and the remaining one remained free of any federal ties.[11]

Apart from the resistance to the Nazi regime by student *corpsiers*, there were a number of corps alumni who played very prominent roles in the German resistance, giving their lives to rid Germany of Hitler's rule. Eduard Brücklmeier, Albrecht von Hagen, Ulrich von Hassell, Herbert Mumm von Schwarzenstein, Fritz Graf von der Schulenburg, Adam von Trott zu Solz, Peter Graf Yorck von Wartenburg – were all executed in connection with their part in the attempted coup of 20 July 1944.[12] Kurt Gerstein worked against the Nazi state and died while in the custody of French partisans.[13] But a number of the conspirators also survived. Hasso von Etzdorf noted that the regular meetings of corps alumni in Berlin during the Third Reich were used as an opportunity to exchange information to aid in efforts against the Nazis.[14] Similarly, Friedrich Freiherr von Münchhausen recounted that the corps alumni network was employed to enlist support and members for the resistance.[15] In both cases, communication was based upon the fact that fraternity brothers were well known and tested so that they could be trusted to keep matters secret, even if they could not directly assist the planned coup.

7 Summary and Conclusions

From the period of the first European universities student organisations existed for the purpose of representing the interests of their members. This perhaps seems a truism, but it must be kept in mind when examining the diversity with which the various organisations of fraternities developed. To the untutored eye in the late twentieth century it is perhaps difficult to see any great difference between the pre- and the post-Reformation student associations, or indeed between those of the mid-nineteenth century. But each of these manifestations resembles certain aspects of the period in which it first appeared. The *Pennalen* and student orders correspond to the continued disquiet and despotism found following the Thirty Years' War; the *Kränzchen* illustrate an application of Enlightenment principles within academe; the *Deutsche Burschenschaft* indicates the rise of German nationalism in its various strains following Napoleon's defeat; and the Reform Movement of the mid-nineteenth century is reflected in the foundation of groups such as the *Deutsche Sängerschaft*. The *Deutsche Wehrschaft* which was constituted after the First World War and antedated its founding to the signing of the Versailles Treaty, gave a resounding indication of the rise of *völkischem* nationalism and in retrospect, can be seen to have served as a precursor in the establishment of the *NSDStB* in 1928.

Prior to German unification the German universities were relatively insulated against party political activity within their academic precincts. But with the loss of their institutional privileges following the reception of German law, the universities became susceptible to political ideologies; a trend which crystallised most dramatically in the Nazi student movement during the 1930s. The corps of the *KSCV* sought to maintain their apolitical stance and attempted to function purely as an organisation of fraternities devoted to the interaction of scholars within the universities. Not surprisingly they clashed radically with the doctrine and racial politics advocated by their Nazi student counterparts. Once the *NSDAP* assumed power certain of its younger leaders such as Baldur von Schirach and Walter Lienau, used their positions of influence to settle old, and often personal, feuds with the corps; organisations which they deemed to be the very essence of conservative and reactionary resistance to the new regime. The corps eventually succumbed to the pressures exerted upon them by the *NSDAP* through its edicts and policies aimed specifically at bringing about their dissolution. Decrees such as the one made by *SA* leader Viktor Lutze in September 1935, were designed to extract retribution from the corps for refusing to expel their non-Aryan members and their demonstrative indifference towards joining the march of the 'Brown Column' into the Thousand-Year Reich.

The leadership of the *NSDAP* placed great significance upon the voluntary acceptance of Nazi precepts. In his conversation with Blunck on the terrace of the *Reichskanzlei*, Hitler stated that only certain concepts were compulsory for everyone. Upon those ideas, Hitler claimed, the new regime would continue to grow and prosper. However, there was not a uniform implementation of Nazi doctrine, with the result that party officials tended to establish their own personal bailiwicks and interpreted *NSDAP* policy to suit their particular prejudices – rather than to further the collective good of the German nation.

The introduction of Nazi doctrine generally was implemented in steps of escalating severity, beginning with what appeared as a relatively limited application and in the end exercised many broadly felt ramifications. Changing definitions played an important role in Nazi tactics, as seen in the altered criteria for determining Jewishness. Mere adherence to the strict guidelines of the new state's regulations was not enough to satisfy its leaders, as the corps learned to their detriment.

Attitudes towards National Socialism were by no means uniform among the corps, as seen in the actions of Walter Lienau and Max Blunck, but the line generally adopted was one of neutrality rather than political ardency. Repeated incidents such as the 'asparagus affair' of Corps Saxo-Borussia in Heidelberg, the activities of the Kameradschaft Misnia in Leipzig and the active programme of *Mensur* fencing practised by many corps after 1937, despite its illegality, all indicate a conservatism which was much less compliant to the Nazi regime than might generally be thought to have been the case. The conservatism demonstrated by the corps was for the retention and continuation of their time-honoured traditions which they wished to conserve so much so that corps members were willing to risk imprisonment, or worse, from the Nazi regime in order to ensure their preservation. This naturally did not hold true for all corps since many lay dormant between the years of 1935 and 1951. But there is an interesting similarity in the development of resistance to Nazi directives which unfolded among the *Kameradschaf-*

Summary and Conclusions

ten established by corps alumni. The corps alumni proved the Nazis correct in their suspicions that the *Alte Herren* would divert student members away from the path of National Socialist orthodoxy. The constancy of the alumni to their corps precepts was admired by the new members, for whom in turn, the *Mensur* became a ritual of resistance to the *völkischer* state; an art form to be cherished and passed on to future generations of corps brothers along with other aspects of the corps ethos. These *corpsiers* illustrated during the Nazi regime, just as their predecessors had in the Weimar period, that they possessed little affinity for any government which attempted to impede the continuity of their traditions.

Germans working against the Nazis found it increasingly difficult to find dependable support among their compatriots and were thrown continually upon their own resources.[1] This meant more and more that only old and well tried friends could be depended upon and the friendship of fraternity brothers became increasingly important as one such bond which proved true and dependable.

While this work has not examined an easily definable organisation within the German Resistance to Nazi domination, it has looked at a specific early affiliation common to a number of the prominent figures within the German Resistance: Eduard Brücklmeier, Albrecht von Hagen, Ulrich von Hassell, Herbert Mumm von Schwarzenstein, Fritz Graf von der Schulenburg, Adam von Trott zu Solz, Peter Graf Yorck von Wartenburg, Kurt Gerstein, Hasso von Etzdorf, Friedrich Hielscher, *et al.* These men all experienced a common academic milieu during their university years as members of a student corps which had as its cornerstone the principle of political and religious tolerance: an attribute rare during the Nazi tenure of power.

In fact, the early conclusions drawn by some of the Nazi leaders would appear to have been correct. The corps alumni did contaminate their younger fraternity brothers with the ideals upon which the corps were founded and thereby tainted many of them against the tenets of National Socialism. 'Ideally the behaviour expected of a *corpsier*, which of course every corps member will not be able to achieve, but which nevertheless should be required of every *corpsier*, is the ability to remain uninfluenced by ideologies and observe strict loyalty to his word of honour.'[2]

Glossary

Allgemeine Deutsche Waffenring. National association fencing fraternities.
Altakademiker. A member of the Nazi-sponsored student alumni association.
Band. A broad ribbon about 30–40 mm in width, in the colours of a specific fraternity, worn over one shoulder and diagonally across the chest, the ends fastened at the hip with a large ornamental button.
Cerevis. A specially embroidered fraternity cap.
Colours. In the most basic sense, the colours which designate a specific fraternity; usually a tricolour – most significant item is the chest band which is given to a candidate when he is received as a full member of the fraternity – in general the term refers to any articles which display the fraternity's insignia and/or designated colours such as caps, flags, etc.
Corpsier. A corps member.
Corpsstudententum. The realm of corps students – corpsier.
Deutsche Studentenschaft. Association of German students – included Austria, Bohemia, etc.
Fuchs. Novice fraternity member.
Gemeinschaft Studentischer Verbände. Organisation of all student federations under the leadership of Secretary of State Lammers for the purpose of bringing them into line with *NSDAP* directives.
Gleichschaltung. Policy of co-ordinating the uniform implementation of Nazi doctrine particularly regarding associations and institutions.
Kommers. A particularly festive fraternity gathering with some formal and ceremonial aspects; much like an officer's mess dinner.
Korporation. A student fraternity recognised as an entity by the authorities of its university – the term is often and incorrectly used as a synonym for corps – a corps is a *Korporation* but not necessarily vice versa.
Landesvater. Founder's Feast.
Leibbursch. The mentor of a fraternity novice (Fuchs).
Leibfuchs. A fraternity novice under the sponsorship and protection of a specific senior student member of the fraternity.
NS-Alteherrenbund. Nazi student alumni association.
Partei. In the student fraternity sense, a fencing match and those persons directly associated with its effectuation.
Satisfaktionsfähig. Able to give armed satisfaction. A man of honour.
Stahlhelm-Studentenring Langemarck. Student militia sponsored by ex-servicemen's association, *Stahlhelm* – student section absorbed by *NSDStB* 15 September 1933.
Stammtisch. Regular informal gathering.
Studentenschaft. Student body.

Glossary

Untersuchungs- und Schlichtungs-Auschüsse. Nazi party disciplinary organisation.
Volksgenosse. Member of the same race.
Vorort. The position of presiding *SC*, rotated annually in alphabetical sequence.
Waffen belegen. The practice whereby a person who does not belong to a local or recognised fencing fraternity is allowed to settle an affair of honour through the sponsorship of a recognised fraternity.
Waffenring. An organisation, usually at the local level, of mutually recognised *satisfaktionsfähig* fraternities.
Waffenschutz. Hospitality offered to a member of another corps (or recognised organisation) enabling him to fence or settle an affair of honour within the jurisdiction of a *SC* to which his corps is not a member – weapons and a second are provided by the host corps.
Waffenverruf. Ban against an individual or group, barring them from satisfaction at arms because of dishonourable behaviour or practices.
Zirkel. The insignia of a fraternity, incorporating the initials and/or its motto or a salutation such as *vivat, crescat, floreat!*

Biographical Notes

Blunck, Max – Führer of the *KSCV* 1933–5 – studied law at University of Jena.
Buch, Walter – left army as Major following the First World War – joined *NSDAP* 1922 – 1927 appointed chairman of the Nazi membership disciplinary organisation *USCHLA* – achieved notoriety for his sadistic behaviour towards prisoners during party purge of the *SA* and later to anyone within his aegis who displeased him.
Feickert, Andreas – active in student politics both in Berlin and Hamburg – 1932 *NSDStB* national executive – 1934–6 National Student Leader (*Reichsführer der DSt*).
Krüger, Gerhard – member of Burschenschaft Arminia and militant *NSDAP* member at the University of Greifswald where he received his PhD in Sociology in 1934 – *NSDStB* executive portfolio for university politics, 1931 – replaced Walter Lienau as chairman of *DSt* in September 1931–3 – numerous publications – taught at the University of Strassburg.
Lammers, Hans Heinrich – studied law at Heidelberg and Breslau – took up post in Reich Ministry of the Interior following the First World War – appointed chief of the Reich Chancellery in 1933 following Nazi victory – became one of Hitler's closest advisers – *Führer* of *GStV* 1934–5.
Lienau, Walter – studied in Munich, where he was very active both in the *NSDStB* and student government – briefly a member of Corps Isaria but expelled for support of Baldur von Schirach against the corps of the Munich *SC* – elected chairman of *DSt* in Graz, 1931 – impeached and removed from office autumn of 1931 – later served in *SS-Leibstandarte*.
Scheel, Adolf – member of a *VDSt* fraternity while completing Dr med. at Heidelberg – held various *NSDStB* and *DSt* offices – 1936–45 National Student Leader (*Reichsstudentenführer*) – 1941–5 *Gauleiter* for Salzburg.
Schirach, Baldur von – studied in Munich – joined *NSDAP* in 1924 – tireless organiser of youth and students for *NSDAP* – 1928–33 *NSDStB Führer* – 1933–40 Reich Youth Leader – 1940–5 *Gauleiter* for Vienna.
Stäbel, Friedrich Oskar – decorated in the First World War – *Freikorps* member – Doctorate in Engineering from Karlsruhe – active in *NSDStB* – 1933 named national leader of both NSDStB and *DSt*.

I would like to express my thanks for the above biographical material to a number of the gentlemen whom I interviewed while researching this work.

Appendix

TABLE A.1 *THE FEDERATIONS OF STUDENT FRATERNITIES IN GERMANY, 1929*

1. KSCV	Hoher Kösener Senioren-Conventen-Verband	
2. DL	Deutsche Landsmannschaft	
3. VC	Vertreter-Convents-Verband der Turnerschaften an deutschen Hochschulen	

1 to 3 all signatories to the Marburg Agreement, 1912–14

4. RSC	Rudolstädter Senioren-Convent	
5. WSC	Weinheimer Senioren-Convent	

1 to 5 all signatories to the Allgemeiner Deutscher Waffenring, 1919

6. DB	Deutsche Burschenschaft – briefly in Marburg Agreement	
7. DS	Deutsche Sängerschaft	
8. VDSt	Kyffhäuser-Verband der Vereine Deutscher Studenten	
9. ADB	Allgemeiner Deutscher Burschenbund	
10. ATB	Akademischer Turn-Bund	
11. DW	Deutsche Wehrschaft	
12. MR	Miltenberger Ring	
13. RVSV	Rothenburger Verband Schwarzer Verbindungen	
14. ARB	Akademischer Ruderbund	
15. KDASV	Kartell-Verband deutsch-akademischer Segler-Vereine	
16. WV	Wernigeroder Verband	
17. NDC	Naumburger Delegierten-Convent akademischer landwirtschaftlicher Verbindungen	
18. SV	Sonderhäuser Verband deutscher Sängerverbindungen	after 1922
19. AIV	Akadem. Ingenieur Verband	
20. VASpV	Verband d. akadem. Sportverbindungen	

1 to 20 all parties to Allgemeiner Deutscher Waffenring Agreement, 1922

21. CV	Cartell-Verband der kath. deutschen Studentenverbindungen
22. KV	Kartell-Verband katholischer deut. Studentenvereine
23. UV	Unitas: Verband d. wissenschaftl. katholischen Studentenvereine
24. DWV	Deutscher Wissenschafter Verband
25. WB	Wingolf
26. SB	Schwarzburgbund
27. RKDB	Ring katholischer deut. Burschenschaften
28. DAG	Deutsche Akademische Gildenschaft

Appendix

29. VDB   Verband Deutscher Burschen
30. HV   Hochlandverband: kath. neustudent. Verbindungen
31. GV   Godesberger Verband deutscher Sportschaften
32. RK   Rüdesheimer Kartell
           1 to 32 all parties to the ADW Erlangen Agreement of 1927
33. RV   Rothenburger Verband akademischer Archit.-Vereine
34. GG   Grossdeutsche Gildenschaft
35. SR   Schwarzer Ring
36. BFW   Bund für wissenschaftl. Vereinigungen
37. WK   Wartburg Kartell d. akademische evangelische Verbindungen
38. AOSt   Arbeitsring ostdeutscher Studenten-Verbände
39. KNMV   Kartell Akad. Natursv.-Med.-Vereine
40. BCC   Bamberger Chargierten-Convent
41. AFIR   Akademischer Fliegerring
42. LV   Leuchtenburg Verband evangelisch.-Studenten-Vereine
43. WJSC   Wernigeroder Jagdcorps Senioren-Convent
44. GGR   Grossdeutscher Gildenring
45. BC   Burschenbunds-Convent
46. KC   Kartell-Convent der Verbindungen deutscher Studenten jüdischen Glaubens
47. KJV   Kartell Jüdischer Verbindungen
48. BJA   Bund Jüdischer Akademiker

TABLE A.2 Selected Major Student Fraternity Federations

Federation	Number of fraternities	%	Number of student members	%	Total of alumni and student members	%
Overall totals	1 582	100	68 487	100	243 302	100
KSCV	125	7.9	5 184	7.5	25 908	10.64
WSC	60	3.79	2 623	3.82	9 328	3.83
RSC	51	3.22	2 701	3.94	8 404	3.45
DL	105	6.63	6 232	9.09	17 041	7.0
VC	89	5.62	4 938	7.21	13 856	5.69
MR	6	0.37	374	0.54	1 625	0.66
DB	175	11.06	8 678	12.67	33 816	13.89
ATB	50	3.16	2 910	4.24	9 352	3.84
DS	43	2.71	2 252	3.28	8 839	3.68
ADB	38	2.40	1 483	2.16	3 541	1.45
DW	36	2.27	3 156	4.60	3 156	1.29
WJäSC	5	0.31	133	0.19	218	0.08
KC	24	1.51	315	0.45	1 511	0.62
KJV	17	1.07	416	0.60	1 394	0.57
BJA	12	0.75	176	0.25	627	0.25
CV	118	7.45	6 232	9.09	17 041	7.0
KV	96	6.06	4 938	7.21	13 856	5.69
WB	39	2.46	1 123	1.63	6 453	2.64
UV	57	3.60	1 808	2.63	5 081	2.08

SOURCE: O. Scheunemann, 'Die zahlenmässigen Entwicklung des Kösener SC-Verbandes 1848–1935', *Einst und Jetzt*, 1958, vol. 3, and H. Weber, 'Die studentischen Korporationsverbände', Wende und Schau, 1930, vol. 1.

TABLE A.3 KSCV (Hoher Kösener Senioren Conventen Verband), 1869–1935

As of annual conference at Pentecost	Total number of Senioren-Conventen	Total number of corps		Student membership (Germany only)			Male students in Germany	Corpstudents as % of total
		Germany	Foreign	Active	Inactive	Total		
1869	19	—	—	740	—	—	13 772	
1879	21	—	—	873	—	—	19 759	
1889	19	83	—	1232	1001	2233	28 982	7.7%
1899	22	87	2	1301	1404	2705	32 955	8.2%
1909	23	93	3	1355	1739	3094	50 483	6.12%
1919	23	96	6	1993	1070	3063	82 330	3.72%
1929	30	124	18	2337	3500	5837	78 167	7.46%
1935	29	111	15	1090	3514	4604	47 272	9.73%

SOURCE: O. Scheunemann, 'Die zahlenmässigen Entwicklung des Kösener SC-Verbandes 1848–1935', *Einst und Jetzt*, 1958, vol. 3, and H. Weber, 'Die studentischen Korporationsverbände', *Wende und Schau*, 1930, vol. 1.

Notes and References

PREFACE

1. H. Weber, 'Die studentischen Korporationsverbände', *Wende und Schau* (Frankfurt am Main: VAC Verlag, 1930), Appendix Ib.
2. J. W. Baird, 'Goebbels, Horst Wessel, and the Myth of Resurrection and Return', *Journal of Contemporary History*, 1982, no. 17, pp. 633–50. Baird mentions that Horst Wessel's corps brothers participated in the ritual at his funeral in 1930: this, however, should not be taken to indicate collaboration on the part of the corps with the Nazis, but rather a corps and the *SA* both honouring a deceased member.
3. H. Weber, 'Die studentischen Korporationsverbände', Appendix Ib.

1 GERMAN STUDENT FRATERNITIES

1. H. Weiruszowski, *The Medieval Universities* (Toronto: Van Nostrand, 1966) p. 36.
2. P. Kibre, *The Nations in the Mediaeval Universities* (Cambridge, Mass.: Mediaeval Academy of America, 1948) p. 9.
3. P. Dietrich, *Historia Academica* 3/4 (Stuttgart-Möhringen: Studentengeschichtliche Vereinigung des Coburger Convents, 1958) p. 12.
4. H. Rashdall, *The Universities of Europe in the Middle Ages* (London: Oxford University Press, 1936) p. 262.
5. From the latin *bursa* = purse, in reference to the weekly room rental in such dormitories. Students who lived in *Bursen* became known as *bursales* or *bursarli* which later became the general term for a student: *Bursche*.
6. Dietrich, *Historia Academica*, p. 13.
7. W. L. Bell (ed.), *The Graduate Studies Prospectus* (Oxford: Oxford University Press, 1981) p. 168 and pp. 163–4.
8. Dietrich, *Historia Academica*, p. 14.
9. F. Schulz and P. Ssymank, *Das Deutsche Studententum* (Munich: Verlag für Hochschulkunde, 1932) p. 68.
10. E. Hunger and C. Meyer, *Studentisches Brauchtum* (Stuttgart: Verlag des AHCC, 1957) p. 17. Bean from *bec jaune* = *Gelbschnabel* = yellow beak.
11. Schulz and Ssymank, *Das Deutsche Studententum*, p. 69.
12. Hunger and Meyer, *Studentisches Brauchtum*, p. 17.
13. Ibid., p. 18.
14. Ibid., p. 17.

15. Dietrich, *Historia Academica*, pp. 14–15.
16. A. B. Cobban, *The Medieval Universities* (London: Methuen & Co. Ltd, 1975) p. 231.
17. Hunger and Meyer, *Studentisches Brauchtum*, p. 70.
18. W. Fabricius, *Die Deutschen Corps* (Frankfurt am Main: Verlag der Deutschen Corpszeitung, 1926) p. 30.
19. Hunger and Meyer, *Studentisches Brauchtum*, p. 71.
20. F. R. Bryson, *The Sixteenth Century Italian Duel* (Chicago: University of Chicago Press, 1938) pp. 13–14.
21. Dietrich, *Historia Academica*, pp. 15–16.
22. Fabricius, *Corps*, p. 28.
23. Dietrich, *Historia Academica*, p. 14.
24. E. Meyer-Camberg, 'Über unbedingt notwendige Grundlagen in der studentenhistorischen Forschung', *Einst und Jetzt*, 1969, vol. 14, p. 47.
25. C. E. McClelland, *State, Society and University in Germany 1700–1914* (London: Cambridge University Press, 1980) pp. 34–5. Also see, F. Paulsen, *German Education. Past and Present*, trans. T. Lorenz (London: T. Fisher Unwin, 1908) pp. 112–16.
26. M. Rassem, 'Der Student als Ritter', *Studium Generale* (Berlin: Springer-Verlag, 1963) vol. 5, p. 278.
27. Meyer-Camberg, 'Über unbedingt', p. 47.
28. Schulz and Ssymank, *Das Deutsche Studentantum*, p. 165.
29. N. Webster, *Secret Societies and Subversive Movements* (London: Boswell Printing & Publishing Co. Ltd, 1924) pp. 137–8.
30. R. F. Gould, *The Concise History of Freemasonry*, 2nd ed. (London: Gale & Polden Ltd, 1951) pp. 237–41.
31. Ibid., p. 283.
32. Hunger and Meyer, *Studentisches Brauchtum*, p. 26.
33. Schulz and Ssymank, *Das Deutsche Studentantum*, p. 166.
34. F. Christian Laukhard, quoted in Fabricius, *Corps*, p. 46.
35. Dietrich, *Historia Academica*, p. 18.
36. Laukhard, in Fabricius, *Corps*, p. 46.
37. Hunger and Meyer, *Studentisches Brauchtum*, p. 27.
38. Ibid., p. 26.
39. W. Fabricius, 'Kösener Senioren-Convents-Verband', *Das Akademische Deutschland* (Berlin: C. A. Weller Verlag, 1930–1) vol. III, p. 259.
40. H. Kessler, 'Orden und Landsmannschaften unter akademischer Gerichtsbarkeit,' *Einst und Jetzt*, 1957, vol. 2, p. 61.
41. Dietrich, *Historia Academica*, pp. 19–20.
42. N. Wilgus, *The Illuminoids* (London: New English Library, 1980) p. 17.
43. E. Röhlke, 'Versuch einer Begründung für Entstehen, Aufgaben, Ziele und Untergehen der Ordenlogen und der Orden', *Einst und Jetzt*, 1976, vol. 21, Sonderheft, p. 62.
44. Ibid., p. 62.
45. F. Yates, *The Rosicrusian Enlightenment* (St Albans, Herts: Paladin, 1975) pp. 62–4.
46. Röhlke, 'Versuch', pp. 61–2.
47. Kessler, 'Orden', p. 54.
48. Röhlke, 'Versuch', p. 61.

Notes and References 179

49. Kessler, 'Orden', p. 59.
50. Ibid., p. 54.
51. E. Bauer, 'Warum verboten eigentlich die Landesherren die Orden und weshalb bleiben diese Verbote erfolglos?' *Einst und Jetzt*, 1957, vol. 3, pp. 69–70.
52. Fabricius, *Corps*, p. 48.
53. J. H. Müller, *Das Corps Silesia zu Breslau* (Breslau: Grass, Barth & Co., 1931: 1971) p. 16.
54. Röhlke, 'Versuch', p. 63.
55. E. Röhlke, 'Über des Kranzianertum an der Viadrina', *Einst und Jetzt*, 1972, vol. 17, p. 119.
56. Röhlke, 'Kranzianertum', p. 120.
57. From the latin *conventus* = the coming together of cloister members. Hunger and Meyer, *Studentisches Brauchtum*, p. 25.
58. Röhlke, 'Kranzianertum', p. 123.
59. *Zur Geschichte und Vordatierung des Stiftungstages der Guestphalia zu Halle* (Halle: n. publ., 1925) p. 4. For an interesting presentation of early corps constitutions including that of Onoldia and twenty others, see E. Meyer-Camberg (ed.), 'Zum Gedenken an Dr med. Albin Angerer – 21 der ältesten Constitution der Corps und Vorläufer bis zum Jahre 1810', *Einst und Jetzt*, 1981, Sonderheft.
60. Onoldia predates Guestphalia of Halle in the use of the prefix 'corps'. However, the constitution of Guestphalia predates that of Onoldia by nine years, giving Guestphalia the distinction of being the oldest corps.
61. Fabricius, *Corps*, p. 215.
62. Fabricius, *Corps*, appendix, p. 15.
63. A. Methner and G. Lustig, *Geschichte des Corps Borussia zu Bresleu* (Breslau: Verlag von Wilh. Gottl. Korn, 1911) pp. 27–8.
64. Ibid., p. 32.
65. Ibid., pp. 32–3.
66. R. Körner, 'Zur Frage der zu Studentenorden allgemeinen', *Einst und Jetzt*, 1969, vol. 14, p. 188.
67. Methner and Lustig, *Geschichte des Corps*, p. 33.
68. Schulz and Ssymank, *Das Deutsche Studententum*, p. 180.
69. Ibid., p. 180.
70. Ibid., p. 181.
71. R. Lutze, ' "Father" Jahn and his Teacher-Revolutionaries from the German Student Movement', *The Journal of Modern History* (University of Chicago Press, On-demand supplement), 1976, vol. 48, no. 2, p. 5.
72. Lutze, *Jahn*, p. 1.
73. G. Heer, 'Deutsche Burschenschaft', *Akademische Deutschland* (Berlin: C. A. Weller Verlag, 1930–1) vol. III, p. 303.
74. Heer, Deutsche Burschenschaft, p. 304. Also see A. G. Whiteside, *The Socialism of Fools: Georg Ritter von Schönerer and Austrian Pan-Germanism* (Berkeley, California: University of California Press, 1975) pp. 43–4.
75. Heer, Deutsche Burschenschaft, p. 304.
76. B. Sommerlad, 'Wartburgfest und Corpsstudenten', *Einst und Jetzt*, 1979, vol. 24, pp. 16–17.
77. Heer, Deutsche Burschenschaft, p. 304.

78. E. Weiss, 'Burschenschaftliche Ideen im Corps', *Einst und Jetzt*, 1978, vol. 23, p. 89. See also F. Schnabel, *Deutsche Geschichte im Neunzehnten Jahrhundert* (Freiburg im Br.: Verlag Herder, 1949) vol. 2, pp. 242–3.
79. Heer, Deutsche Burschenschaft, p. 305.
80. Lutze, *Jahn*, p. 2.
81. G. Heer, 'Die Demagogenzeit. Von den Karlsbader Beschlüssen bis zum Frankfurter Wachsturm 1820–33', *Geschichte der Deutsche Burschenschaft* (Heidelberg: Carl Winter Verlag, 1927), vol. 2, p. 24.
82. R. Lutze, 'The German Revolutionary Student Movement 1819–1833', *Central European History*, 1971, vol. IV, pp. 230–1.
83. K-W. v. Uhlenhorst-Ziechmann, *Die Deutsche Burschenschaften* (Cleveland, Ohio: unpubl. ms., 1972) p. 3.
84. Lutze, *Student Movement*, p. 236.
85. Ibid., pp. 240–1.
86. Heer, Deutsche Burschenschaft, pp. 311–12.
87. Uhlenhorst-Ziechmann, *Die Deutsche Burschenschaften*, p. 3.
88. G. Schaefer-Rolffs and O. Scheunemann, *Handbuch des Kösener Corpsstudenten*, 5th ed. (Bochum: VAC Verlag, 1965) p. 47.
89. Fabricius, *Kösener Verband*, p. 261.
90. R. Paschke, 'Die Einigungsbestrebungen der deutschen Corps bis 1848', *Einst und Jetzt*, 1958, vol. 3, pp. 16–17.
91. Schulz and Ssymank, *Das Deutsche Studententum*, p. 300.
92. E. Bauer, 'Die Jenaer Corpsversammlung, 15–17 Juni 1848', *Einst und Jetzt*, 1958, vol. 3, p. 22.
93. Fabricius, Kösener Verband, p. 262.
94. Bauer, *Jena 1848*, p. 23. See also W. Fabricius, *Geschichte und Chronik des Kösener SC-Verbandes* (Frankfurt am Main: Verlag der Deutschen Corpszeitung, 1921) pp. 26–7.
95. Schaefer-Rolffs and Scheuhemann, *Handbuch*, p. 48.
96. Bauer, *Jena 1848*, pp. 29–32.
97. Fabricius, *Geschichte und Chronik*, p. 25.
98. Schaefer-Rolffs and Scheunemann, *Handbuch*, p. 48.
99. F. Nachreiner, 'Der Kösener Seniorenconventsverband', in W. Ranz and E. Bauer (eds), *Handbuch des Kösener Corpsstudenten 1953* (Hamburg: Selbstverlag des Verbandes Alter Corpsstudenten, 1953) p. 106.
100. Fabricius, *Geschichte und Chronik*, pp. 88–9.
101. Ranz and Bauer, *Handbuch*, p. 106.
102. Fabricius, *Geschichte und Chronik*, pp. 88–9.
103. Dietrich, *Historia Academica*, pp. 26–8.
104. K. H. Jarausch, *Students, Society and Politics in Imperial Germany* (Princeton, New Jersey: Princeton University Press, 1983) pp. 321–5.
105. O. Gerlach, *Kösener Corpslisten – 1960* (Bochum: Selbstverlag des Verbandes Alter Corpsstudenten, 1961) p. 479 and p. 88. See also for the role of the corps during the Wilhelmine Period, M. Studier, 'Der Corpsstudent als Idealbild der Wilhelminischen Ära' (Diss., University of Erlangen, 1965).
106. H. Schüler, 'Weinheimer Senioren-Convent', *Das Akademische Deutschland* (Berlin: C.A. Weller Verlag, 1930–1) p. 278.
107. Ibid., p. 281.

Notes and References 181

108. A. Bundle, 'Rüdolstädter Senioren-Convent', *Das Akademische Deutschland* (Berlin: C. A. Weller Verlag, 1930–1) p. 287.
109. W. Bushmann, 'Naumburger Senioren-Convent', *Das Akademische Deutschland* (Berlin: C. A. Weller Verlag, 1930–1) p. 347. See also P. Gladin, 'Die Naumburger Senioren-Convent', *Die Wachenburg: Nachrichten des Weinheimer Senioren-Convents*, 1977, Nr. 3, pp. 91–3.
110. Fabricius, *Corps*, pp. 445–6.
111. H. Leupold, 'Der Kartellvertrag zwischen Bavaria-Landshut und Bavaria-Erlangen vom 30.V. 1822,' *Einst und Jetzt* 1982, vol. 27.
112. Fabricius, *Corps*, p. 445.
113. Schaefer-Rolffs and Scheunemann, *Handbuch*, p. 134.
114. Fabricius, *Corps*, p. 448.
115. Schaefer-Rolffs and Scheunemann, *Handbuch*, p. 135.

2 STUDENTS, LAW AND CODES

1. C. Bornhak, *Geschichte der preussischen Universitätsverwaltung bis 1810*, cited in Kessler, 'Orden', p. 54.
2. O. Götze, *Die Jenaer akademischen Logen und Studentenorden des 18 Jahrhunderts* (Jena: n. publ., 1932) pp. 166–7.
3. Kessler, 'Orden', p. 54.
4. Ibid., pp. 54–5.
5. Ibid., p. 55.
6. Ibid., p. 66.
7. G. Neuenhoff, 'Ehrenwort und Ehrenschein', *Einst und Jetzt*, 1979, vol. 24, p. 60.
8. Kessler, 'Orden', p. 66.
9. Ibid., p. 67.
10. E. Weiss, *Festschrift zum 170 jährigen Bestehen Corps Lusatia* (Berlin: pri. publ., 1977), p. 48.
11. Kessler, 'Orden', p. 67.
12. A. Angerer, 'Die Entwicklung des Toleranzgedankens in studentischen Zusammenschlüssen', *Einst und Jetzt*, 1958, vol. 3, p. 35.
13. Schaefer-Rolffs and Scheunemann, *Handbuch*, p. 141.
14. Schultz and Ssymank, *Das Deutsche Studentum*, p. 191.
15. Neuenhoff, *Ehrenwort*, p. 58.
16. Schaefer-Rolffs and Scheunemann, *Handbuch*, p. 139.
17. T. Ziegler, *Der deutsche Student am Ende des 19. Jahrhunderts* (Leipzig: G. J. Göschen'sche Verlagshandlung, 1902) pp. 99–100.
18. 'Zweck und Ziele des deutschen Korpsstudentums', *Academische Monatshefte*, Mar. 1911, pp. 365–6.
19. Ibid., p. 367.
20. 'Zur Duellfrage', *Academische Monatshefte*, Mar. 1902, p. 300.
21. Ibid., p. 300.
22. F. Hielscher and W. Barthold, *Die Mensur: Herkunft, Recht und Wesen: Vierte Denkschrift des KSCV* (Bochum: VAC Verlag, 1968) p. 12.
23. Ibid., p. 14.

24. Ibid., p. 13.
25. Ibid., p. 14.
26. 'Zweck und Ziele', pp. 365–6.
27. F. Hielscher, 'Zweikampf und Mensur', *Einst und Jetzt*, 1966, vol. 11, p. 190.
28. F. Hielscher, 'Das kanonische Urteil der katholischen Kirke über die Mensur im 19. Jahrhundert', *Einst und Jetzt*, 1962, vol. 7, p. 100.
29. Hielscher, Kanonische Urteil, p. 100.
30. R. Assmann (ed.), 'Constitutionen der Corps und ihrer Vorläufer 1810–1820', *Einst und Jetzt*, Sonderheft (1983).
31. F. Hielscher, *Festschrift zum Kösener Congress 1960* (Würzburg: J. M. Richter's Buch- und Steindruckerei, 1960) p. 58.
32. F. Hielscher, *Recht und Ethik der Mensur: Fünfte Festschrift des HKSCV* (Würzburg: J. M. Richter's Buch und Steindruckerei, 1958) p. 18.
33. Hielscher, *Zweikampf und Mensur*, p. 199.
34. Bryson, *The Sixteenth Century Italian Duel*, pp. 10–11.
35. Fabricius, *Corps*, pp. 136–7.
36. Schaefer-Rolffs and Scheunemann, *Handbuch*, p. 138.
37. Hielscher, *Festschrift 1960*, pp. 10–11.
38. Ibid., p. 12.
39. E. Bauer and H. Schorr, 'Das Erscheinungsbild unserer Mensuren seit 1800 im Wandel der Zeit', *Einst und Jetzt*, 1961, vol. 7, p. 84.
40. F. and C. Seemann-Kahne, *Akademische Fechtschule* (Leipzig: J. J. Weber, 1926).
41. Hielscher, *Festschrift 1960*, pp. 13–14.
42. Ibid., p. 16.
43. J. Huizinga, *The Waning of the Middle Ages* (Harmondsworth, Peregrine Books, 1976) p. 224.
44. R. Baldick, *The Duel* (London: Chapman & Hall, 1965) p. 144b.
45. W. Meissner and F. Nachreiner, *Handbuch des deutschen Corpsstudenten 1930* (Frankfurt am Main: VAC Verlag, 1930) pp. 334–5.
46. Fabricius, *Geschichte und Chronik*, p. 167.
47. W. Teutloff, *Historia Academica* 6/7 (Stuttgart-Möhringen: Studentengeschichte Vereinigung des Coburger Convents, 1968) p. 114.
48. A. Sack, *Die Begründung des Allgemeinen Deutschen Waffenringes* (Berlin, n. publ., 1919) pp. 43–4.
49. Ibid., pp. 44–6.
50. Ibid., p. 46.
51. Teutloff, *Historia Academica*, p. 117.
52. T. Hammerich, *Handbuch für den Weinheimer Senioren-Covent* (Bochum: Laupenmühlen & Dietrichs, 1971) p. 8.
53. Schaefer-Rolffs and Scheunemann, *Handbuch*, p. 84.
54. O. Gerlach, *Kösener Corpslisten 1798–1960* (Bochum: VAC Verlag, 1961)
55. M. Steinberg, *Sabers and Brown Shirts* (Chicago: University of Chicago Press, 1977) pp. 51–2.
56. Meissner and Nachreiner, *Handbuch*, p. 177.
57. Ibid., pp. 296–9.
58. Fabricius, *Geschichte und Chronik*, p. 171.
59. Meissner and Nachreiner, *Handbuch*, pp. 298–9.

60. Sack, *Die Begründung*, p. 49.
61. A. Lohmann, 'Chronik des SC-Verbandes 1918–1933', *Einst und Jetzt*, 1960, vol. 5, pp. 6–7.
62. Meissner and Nachreiner, *Handbuch*, pp. 335–7.
63. *Ehrenschutz-Abkommen zwischen dem HKSCV, dem Gesamtausschuss des Verbandes alter Corpsstudenten, und dem Deutschen Offizierbund und Nationalverband Deutscher Offizier (DOB und NDO)* (Frankfurt am Main: VAC Verlag, 1926) p. 6.
64. Teutloff, *Historia Academica*, p. 136.
65. Lohmann, 'Chronik des SC-Verbandes', p. 14.
66. Ibid., p. 15.
67. Ibid., pp. 16–17.
68. Teutloff, *Historia Academica*, pp. 143–4.
69. Lohmann, 'Chronik des SC-Verbandes', pp. 20–1.
70. Deutsche Studentenschaft, *Akademische Korrespondenz*, 9 April 1930, Kob., R 129, f.183.
71. A. Asch, 'Der Kampf des Kartellverbandes jüdischer Korporationen (KC) gegen den Antisemitismus,' *Einst und Jetzt*, 1971, vol. 16, p. 148. Also see J. Katz, *Out of the Ghetto* (Cambridge, Mass.: Harvard University Press, 1973) pp. 191–2.
72. Ibid., p. 148.
73. Angerer, Toleranzgedanken, pp. 93–8.
74. F. Moldenhauer, *Das deutsche Corpsstudententum und seine Bedeutung* (Berlin: Verlag von Albert Ahn, 1897) p. 19
75. Ibid., p. 22.
76. Schulz and Ssymank, *Das Deutsche Studententum*, pp. 370–1.
77. F. L. Carsten, *Fascist Movements in Austria: From Schönerer to Hitler* (London: Sage Publications, 1977) p. 11.
78. O. Scheuer, *Burschenschaft und Judenfrage: Der Rassenantisemitismus in der deutschen Studentenschaft* (Berlin: Verlag Berlin-Wien, 1927) pp. 40–1. See also H. Becker, *Antisemitismus in der Deutschen Turnerschaft* (Sankt Augustin, BRD: Verlag Hans Richarz, 1980) pp. 17–30.
79. Scheuer, *Burschenschaft*, p. 43.
80. Whiteside, *The Socialism of Fools*, pp. 153–4. Compare with P. G. J. Pulzer, *The Rise of Political Anti-Semitism in Germany and Austria* (New York: John Wiley and Sons, Inc., 1964) pp. 253–4.
81. Scheuer, *Burschenschaft*, p. 55.
82. Schulz and Ssymank, *Das Deutsche Studententum*, p. 372.
83. Scheuer, *Burschenschaft*, p. 55.
84. Ibid., pp. 57–8.
85. G. Mosse, *German and Jews* (New York: Howard Fertig, 1970) pp. 94–5.
86. Meissner and Nachreiner, *Handbuch*, pp. 156–7.
87. Asch, 'Der Kampf', pp. 150–1.
88. Angerer, Toleranzgedanken, p. 97.
89. Scheuer, *Burschenschaft*, p. 59.
90. Lohmann, 'Chronik des SC-Verbandes', pp. 9–10.
91. *Monatschrift des Rudolstädter SC*, 1921, nr. 7, p. 125.
92. Ibid.
93. Scheuer, *Burschenschaft*, p. 57.

94. Lohmann, 'Chronik des SC-Verbandes', pp. 7-9.
95. Asch, 'Der Kampf', p. 153.
96. *Monatschrift des RSC*, 1921, nr. 7, p. 125.
97. *Niederschrift, ADW Tagung 25.02.1931*, Kös. Arch.
98. 'Auf Mensur', *Der Wehrschafter: Zeitschrift der Deutschen Wehrschaft an den Hochschulen des deutschen Sprachgebiets* (Hornung: Feb. 1931) p. 9.
99. A. Faust, 'Die "Eroberung" der Deutschen Studentenschaft durch den Nationalsozialistischen Deutschen Studentenbund', *Einst und Jetzt*, 1975, vol. 10, p. 53.
100. *Deutsche Wehrschaft* was founded in 1919/20 as a federation of fencing fraternities centring on an extreme *völkischen* nationalism which made the *Deutsche Burschenschaften* almost pale as moderate in comparison.
101. J. Fest, *Das Gesicht des Dritten Reiches* (Munich: Piper Verlag, 1964) p. 309, cited in M. Kater, *Studentenschaft und Rechtsradikalismus in Deutschland 1918-1933* (Hamburg: Hoffman & Campe, 1975) p. 132.
102. Author's correspondence with *KSCV* members.
103. Faust, Eroberung, p. 49.
104. H. Jescheck, 'Die Behandlung des Zweikampfs in der Strafrechtsreform,' *Juristenzeitung*, 1957, vol. 4, p. 110.
105. Lohmann, 'Chronik des SC-Verbandes', p. 23.
106. Ibid.
107. B. von Schirach, 'Ehrenordnung des Nationalsozialistischen Deutschen Studentenbundes', *Die Bewegung*, 8 July 1930, p. 4.
108. Ibid.
109. Ibid.
110. Ibid.
111. Ibid.
112. A. Faust, *Der Nationalsozialististische Studentenbund* (Düsseldorf: Verlag Schwann, 1973), vol. II, pp. 152-5.
113. *Ehrenordnung des NSDStB*, Ins.RstF. F.I*04C3.
114. Ibid.
115. Faust, *NSDStB*, vol. 2, p. 156.
116. *Ehrenordnung des NSDStB*, Ins.RStF. F.I*04C3.

3 THE CORPS VERSUS THE *NSDStB*

1. B. von Schirach, *Ich glaubte an Hitler* (Hamburg: Mosaik Verlag 1966) p. 122.
2. A. Wagner, *NSDAP Denkschrift, Betrifft: Streitfall NSDAP - Korps Franconia, München* (Munich, NSDAP Gau München, Münchener Buchgewerbhaus M. Müller & Sohn, 1931); also Münchener SC, *Denkschrift Münchener SC contra Münchener NSDStB und Reichsleitung der NSDAP* (Frankfurt am Main: VAC Verlag, 1931) - both works - Kös. Arch.
3. Wagner, *NSDAP Denkschrift*, p. 1.
4. W. Hachenberger to F. Landfried, February 1931, Kös. Arch.
5. Wagner, *NSDAP Denkschrift*, p. 1.
6. W. Gottwald, 'Hitlers Einstellung zum Waffenstudententum vor der

Machtübernahme. Ein Brief Hitlers a. d. J. 1931', *Einst und Jetzt*, vol. 19, 1974, p. 112.
7. MSC, *Contra NSDStB*, p. 3.
8. Ibid., p. 4.
9. Ibid., p. 5.
10. Wagner, *NSDAP Denkschrift*, p. 3.
11. MSC, *Contra NSDStB*, p. 5.
12. Ibid., p. 6.
13. Ibid., pp. 8-9.
14. Ibid., p. 6.
15. Ibid., p. 8.
16. Ibid.
17. Ibid., p. 9
18. Ibid., pp. 9-10.
19. Ibid., p. 10.
20. v. Schirach, *Hitler*, pp. 123-4.
21. Hachenberger to Landfried.
22. MSC, *Contra NSDStB*, p. 14.
23. Ibid.
24. Ibid.
25. Ibid., pp. 15-16.
26. According to William Carr, *History of Germany*, 2nd ed. (London: Edward Arnold, 1979) p. 331, Röhm only reached the rank of Captain in the *Reichswehr* and as *SA* ranks did not include *Oberstleutnant* according to L. Hamilton, *The BBC German Vocabulary* (London: Longmans, Green & Co., 1947) p. 92, it is difficult to know upon what this reference by the Munich *SC* was based unless Röhm was given an honorary rank of Lt.-Colonel by the *NSDAP*.
27. MSC, *Contra NSDStB*, pp. 16-17.
28. Walter Lienau to Corps Isaria, 24 April 1931, Kos. Arch.
29. MSC, *Contra NSDStB*, p. 18.
30. Ibid., p. 19.
31. Ibid., p. 21.
32. Wagner, *NSDAP Denkschrift*, p. 4.
33. Gottwald, 'Hitlers Einstellung', p. 120.
34. Ibid.
35. Allgemeiner Deutscher Waffenring, *Niederschrift über die Behandlungen des ordentlichen Waffenstudententages am 4. und 25. Januar 1931 zu Erfurt* (Frankfurt am Main: Englert und Schlosser, 1931) pp. 2-3.
36. ADW, *Niederschrift Januar 1931*, p. 3.
37. ADW, *Vor der Zertrümmerung des waffenstudentischen Ehrbegriffes durch 'Revolutionierung'?*, Wehrschrift der anerkannten ADW-Verbände (Berlin: February 1935).
38. ADW, *Niederschrift Januar 1931*, pp. 12-13.
39. W. Teutloff, 'Die wichtigsten Ereignisse, Tagungen und Beschlüsse zur Geschichte des Allgemeinen Deutschen Waffenringes – Anlage zum Referat auf der 18. Studenten-Historiker-Tagung zu Darmstadt am 13. und 14. September 1958' MS., Ins. HK., p. 48.
40. Faust, *NSDStB*, vol. II, p. 157.

41. v. Schirach, *Hitler*, pp. 99–100.
42. W. Lienau (psdn. L. Retlaw), 'Der Pfahl im Fleisch', *Die Sturmfahne* (Berlin, Kreis IV des NSDStB, 1931).
43. ADW Verhandlungsausschuss, *An die studentischen Verbände* (Berlin: Montanus-Druckerei, 19 December 1931), Kobl. R 129, f.26, p. 2.
44. ADW, *Dec. 19, 1931*, p. 1.
45. Ibid., p. 4.
46. Faust, *NSDStB*, vol. II, p. 25.
47. W. Lienau, 'Erklärung', ADW, *Dec. 19, 1931*, p. 6.
48. Lienau, Erklärung, p. 8.
49. Lienau, Erklärung, pp. 7–8.
50. Kös. Arch.
51. Teutloff, *Geschichte ADW*, p. 49.
52. Ibid.
53. Ibid., p. 50.
54. ADW, *Bericht* (5 April 1932) Kobl. R 129, f.26, pp. 3–5.
55. Ibid., p. 1.
56. ADW, *Rundschreiben an die deutschen Korporationen* (Berlin, 23 February 1932) Kobl. R 129, f.26, p. 2.
57. ADW, *Bericht* (5 April 1932), p. 3.
58. ADW, *Rundschreiben* (23 February 1932), pp. 1–2 ii.
59. Ibid., p. 3. See also Krüger to Kraaz, Corps Bremensia, KSCV Vorort, 18 March 1932, Kös. Arch.
60. ADW, *Bericht* (5 April 1932) p. 3.
61. Krüger to Kraaz (18 March 1932).
62. ADW, *Bericht* (5 April 1932) pp. 5–6.
63. Vorstand der Deutschen Studentschaft, *Rundschreiben A* 28 WS 31/32 (Berlin: 22 March 1932) Kobl. R 129, f.26, p. 1.
64. Teutloff, *Geschichte ADW*, p. 50.
65. Faust, *NSDStB*, vol. II, p. 35.
66. Ibid., p. 37.
67. G. Kraaz, 'Der 15. Deutsche Studententag in Königsberg', *Deutsche Corpszeitung*, September 1932, p. 119.
68. Faust, *NSDStB*, vol. II, p. 39.
69. Ibid., pp. 38 and 40.
70. Faust, *NSDStB*, vol. II, p. 40.
71. Lohmann, 'Chronik des SC-Verbandes', p. 27.
72. Kraaz, DCZ, September 1932, pp. 121–2.
73. Lohmann, 'Chronik des SC-Verbandes', pp. 25–6.
74. Ibid., p. 27.
75. Ibid., p. 15.
76. Ibid., p. 27.
77. Ibid., p. 27.
78. Ibid., p. 27–8.
79. Ibid., p. 27.
80. Corps Bremensia, KSCV Vorort, to ADW, 5 November 1932, Kös. Arch.
81. Bremensia to ADW, pp. 2–3.
82. Ibid., pp. 3–7.
83. 'Mitteilung der V.L.,' *Der Wehrschafter*, Nebelmond/Julmond (Nov/Dec),

1932, pp. 51–2.
84. Corps Bremensia, KSCV Vorort, *Erklärung des KSCV auf dem Waffenstudententag in Goslar*, December 1932, Kös. Arch.
85. Teutloff, *Historia Academica 6/7*, p. 157.
86. Bremensia to ADW, pp. 1–2.
87. Lohmann, 'Chronik des SC-Verbandes', p. 28.
88. K. F. Mohr, *Bericht über die Vorortgeschäfte 1933*, Kös. Arch.
89. Lohmann, 'Chronik des SC-Verbandes', p. 29.
90. Mohr, *Bericht*, p. 27.
91. *Reichsgesetzblatt*, Jahrgang 1933, Teil I, par. 210a, p. 296; also pp. 295–8.
92. Mohr, *Bericht*, p. 25.
93. G. Krüger. *An die Studentischen Verbände*, 20 March 1933, Kos. Arch.
94. J. Haupt, *Neuordnung im Schulwesen und Hochschulwesen* (Berlin: 1933) p. 17.
95. Ibid., p. 10.
96. *Satzung der Mannheimer Studentenschaft – Mai 1933*, Kobl. R 129, f.140.
97. *Preussische Studentenrechtsverordnung* (Berlin: April 1933), cited *DCZ*, May 1933, pp. 37–9.
98. *Preussische Studentenrechtsverordnung*, *DCZ*, p. 38.
99. H. Schlömer, *Die allgemeine Entwicklung der Studentenschaft im Früjahr, 1933*, MS. (n.p.: n.p., n.d.), Ins. HK.
100. Ibid.
101. H. C. Mahrenholz, 'Einführung des Arierprinzips im Wingolf nach 1933', *Einst und Jetzt*, 1982, vol. 27, p. 128.
102. ADW, *Bundesgesetz – Allgemeiner Deutscher Waffenring vom 20.05. 1933* (n.p.: Arbeitskreis des ADW, September 1933) Kös. Arch.
103. ADW, *Bundesgesetz*, p. 5.
104. ADW, *Sitzungsbericht des ausserordentlichen Waffenstudententages am 20 Mai 1933, zu Goslar* (Berlin: Arbeitskreis des ADW, n.d.) Kös. Arch.
105. ADW, *20. Mai 1933*, pp. 5–6.
106. Mohr, *Bericht*, p. 26.
107. Ibid.
108. Ibid., p. 30.
109. Ibid., p. 32.
110. Ibid.
111. Ibid., p. 34.
112. Ibid., pp. 36–7.
113. Ibid., pp. 34–5.
114. 'Die Naumburger Feier am 31. Mai 1933', *DCZ*, June 1933, p. 63.
115. C. Otto, *Bericht Otto-Kösener Congress 1933*, Kös. Arch.
116. Ibid., p. 3. See also G. Neuenhoff, 'Die Auflösung des KSCV und VAC', *Einst und Jetzt, Beilageheft zum Jahrbuch 1968*, 1968, pp. 6–7.
117. Otto, *Bericht Otto-Kosener Congress*, pp. 6–7.
118. Mohr, Corps Guestphalia zu Greifswald, KSCV Vorort to Reichsinnenministerium, 1 June 1933, Kös, Arch.
119. Mohr, Corps Guestphalia zu Greifswald, KSCV Vorort, *Absage des ordentlichen Kösener Congress 1933*, Kös. Arch.
120. Otto, *Bericht Otto-Kosener Congress*, p. 16.
121. Ibid., pp. 19–21.

4 BLUNCK AS *FÜHRER* OF THE *KSCV*

1. Otto, *Berichte Otto-Kosener Congress*, pp. 5-6.
2. *Bericht über Sitzung vom 19. Juli 1933*, Kös. Arch.
3. Blunck, *Anordnungen und Bekanntmachen des Führers der deutschen Corpsstudenten und seiner Beauftragten*, DCZ, June 1933, pp. 71-3.
4. Neuenhoff, *Auflösung*, p. 7.
5. Blunck, *DCZ*, June 1933, pp. 72-3.
6. Neuenhoff, *Auflösung*, p. 7.
7. Blunck of KSCV to Stäbel of NSDStB, 12 July 1933, Inst. Ztgt. MA 228, pp. 24688-9.
8. D. M. McKale, *The Nazi Party Courts* (Wichita: University of Kansas Press, 1974) pp. 112-14.
9. Blunck, *KSCV Circular Number 3*, June 1933, Kös Arch.
10. Ibid.
11. Blunck to Sauermann of ADW, 12 July 1933, Inst. Ztgt. MA 228, pp. 4666-9.
12. Blunck, *KSCV Circular Number 4*, June 1933, Kös. Arch.
13. Sauermann, *ADW Forms I, II, III*, 1933, Kös. Arch.
14. Corps Rhenania-Strassburg zu Marburg to Blunck, 25 June 1933, Kös. Arch.
15. Corps Palaiomarchia zu Halle to Blunck, 4 July 1933, Kös. Arch.
16. Blunck to Sauermann, 12 July 1933, Inst. Ztgt, MA 228, pp. 4666-9.
17. Blunck to Stäbel, 12 July 1933, Inst. Ztgt, f.MA 228, pp. 4661-5.
18. Corps Moenania zu Würzburg to Blunck, 20 August 1933, Kös. Arch.
19. Die Kieler Waffenstudenschaft to Rust, Stäbel, Sauermann, Krüger, 14 July 1933, Inst. RStFü., f.I*04g314.
20. Blunck, *KSCV Circulars Number 4, 5, 6*, July 1933, Kös. Arch.
21. Blunck, *KSCV Circular Number 7*, 8 August 1933, Kös. Arch.
22. M. Franze, *Die Erlanger Studentenschaft 1918-1945*, 1972, pp. 230-2.
23. Blunck, *KSCV Circular Number 5*, 10 July 1939. Kös. Arch.
24. F. Stadtmüller, *Geschichte des Corps Hannovera zu Göttingen 1809-1959* (Göttingen: Verein Göttinger Hannoveraner e.V., 1969) p. 270.
25. Blunck, *KSCV Circular Number 9*, 1 September 1933, Kös. Arch.
26. Stadtmüller, *Hannovera*, pp. 270-1.
27. Blunck, *Number 9*.
28. Blunck, *KSCV Circular Number 10*, 12 September 1933, Kös. Arch.
29. Blunck, *Number 9*.
30. Ibid.
31. Druckery, *KSCV Circular Number 11*, September 1933, Kös. Arch.
32. *NSGCV Vereinbarung*, 22 September 1933, Kös. Arch.
33. Druckery, 'Corpsstudentisches Bekenntnis', *DCZ*, October 1933, p. 140.
34. Druckery to Stäbel, 3 October 1933.
    Druckery to Zaeringer of WSC, 5 October 1933.
    Stäbel to Druckery, 7 October 1933, all Inst. RStFü. f.I*0406.
35. '45. Treffen der norddeutschen Korpsstudenten', *Lübecker Generalanzeiger*, 10 October 1933.
36. 'Der Corpsstudent im Dritten Reich', *Deutsche Allgemeine Zeitung*, 11 October 1933.

37. 'Rede des Führers Dr Max Blunck am 7. Oktober 1933', *DCZ*, October 1933, p. 147.
38. *Sitzung des Führerkreises der N-S Gemeinschaft corpsstudentischer Verbände vom 4. November 1933*, Kös. Arch.
39. N-SGCV, *4.11.33.*
40. Blunck, *KSCV Circular Number 15*, November 1933, Kös. Arch.
41. Heringhaus to Kraaz, 5 September 1933, Kös. Arch.
42. Blunck, *Number 15*.
43. *Stitzung des Führerkreises der N-S Gemeinschaft Corpsstudentischer Verbände vom. 18 November 1933*, Kös. Arch.
44. N-SGCV, *18.11.33.*
45. Druckery (N-SGCV) to Stäbel, 23 November 1933, Inst. RStFü, f.I*0406.
46. *Kameradschaft Waffenstudentischer Verbände*, Kölnische Zeitung, 18 November 1933, Kös. Arch.
47. *Sitzung N-SGCV November 18, 1933*, Kös. Arch.
48. *Schwab Rede*, Erlangen, 1 December 1933. Kös. Arch.
49. 'Corps und Burschenschaft', *Deutsche Zukunft*, Berlin, Nr 9, 10 December 1933; as well as, 'Studentenschaft und Korporationen', *Breslauer Neueste Nachrichten*. Breslau, 7 December 1933. Kös. Arch.
50. Druckery, *Vereinbarung zwischen der nationalsozialistischen Gemeinschaft corpsstudentischer Verbände und der Deutschen Burschenschaft*, 1 January 1934, as well as Druckery to Schwab, 8 January 1934, both in Kös. Arch.
51. Franze, *Erlanger Stud.*, p. 239.
53. H. Weber, 'Die studentischen Korporationsverbände 1930', *Wende und Schau*, Kösener Jahrbuch 1930, Frankfurt am Main, Appendix I.b.
55. Langhoff, *ADW Circular 4/1934*, Berlin, March 1934. Kös. Arch.
56. 'Neuer ADW-Verband', *DCZ*, Jan. 1934, p. 238.
57. 'Aus anderen Verbänden', *DCZ*, Jan. 1934, pp. 238-9.
58. H. Bernhardi, *Frisia Gottingensis 1931-1956* (Heide in Holstein: Boyens and Co., 1956) p. 41.
59. Ibid., pp. 40-1.
60. 'Auflösung der nationalsozialialistischen Gemeinschaft corpsstudentischer Verbände', *DCZ*, Mar. 1934, pp. 300-301; also see Jockusch, 'Zur Geschichte der landwirtschaftlichen Verbindungen an deutschen Hochschulen', *Pflug und Schwert; Monatsschrift des Naumburger Verbandes landständischer Verbindungen an deutschen Hochschulen*, Eismond (Jan.) 1934, pp. 7-8.
61. 'Deutsche Bauernschaft', *DCZ*, February 1934, pp. 238-9.
62. Jockusch, 'Zur Geschichte', p. 238.
63. Langhoff, *ADW Circular 4/34*, March 1934, Kös. Arch.
64. Blunck, *KSCV Circular Number 23*, 20 January 1934, Kös. Arch.
65. Teutloff, *Geschichte des Allgemeinen Deutschen Waffenringes*, pp. 158-9.
66. Fillibeck, *Denkschrift des Corps Suevia zu München*, 1934.
67. Blunck to Corps Suevia zu Munchen, in Fillibeck, *Corps Suevia Denkschrift*, 19.
68. Fillibeck, *Corps Suevia Denkschrift*.
69. Gottwald, 'Der Kösener-Verband und die Versipptenfrage im 3. Reich', *Einst und Jetzt*, vol. 12, 1967, pp. 60-3.
70. Fillibeck, *Corps Suevia Denkschrift*.

71. E. Weiss, 'Lusatia kontra NSDStB; Die Auseinandersetzung mit dem NS-Studentenbund Leipzig 1934', *Einst und Jetzt*, vol. 17 1972, pp. 149–51.
72. Ibid., pp. 152–3.
73. *Osnabrücker Zeitung*, Osnabruck, 8 June 1934; see also *Flensburger Nachrichten*, Flensburg, 8 June 1934; and *Westfälischer Kurier*, Hamm, 8 June 1934, Kös. Arch.
74. 'Ueberempfindlich', *Film-Journal*, Berlin, 10 June 1934, Kös. Arch.
75. 'Die Goldene Gans', *Königsberger Zeitung*, 17 June 1934, Kös. Arch.
76. Blunck, *KSCV Special Circular*, Berlin, 13 July 1934, Kös. Arch.
77. Blunck, 'Schutz den Farben', *DCZ*, 15 July 1934, pp. 215–16.
78. Heringhaus, 'Die unentbehrlichen Verbände', *DCZ*, 11 August 1934, p. 267.
79. 'Aufgehen des Rudolstädter SC im Weinheimer SC', in *Corpsstudentische Monatsblätter*, April 1934, pp. 185–6.
80. Reick, 'Geschichte des Rudolstädter Senioren-Convent', *100 Jahre Weinheimer Senioren-Convent* (Bochum: WSC Historische Komission, 1963) p. 74.
81. Feickert, *Studenten Greifen an: Nationalsozialistische Hochschulrevolution*, Hamburg, 1934, Inst Ztgt, WK 360.
82. Feickert, 'Anordnung über Kameradschaftserziehung', *DCZ*, October 1934, pp. 305–306.
83. Corps Turingia zu Leipzig to Stadtsteueramt Leipzig, 30 November 1934, Kös. Arch.
84. Blunck to Hermann Fischer Corps Suevia Strassburg zu Marburg, 26 March 1934, Kös. Arch.
85. Blunck to Kraaz, Internal Memo, 30 October 1934, Kös. Arch.
86. Blunck/Heringhaus, *Bericht a.o. Kösener Congress 1934*, Kös. Arch.
87. Segler, DSt Amt für Kameradschaftserziehung. *DST Circular Number A 12/1934*, 5 October 1934, RStFü. f.I*5g398.
88. Blunck, *KSCV Circular Number 33*, 26 October 1934, Kös. Arch.
89. 'Freiwillige Kameradschaft', *Berliner Tageblatt*, Berlin, 27 October 1934.
90. 'Umstellung der Erziehung auf den Gemeinschaftsgedanken', *Cottbuser Anzeiger*, Cottbus, 16 November 1934; also see 'Korporationsfrage geklärt', *Neue Preussische Kreuzzeitung*, Berlin, 17 November 1934.
91. Kraaz to Blunck, 17 October 1934, Kös. Arch.
92. Teutloff, *ADW*, pp. 158–9.
93. Blunck to Kraaz, 30 October 1934 Kös. Arch.
94. 'Verlautbarung des Völkischen Waffenrings', *DCZ*, January 1935, p. 389.
95. Blunck to Lammers, 29 December 1934, Kobl. R 128, f.27.
96. 'Zur Lage', *DCZ*, December 1934, p. 368.
97. Blunck, 'Was trennt uns von der Schwab'schen Burschenschaft?', *DCZ*, January 1935, pp. 369–71.
98. Meissner, *Die corpsstudentische Idee* (Frankfurt am Main, VAC Verlag, 1934) p. 62.
99. Ibid., p. 83.
100. Weiss, *Corps Lusatia kontra NSDStB*, 1972, pp. 145–7; see also *Völkischer Beobachter*, 25 April 1934.
101. Blunck, Personal note, 5 November 1934, Kös. Arch.
102. Frommel, Archivist's note, Kös. Arch.
103. Langhoff, *ADW Niederschrift vom ordentlichen Waffenstudententag 1935*,

pp. 3-4, Kös. Arch.
104. Lammers, *Gemeinschaft Studentischer Verbände*, Berlin, 12 January 1935, Kolb. R 128 f.6, pp. 103-104.
105. Heringhaus to Lammers, Kös. Arch.
106. Bormann to Lammers, 14 March 1935, Kobl. R 128 f.1026, p. 56; see also, Lammers to Schmidtkampf, 4 April 1935, Kobl. R 128, f.1026, p. 83.
107. Glatzer to Hitler, Kobl. R 128 f.1026, pp. 92-3.
108. Wagner, quoted in Lammers, *GStV Circular*, 28 January 1935, Kobl. R 128 f.6, p. 103 B.
109. Teutloff, *ADW Geschichte*, p. 160.
110. Lammers, *GStV Circular*, 28 January 1935, Kobl. R 128, f.6, p. 103.
111. Witthauer, *GStV Protocol*, 30 January 1935, Kobl. R 128 f.1, pp. 55-6.
112. GStV, *Vereinbarung*, 12 March 1935, Kobl. R 128 f.93.
113. Hitler to Lammers, 30 March 1935, Kobl. R 128, f.5.
114. Lammers, *Speech - GStV Conference*, 30-31 March 1935, Kobl. R 128, f.6, p. 4.
115. 'Gemeinschaft Studentischer Verbände', *DCZ*, April 1935, pp. 28-9.
116. Blunck to Corps Bavaria zu München, June 1935, Kös. Arch.
117. 'Das Heidelberger Urteil', *DCZ*, July 1935, p. 117.
118. *Jüdische Korpsbrüder bei Palaiomarchia: Nationalsozialisten verlassen unter Protest das Korps*, Mitteldeutsche National-Zeitung Halle, 29 August 1935, Kobl. R 128, f.74 and Kös. Arch.
119. Blunck to Herrmann GStV, Kös. Arch.
120. Lammers, *Vom Fall Palaiomarchia bis zum Ausschluss des Kösener SC*, Kobl. R 128, 101.
121. Wagner, *Burschentag-Eisenach 1935*, Kobl. R 128, f.1027.
122. Blunck to Lammers, 11 May 1935, Kös. Arch.
123. Blunck to Lammers, 25 June 1935, Kös. Arch.
124. GStV. *Vermerk*, Lammers, Wagner, Derichsweiler meeting, Berlin, 21 June 1935, Kobl. R 128, f.37; see also, 'Die Richtlinien des NSDStB vom 25. Juni 1935', *DCZ*, July 1935, pp. 136-7.
125. Lammers to Derichsweiler, 1 July 1935, Kös. Arch; see also, Lammers to GStV Verbände Führer, 3 July 1935, Kös. Arch.
126. Herrmann, *Verbändeführer Sitzung der GStV am 14, Juli 1935 in Berchtesgaden*, Kobl. R 128, f.13, pp. 9-19.
127. Herrmann, *14 Juli 1935*, pp. 117-18.
128. Faust, 'Göttinger Burschenschaft Holzminda', *Westdeutscher Beobachter*, quoted in *DCZ*, 25 July 1935, p. 124.
129. Hermann, *Bericht - Juli 24, 1935*, 24 July 1935, Kobl. R 128, f14, pp. 50-1.
130. Hermann, *Niederschrift der Verbändeführer-Sitzung der GStV vom 24 Juli 1935, Berlin Nationaler-Klub*, Kobl. R 128, f.14, pp. 85-8.
131. Herrmann, *Sitzung 24, Juli 1935*, pp. 14-15.
132. Herrmann, *24 Juli 1935*, pp. 89-100.
133. Blunck to Nordmann, 16 July 1935, Kös. Arch and Kobl. R 128, f.30.
134. Nordmann to Blunck, 22 July 1935, Kös Arch. and Kobl. R 128, f.38.
135. Lammers, *GStV - [Resignation Speech], Nationaler-Klub*, 8 September 1935, Berlin, 9 September 1935, Kobl. R 128, f.18, pp. 17-21.
136. Lammers, *GStV Circular 23/25*, 6 September 1935, Kobl. R 128, f.24, pp. 71-2.
137. Lammers, *Speech September 8, 1935*, Kobl. R 128, f.18, pp. 21-3.

138. Blunck to Lammers, 13 August 1935, Kös. Arch.
139. Lammers to Blunck, Telegram, 28 August 1935, Kös. Arch.
140. Blunck to Lammers, 28 and 29 August 1935, Kös. Arch.
141. Blunck to Nordmann, 31 August 1935, Kös. Arch.
142. Lammers, *Speech September 8, 1935*, Kobl. R 128, f.18, pp. 29–34.
143. Lammers to Blunck, Telegram, 5 September 1935, *DCZ*, September 1935, p. 156.
144. Lammers, *GStV Circular 23/25*, 6 September 1935, Kobl. R 128, f.24, pp. 71–2.
145. Lammers, *Speech September 8, 1935*, pp. 35–40.
146. Ibid., p. 44 and p. 109.
147. Ibid., pp. 41–53.
148. Hermann, *GStV Circular 24/35*, Kobl R 128, f.24, pp. 73–4.
149. Heringhaus, *An die Corps im KSCV*, special KSCV Circular, 28 September 1935, Kös. Arch; see also Blunck, 'Vertrauliche Mitteilungen der Verbandsführer des KSCV und VAC', *DCZ*, September 1935, pp. 149–50.
150. Heringhaus, *DCZ*, September 1935, p. 150.
151. H. Krausnick, *The Nuremberg Laws and Their Consequences*, in *Anatomy of the SS State* (London: Paladin, 1970) pp. 49–50.
152. *Lutze-Erlass*, 28 September 1935, Kös. Arch.
153. Neuenhoff, *Auflösung*, p. 26.
154. Heringhaus, *KSCV Circular Number 46*, 9 October 1935, Kös. Arch.
155. Grosche, 'Juden, Freimaurer und Cösener SC', *Deutsche Wollen*, Number 175, 11 October 1935.
156. Neuenhoff, *Auflösung*, p. 27.
157. *Nachrichtenblatt der Deutschen Burschenschaft*, 2 November 1935, pp. 1–2 compliments of the Burschenschaftlichen Archivs, Frankfurt am Main.
158. Interview with participants.

5 THE *VERBOTZEIT*, 1936–45

1. A. Derichsweiler, *Deutsche Studenten-Zeitung*, 1935, no. 25.
2. L. A. Ricker, 'Freiburger Mensuren in der nationalsozialistischen Verbotzeit', *Einst und Jetzt*, vol. 10, 1965, p. 72.
3. Hess, *Die Bewegung*, January 1936.
4. Ricker, 'Freiburger Mensuren', p. 72.
5. H. Scherer, 'Die WSC-Corps in der Verbotzeit (1935–1945)', *Einst und Jetzt*, vol. 5, 1960, p. 86.
6. H. Bernhardi, *Die Göttinger Burschenschaft 1933–1945* (Heidelberg: Winter Verlag, 1957) pp. 224–5.
7. E. Bauer, 'Die Kameradschaften im Bereiche des Kösener SC in den Jahren 1935–1945', *Einst und Jetzt*, vol. 1, 1956, p. 17.
8. G. Neuenhoff *Auflösung des KSCV*, p. 25.
9. E. Schlange, 'Mitteilungen des Verbandsführers', *DCZ*, March 1936, p. 250.
10. Ibid., p. 251.
11. Ibid., p. 253.

12. Ibid., pp. 253-4.
13. R. Hess, 'Kein Nationalsozialist kann Verbindungsstudent sein!' *Die Bewegung*, 20 May 1936, p. 1.
14. R. Hess, 'Student-Kampfhilfe neu gegründet', *Die Bewegung*, 20 May 1936, p. 1.
15. Bernhardi, *Burschenschaft*, p. 224.
16. 'Abkommen zwischen SA und NSDStB', *Die Bewegung*, 15 April 1936, p. 2.
17. 'Der dicke Strich', *Die Bewegung*, 20 May 1936, p. 1.
18. Ibid.
19. As an indication of student lethargy toward the new system of *Kameradschaften* the University of Göttingen had only two *Stamm-Kameradschaften* during the summer semester of 1936 and no other student organisation. Bernhardi, *Burschenschaften*, p. 227.
20. Nationalsozialistische Studentenkampfhilfe, *Richtlinien für die Beitragsselbsteinschätzung...*, Munich, 23 July 1936.
21. NS Studentenkampfhilfe, *Richtlinien*.
22. Verein Deutscher Studenten (VdSt).
23. Bauer, *Kösener SC 1935-1945*, pp. 8-9.
24. Bernhardi, *Burschenschaft*, p. 227. This agreement differed from the Erfurt Agreement by which *NSDStB* members had been given the choice between armed or *verbriefte* satisfaction.
25. Interview with Dr Karl-Heinz Herberger, Mannheim, June 1977.
26. 'Stammhochschulerlass des Reichswissenschaftsministers', *Die Bewegung*, 3 March 1937, p. 9.
27. '14000 an der Front!', *Die Bewegung*, 3 March 1937, p. 4, Sanderberg.
28. 'Die Ehrenerklärung der Partei', *Die Bewegung*, 27 April 1937, p. 2.
29. A. Scheel, 'Ehren- und Dienststrafordnung verkündet und in Kraft gesezt', *Die Bewegung*, 29 June 1937, p. 2.
30. 'Die neuen Dienststrafordnungen', *Die Bewegung*, 8 June 1937, p. 6.
31. 'Aufruf an die alten Waffenstudenten!', *Die Bewegung*, 8 June 1937, p. 1.
32. Originally 60 per cent of a fraternity's *Alteherrenschaft* was required in order to qualify under the programme but the prerequisite was later changed to a standard total number of 200.
33. Bauer, *Kösener SC 1935-1945*, footnote 26, p. 12.
34. G. A. Scheel, *Die Reichstudentenführung*, 1938, p. 13.
35. Herberger interview.
36. Scheel, *Reichstudentenführung*, p. 14.
37. One such affair of honour is propounded to have taken place at Freiburg i.Br. in 1939.
38. Bauer, *Kösener SC 1935-1945*, p. 12.
39. R. Assmann, 'Die Suspensionszeit des Tübinger SC im Dritten Reich', *Einst und Jetzt*, vol. 21, 1976, pp. 153-4.
40. Ricker, 'Freiburger Mensuren', pp. 74-5.
41. E. Bauer, 'Von Kameradschaft zum Corps', Die Gründungsgeschichte der Misnia zu Leipzig', *Einst und Jetzt*, vol. 18, 1973, p. 115.
42. Stadtmüller, *Hannovera*, p. 277.
43. A. Scheel, 'Namen der Kameradschaften', *Die Bewegung*, 16 November 1937, p. 8.

44. C. Mehring, interviewed, Bielefeld, November 1978.
45. C. Mehring, *Die Kameradschaftszeit in Bonn* (Bonn: Corps Rhenania zu Bonn, 1971).
46. G. Bartels, interviewed, Göttingen, November 1978.
47. Stadtmüller, *Hannovera*, pp. 286–7.
48. *Zur Geschichte und Vordatierung des Stiftungstages der Guestphalia zu Halle* (Halle: priv. 1925).
49. W. Schutze, *Geschichte des Corps Guestphalia zu Jena* (Cologne: priv. 1952) p. 137.
50. Stadtmüller, *Hannovera*, p. 285.
51. Ricker, *Freiburger Mensuren*, p. 75.
52. Stadtmüller, *Hannovera*, p. 284.
53. Possibly connected with Hitler's campaign against homosexuals or anything associated with the *NSDAP* which remotely suggested close male relationships. See R. G. L. Waite, *The Psychopathic God: Adolf Hitler* (New York: Basic Books, Inc., 1977) pp. 234–5.
54. H. Scherer, 'Der Weg durch die Krise (1933–1945)', *100 Jahre Weinheimer Senioren-Convent* (Bochum: Weinheimer Verband Alter Corpsstudenten e.V., 1963) p. 112.
55. E. Bauer, 'Eine Rekonstitution des KSCV im Juni 1944', *DCZ*, February 1953, p. 8.
56. Ibid., p. 8.
57. Ibid., p. 9.
58. Ibid., p. 10.
59. Scherer, *Der Weg*, pp. 113–14.

6 EPILOGUE

1. *Military Government of German Fragebogen* – American Forces Form MG/PS/G/9a. 15 May 1945, Wiener Library, London.
2. *Reichsgesetzblatt 26. Mai 1933*, Sect. I, quoted in Hielscher and Barthold, *Die Mensur: Herkunft, Recht und Wesen*, p. 73.
3. J. Küper, 'Die Erneuerung der HKSCV im Jahre 1951', *Einst und Jetzt*, vol. 3, 1958, p. 42.
4. J. Küper, 'Die Interessengemeinschaft von 1950 als Vorstufe der Erneuerung des HKSCV im Jahre 1951', *Einst und Jetzt*, vol. 2, 1957, p. 5.
5. Küper, *Interessengemeinschaft*, p. 7.
6. Küper, *Erneuerung*, p. 47.
7. Ibid., pp. 48–9.
8. Hielscher and Bartold, *Die Mensur*, pp. 74–5.
9. Scherer, *Der Weg*, pp. 111–14.
10. W. Rieck, 'Geschichte des Rudolstädter Senioren-Convents', *100 Jahre Weinheimer Senioren-Convent* (Bochum: Weinheimer Verband Alter Corpsstudenten e.V., 1963) pp. 73–4.
11. P. Gladen, 'Der Naumburger Senioren-Convent', *Die Wachenburg*, May/June, 1977, pp. 91–3.

12. Schaefer-Rolffs and Scheunemann, *Handbuch des Kösener Corpsstudenten*, 1965, p. 189.
13. Correspondence with Elfriede Gerstein, widow of Kurt Gerstein, 10 May 1977. Also see H. Rothfels and T. Eschenburg, 'Augenzeugenbericht zu den Massenvergasungen', *Vierteljahrshefte für Zeitgeschichte*, no. 1 (1953) pp. 177–94.
14. H. von Etzdorf, interviewed, Eichtling, Bavaria, June 1977.
15. F. Freiherr von Münchhausen, interviewed, Mannheim, March 1977.

7 SUMMARY AND CONCLUSIONS

1. F. L. Carsten, 'The Introduction', in H. Graml *et al.*, *The German Resistance to Hitler* (London: B. T. Batsford Ltd, 1966) p. viii.
2. W. Barthold, 'Macht und Ohnmacht der Ideologien in den Corps', *Einst und Jetzt*, vol. 27, 1982, p. 83.

Bibliography

A UNPUBLISHED PRIMARY SOURCES

Archiv der Ehem. Reichsstudentenführung (Inst RStF), Würzburg: NSDStB, DSt, RStF.
Bundesarchiv (Kobl), Koblenz: DSt, RStF, GStV, Reichserziehungsministerium.
Institut für Hochschulkunde (Inst HK), Würzburg: Student periodicals, fraternity and federation publications and histories.
Institut für Zeitgeschichte (Inst ZIG), Munich: NSDAP and NSDStB literature.
Kösener Archiv (Kös Arch), Würzburg: Documents, press clippings, etc. of the KSCV.
Weiner Library (WL), London: Student press clippings, NSDAP publications.

B PUBLISHED SOURCES

Allgemeine Deutsche Waffenring, 'Vor der Zertrümmerung des waffenstudentischen Ehrbegriffes durch "Revolutionierung"?'. *Wehrschrift der anerkannten ADW Verbände*. Berlin, February 1935.
Baird, J. W., 'Goebbels, Horst Wessel, and the Myth of Resurrection and Return', *Journal of Contemporary History*, no. 17 (1982), pp. 633–50.
Baldick, R., *The Duel* (London: Chapman & Hall, 1965).
Becker, H., *Antisemitismus in der Deutschen Turnerschaft*, Band 3, Schriften der Deutschen Sportshochschule Köln (Sankt Augustin: Verlag Hans Richarz, 1980).
Bell, W. L. (ed.), *The Graduate Studies Prospectus 1981–1983* (Oxford: Oxford University Press, 1981).
Bernhardi, H., *Frisia Gottingensis 1983–1951* (Heide in Holstein: Westholsteinische Verlagsdruckerei Boyens & Co., 1956).
Bernhardi, H., 'Die Göttinger Burschenschaft 1933 bis 1945', in Wentzcke, P. (ed.), *Darstellungen und Quellen zur Geschichte der deutschen Einheitsbewegung* (Heidelberg: Carl Winter Universitätsverlag, 1957).
Bryson, F., *The Sixteenth Century Italian Duel* (Chicago: University of Chicago Press, 1938).
Bundle, A., 'Rüdolstädter Senioren-Convent', in *Das Akademische Deutschland*, vol. III (Berlin: C. A. Weller Verlag, 1981) pp. 287–302.
Bushmann, W., 'Naumburger Senioren-Convent', in *Das Akademische Deuts-*

chland, vol. III (Berlin: C. W. Weller Verlag, 1931) pp. 346–50.
Carr, W., *A History of Germany*, 2nd ed. (London: Edward Arnold, 1979).
Carsten, F. L. et al., *The German Resistance to Hitler* (London: B. T. Batsford Ltd, 1970).
Carsten, F. L., *Fascist Movements in Austria: From Schönerer to Hitler*, vol. VII of Sage Studies in 20th Century History (London: Sage Publications, 1977).
Chaste, R., *Der Kameradschaftsabend*, vol. X of *Der Appell* (Munich: Zentralverlag der NSDAP, nd).
Cobban, A. B., *The Medieval Universities* (London: Methuen & Co. Ltd, 1975).
Das Corps Onoldia zu Erlangen 1798–1898. Germany: n.p., n.d.
Dietrich, P., *Die Deutsche Landsmannschaft*, vol. 3/4 of *Historia Academica* (Stuttgart: Studentengeschichtlichen Vereinigung des Coburger Convents, 1958).
Fabricius, W., *Geschichte und Chronik des Kösener S.C. Verbande*, 3rd ed. (Frankfurt am Main: Verlag der Deutschen Corpszeitung, 1921).
Fabricius, W., *Die Deutschen Corps* (Verlag der Deutschen Corpszeitung, Frankfurt am Main: 1926).
Fabricius, W., 'Kösener Senioren-Convents-Verband', in *Das Akademische Deutschland*, vol. III (Berlin: C. A. Weller Verlag, 1931) pp. 259–76.
Faust, A., *Der Nationalsozialistische Studentenbund*. 2 vols (Düsseldorf: Verlag Schwann, 1973).
Feickert, A., *Studenten Greifen an* (Hamburg: Hanseatische Verlaganstalt, 1934).
Fest, J., *Das Gesicht des Dritten Reiches* (Munich: Piper, 1964).
Gerlach, O., *Kösener Corpslisten 1960* (Bochum: Selbstverlag des Verbandes Alter Corpsstudenten, 1961).
Giles, G. J., *Der NSD-Studentenbund und der Geist der studentischen Korporationen*. Annual Meeting, Deutsche Gesellschaft für Hochschulkunde, Würzburg. 4 October 1975.
Giles, G. J., 'The Rise of the National Socialist Students' Association and the Failure of Political Education in the Third Reich', in Strachura, P. (ed.) *The Shaping of the Nazi State* (London: Croom Helm, 1978).
Götze, O., *Die Jenaer akademischen Logen und Studentenorden des 18. Jahrhunderts* (Jena: np, 1932).
Gould, R. F. and Crowe, F. J., *The Concise History of Freemasonry*, 2nd ed. (London: Gale & Polden Ltd, 1951).
Hamilton, L., *The BBC German Vocabulary* (London: Longmans, Green & Co., 1947).
Hammerich, T., *Handbuch für den Weinheimer Senioren-Convent* (Bochum: Laupenmühlen and Dierichs, 1971).
Haupt, J., *Neuordnung im Schulwesen und Hochschulwesen* (Berlin: np, 1933).
Heer, G., 'Deutsche Burschenschaft', vol. III (Berlin: C. A. Weller Verlag, 1931) pp. 303–22.
Huizinga, J., *The Waning of the Middle Ages*, 2nd ed. (Harmondsworth: Peregrine Books, 1976).
Hunger, E. and Meyer, C., *Studentisches Brauchtum* (Bonn und Stuttgart: Verlag des AHCC, 1957).
Jarausch, K. H., *Students, Society and Politics in Imperial Germany* (Princeton, New Jersey: Princeton University Press, 1982).

Jescheck, H., 'Die Behandlung des Zweikampfs in der Strafrechtsreform', *Juristenzeitung*, no. 4 (1957) pp. 109–13.
Kater, M., *Studentenschaft und Rechtsradikalismus in Deutschland 1918–33* (Hamburg: Hoffmann & Campe, 1975).
Katz, J., *Out of the Ghetto* (Cambridge, Mass.: Harvard University Press, 1973).
Kibre, P., *The Nations in the Mediaeval Universities* (Cambridge, Mass.: Mediaeval Academy of America, 1948).
Krausnick, H. and Broszat, M., *Anatomy of the SS State* (London: Paladin, 1970).
Lutze, R., 'The German Revolutionary Student Movement 1819–1833', *Central European History*, no. 4 (1971) pp. 215–41.
Lutze, R., '"Father" John and His Teacher – Revolutionaries from the German Student Movement', *The Journal of Modern History*, On-Demand Supplement, vol. 48, no. 2 (June 1976).
McClelland, C. E., *State, Society and University in Germany 1700–1914* (London: Cambridge University Press, 1980).
McKale, D. M., *The Nazi Party Courts* (Wichita: University of Kansas Press, 1974).
Mehring, C., *Die Kameradschaftszeit in Bonn* (Bonn: Corps Rhenania zu Bonn, 1971).
Meissner, C., *Die corpsstudentische Idee* (Frankfurt am Main: Verlag der Deutschen Corpszeitung, 1934).
Meissner, W. and Nachreiner, F., *Handbuch des deutschen Corpsstudenten*, 3rd ed. (Frankfurt am Main: Selbstverlag des Verbandes Alter Corpsstudenten, 1930).
Methner, A. and Lustig, G., *Geschichte des Corps Borussia zu Breslau* (Breslau: Verlag von Wilh. Gottl. Korn, 1911).
Meyburg, G., *50 Jahre Corps Rheno-Guestphalia* (Bremen: np, 1968).
Moldenhauer, F., *Das deutsche Corpsstudententum und seine Bedeutung* (Berlin: Verlag von Albert Ahn, 1897).
Mosse, G., *Germans and Jews* (New York: Howard Fertig, 1970).
Müller, J. H., *Das Corps Silesia zu Breslau* (Breslau: Grass, Barth and Comp., 1931), reprinted 1971.
Nachreiner, F., 'Der Kösener Senioren Convent', in *Handbuch des Kösener Corpsstudent*, 4th ed. (Hamburg: VAC Verlag, 1953).
Olenhusen, A. G. von, 'Die "nichtarischen" Studenten an den deutschen Hochschulen: Zur nationalsozialistischen Rassenpolitik, 1933–1945', *Vierteljahrschefte für Zeitgeschichte*, vol. 14, no. 2 (1966) pp. 175–206.
Paulsen, F., *German Education, Past and Present*, trans. T. Lorenz (London: T. Fisher Unwin, 1908).
Pulzner, P. G. J., *The Rise of Political Anti-Semitism in Germany and Austria* (New York: John Wiley & Sons, Inc., 1964).
Ranz, W. and Bauer, E., *Handbuch des Kösener Corpsstudenten* (Hamburg: VAC Verlag, 1953).
Rashdall, H., *The Universities of Europe in the Middle Ages* (London: Oxford University Press, 1895), reprint 1936.
Rassem, M., 'Der Student als Ritter', *Studium Generale*, no. 5 (1963) pp. 274–9.
Rieck, W., 'Geschichte des Rudolstädter Senioren Convents', in *100 Jahre Weinheimer Senioren-Convent* (Bochum: Weinheimer Verband Alter Corp-

studenten e.V., 1963).
Rothfels, H. and Eschenburg, T., 'Augenzeugenbericht zu den Massenvergasungen', *Vierteljahrshefte für Zeitgeschichte*, no. 1 (1953) pp. 177-94.
Sack, A., *Die Begründung des Allgemeinen Deutschen Waffenringes* (Berlin: ADW, 1919).
Schaefer-Rolffs, G. and Scheunemann, O., *Handbuch des Kösener Corpsstudenten*, 5th ed. (Bochum: VAC Verlag, 1965).
Scheel, G. A., *Die Reichsstudentenführung* (Berlin: Junker und Dunnhaupt Verlag, 1938).
Scheel, G. A., *Grundsätze der Kameradschaftsarbeit* (Munich: NSDStB, 1942).
Schere, H., 'Der Weg durch die Krise, 1933-1952' in *100 Jahre Weinheimer Senioren-Convent* (Bochum: Weinheimer Verband Alter Corpsstudenten e.V., 1963).
Scheuer, O. F., *Burschenschaft und Judenfrage: Der Rassenantisemitismus in der deutschen Studentenschaft* (Berlin – Vienna: Verlag Berlin – Wien, 1927).
Schirach, B. von, *Wille und Weg des Nationalsozialistischen Deutschen Studentenbundes* (Munich: Abteilung für Propaganda in der Reichsleitung des NSDStB, 1929).
Schirach, B. von, *Ich glaubte an Hitler* (Hamburg: Mosaik Verlag, 1966).
Schnabel, F., *Deutsche Geschichte im Neunzehnten Jahrhundert*, vol. II, 2nd ed. (Freiburg im Br.: Verlag Herder, 1949).
Schüler, H., 'Weinheimer, Senioren-Convent', in *Das Akademische Deutschland*, vol. III (Berlin: C. A. Weller Verlag, 1931) pp. 277-86.
Schulze, F. and Ssymank, P., *Das deutsche Studententum: von den ältesten Zeiten bis zur Gegenwart – 1931* (Munich: Verlag für Hochschulkunde, 1932).
Schütze, W., *Geschichte des Corps Guestphalia zu Jena* (Cologne: np, 1952).
Seemann-Kahne, F. and C., *Akademische Fechtschule* (Leipzig: Verlagsbuchhandlung J. J. Weber, 1926).
Stadmüller, F., *Geschichte das Corps Hannovera zu Göttingen 1809-1959* (Göttingen: Erich Golze KG, 1963).
Steinberg, M. S., *Sabers and Brown Shirts* (Chicago: University of Chicago Press, 1977).
Teutloff, W., *Die Geschichte des Allgemeinen Deutschen Waffenrings*, vol. 6/7, of *Historia Academica* (Stuttgart: Studentengeschichtlichen Vereinigung des Coburger Convents, 1968).
Waite, R. G. L., *The Psychopathic God – Adolf Hitler* (New York: Basic Books, Inc., 1977)
Webster, N., *Secret Societies and Subversive Movements* (London: Boswell Printing & Publishing Co. Ltd, 1924).
Weiruszowski, H., *The Medieval Universities* (Toronto: D. van Nostrand Company, Inc., 1966).
Weiss, E., *Festschrift zum 170 jährigen Bestehen Corps Lusatia* (Berlin: priv. publ., 1977).
Whiteside, A. G., *The Socialism of Fools: Georg Ritter von Schönerer and Austrian Pan-Germanism* (Berkeley, California: University of California Press, 1975).
Wilgus, N., *The Illuminoids: Secret Societies and Political Paranoia* (London: New English Library, 1980).
Yates, F. A., *The Rosicrucian Enlightenment* (St Albans, Herts: Paladin, 1975).

Ziegler, T., *Der deutsche Student am Ende des 19. Jahrhunderts*, 7th ed. (Leipzig: G. J. Göschen'sche Verlagshandlung, 1902).

C *KSCV* PUBLICATIONS

1. *Einst und Jetzt*. Jahrbuch des Vereins für corpsstudentische Geschichtsforschung (Munich: Ernst Vogel). The following articles appeared in *Einst und Jetzt*:

Angerer, A., 'Die Entwicklung des Toleranzgedankens in studentischen Zusammenschlüssen', vol. 3 (1958) pp. 92–101.
Asch, A., 'Der Kampf des Kartellverbandes jüdischer Korporationen gegen den Antisemitismus', vol. 16 (1971) pp. 147–54.
Assmann, R., 'Die Suspensionszeit des Tübinger SC im Dritten Reich und während der Besatzungszeit', vol. 21 (1976) pp. 153–72.
Assmann, R. (ed.), 'Constitutionen der Corps und ihrer Vorläufer 1810–1820', Sonderheft (1983)
Barthold, W., 'Macht und Ohnmacht der Ideologien den Corps', vol. 27 (1982) pp. 67–84.
Bauer, E., Die Kameradschaften im Bereiche des Kösener SC in den Jahren 1937–1945, vol. 1 (1956) pp. 5–40.
Bauer, E., 'Warum verboten eigentlich die Landesherren die Orden und weshalb bleiben diese Verbote erfolglos?' vol. 2 (1957) pp. 68–70.
Bauer, E., 'Die Jenaer Corpsversammlung (15. bis 17.7.1848), die Wiege des Kösener Seniorenconventsverbandes', vol. 3 (1958) pp. 20–41.
Bauer, E. and Schorr, H., 'Das Erscheinungsbild unserer Mensuren seit 1800 im Wandel der Zeiten', vol. 7 (1961) pp. 80–90.
Faust, A., 'Die "Eroberung" der Deutschen Studentenschaft durch den Nationalsozialistischen Deutschen Studentenbund', vol. 20 (1975) pp. 49–59.
Gottwald, W., 'Der Kösener SC-Verband und die Versipptenfrage im 3. Reich', vol. 12 (1967) pp. 54–68.
Hielscher, F., 'Das kanonische Urteil der Katholischen Kirke über die Mensur im 19. Jahrhundert', vol. 7 (1962) pp. 91–117.
Hielscher, F., 'Zweikampf und Mensur'. vol. 11 (1966) pp. 171–99.
Kessler, H., 'Orden und Landsmannschaften unter akadmischer Gerichtsbarkeit', vol. 2 (1957) pp. 53–68.
Körner, R., 'Zur Frage der Studentenorden allgemeinen', vol. 14 (1969) p. 188.
Küper, J., 'Die Interessengemeinschaft von 1950 als Vorstufe der Erneuerung des HKSCV im Jahre 1951', vol. 2 (1957) pp. 5–11.
Küper, J., 'Die Erneuerung der HKSCV im Jahre 1951', vol. 3 (1958), pp. 41–9.
Leupold, H., 'Der Kartellvertrag zwischen Bavaria-Landshut und Bavaria-Erlangen vom 30.V.1822', vol. 27 (1982) pp. 85–110.
Lohmann, A., 'Chronik des Kösener SC – Verbandes 1918–33', vol. 5 (1960) pp. 5–31.
Mahrenholz, H. C., 'Einführung des Arierprinzips im Wingolf nach 1933', vol. 27 (1982) pp. 127–34.
Meyer-Camberg, E., 'Über unbedingt notwendige Grundlagen in der studentenhistorischen Forschung', vol. 14 (1969) pp. 44–61.

Meyer-Camberg, E., 'Zum Gedenken an Dr. med. Albin Angerer' - 21 der ältesten Constitutionen der Corps und ihrer Vorläufer bis zum Jahre 1810. Sonderheft (1981).
Neuenhoff, G., 'Die Auflösung des KSCV und VAC', Beilageheft (1968).
Neuenhoff, G., 'Ehrenwort und Ehrenschein', vol. 24 (1979) pp. 55-73.
Paschke, R., 'Die Einigungsbestrebungen der deutschen Corps bis 1848', vol. 3 (1958), pp. 5-19.
Ricker, L. A., Aus der Zeit der Kameradschaften, Sonderheft (1960), pp. 47-50.
Ricker, L. A., 'Freiburger Mensuren in der nationalsozialistischen Verbotzeit', vol. 10 (1965) pp. 70-82.
Röhlke, J. H., Über das Kränzianertum an der Viadrina', vol. 17 (1972), pp. 113-125.
Röhlke, E., Versuch einer Begründung für Entsehen, Aufgaben, Ziele und Untergehen der Ordenlogen und der Orden. Sonderheft (1976), pp. 59-66.
Scherer, H., 'Die WSC Corps in der Verbotzeit 1935-1945', vol. 5 (1960) pp. 82-93.
Scheunemann, O., 'Die zahlenmässigen Entwicklung des Kösener SC-Verbandes 1848-1935', vol. 3 (1958) pp. 50-73.
Sommerland, B. 'Wartburgfest und Corpsstudenten', vol. 24 (1979) pp. 16-42.
Weiss, E., 'Lusatia kontra NSDStB - Leipzig 1934', vol. 17 (1972) pp. 145-53.
Weiss, E., 'Burschenschaftliche Ideen im Corps', vol. 22 (1977) pp. 89-98.

2. *Wende und Schau*. Kösener Jahrbuch (pre-1934) (Frankfurt am Main: DCZ Verlag).

Weber, H., Die studentischen Korporationsverbände 1930', vol. I (1930) pp. 196-230.

3. *Festschriften*

Hielscher, F., *Recht und Ethik der Mensur: - Fünfte Festschrift des HKSCV* (Würzburg: HKSCV Vorort, 1958).
Hielscher, F., *Geschichte und Wesen der Mensur - Festschrift zum Kösener Congress 1960* (Würzburg: KSCV Vorort, 1960).
Hielscher, F. and Barthold, W., *Die Mensur: Herkunft Recht und Wesen - Vierte Denkschrift des KSCV* (Bochum: VAC Verlag, 1968).

D PERIODICALS

Akademische Blätter - Zeitschrift des Kyffhäuserverbandes (Tübingen: Bernd & Graefe).
Corpsstudentische Monatsblätter - Zeitschrift des Weinheimer Senioren-Convents (Munich: Verlag: Weinheimer Verband Alter Corpsstudenten e.V).
Deutsche Corpszeitung - Amtliche Zeitschrift des Kösener SC-Verbandes (Frankfurt am Main: Verlag der Deutschen Corpszeitung).
Deutsche Studenten - Zeitung, Zeitschrift der Deutschen Studentenschaft.
Die Bewegung - Zentralorgan des NSD - Studentenbündes (Munich: NSDStB).
Die Wachenberg - Nachrichten des Weinheimer Senioren-Convents (Bochum: Weinheimer Verband Alter Corpsstudenten e.V).

E UNPUBLISHED DISSERTATIONS AND MANUSCRIPTS

Studier, M., 'Der Corpsstudent als Idealbild der Wilhelminischen Ära', Diss. University of Erlangen, 1965.

Teutloff, W., 'Die wichtigsten Ereignisse, Tagungen und Beschlüsse zur Geschichte des Allgemeinen Deutschen Waffenringes', ms., Inst. HK, Würzburg.

Uhlenhorst-Zeichmann, K. W., 'Die Deutsche Burschenschaft', Cleveland, Ohio: unpubl. ms., 1972.

F INTERVIEWS SPECIFICALLY CITED

Bartels, G., personal interview. Göttingen, November 1979.
Etzdorf, H. von, personal interview. Eichtling, Bavaria, June 1977.
Herberger, K. H., personal interview. Mannheim, June 1977.
Mehring, C., personal interview. Bielefeld, November 1979.
Münchhausen, F. F. von, personal interview. Mannheim, March 1977.

Index

academic courts, 27
academic law, 28
accolade cross, 9
Akademischer Turnbund (ABT), 78, 123
Aktive Wehrstudenten-Korps, 156
alla marchia, 36
Allgemeiner Deutscher Senioren-Conventen Verband, 42
Allgemeiner Deutscher Waffenring (ADW), 42–8, 53–4, 58–9, 71, 75–8, 80, 82–91, 97–8, 103–6, 109, 113–19, 122–6, 149 (*et passim*)
Allgemeiner Landsmannschaftliche-Convent, 22
Allied Occupation Forces, 163
Alte Kämpfer (NSDAP), 103, 111
Ambulance Medical Corps, 156
American Military Government Questionnaire, 163
Amicitia, student order, 7
Amtsmann, 27
anti-semitism, 48–55
see also Jewish students
Aryan regulations, 116, 125, 134–5, 139, 142
Austrian corps, 49

Bad Wimpfen, 165
Baden Student Ordinance, 94
Balgerei, 36
see also fencing
Ban, 13, 30, 31, 69
see also Verruf
Bannenstrahl, 30
Bavarian Mensurverbot, 93

Bavarian Student Ordinance, 94
beadles, 27
bean, 2–3
Bebel, A., 32
Berchtesgaden, 132–4, 136–7
Bestimmungsmensur, 21, 44, 46–7
see also Mensur
Beurer, Rittmeister, 73
Bewegung, Die, 59, 60, 72, 143, 146–50
Bismarck Kommers, 53
Bismarck, Otto von, 16, 21–2, 31, 155
Blau-Weiss, 51
Blood Protection Act, 139
Blunck, M. (KSCV), 100–41, 145, 168
Bologna, university of, 1
Bonn, university of, 156
Borman, M., 126
Breslau, university of, 51, 108
Brücklmeier, E., 166, 169
Brückner, Oberpräsident, 100–1
Buch, Major Walter, 64, 66–9, 73–4
Bund Jüdischer Akademiker, 51
Burschen Heraus, 36, 127
Burschenschaft (DB), 17–8, 22, 24, 29, 31–2, 39–41, 44, 48–51, 53, 55–6, 59, 78, 82, 97–8, 105, 108, 111–15, 120, 123–4, 127, 130, 133–4, 137, 140–3, 167
Allgemeine Deputierten-Conventen, 16
Arminia movement, 16
Burschenschaftliche Blätter, 50, 112
early structure and ideas, 14–16
Eisenach, 16, 130
Eisenach Resolutions (1920), 50

Burschenschaft (DB)—(cont.)
  Follen Brothers, 15
  Frankfurter Wachturm, 16
  Germania movement, 16
  Giessen Blacks, 15
  Jena Burschenschaft, 14
  Junglingbund plot, 16
  pan- Germanism, 14
  Streitberg amendments, 16
  Wartburg, 140–1
  Wartburgfest, 15
Burschenschaft
  Alemannia – Bonn, 115
  Bubenruthia – Erlangen, 115
  Franconia – Bonn, 50, 115
  Gaudeamus – Stuttgart, 115
  Holzminda – Göttingen, 132
  Königsgesellschaft – Tübingen, 115
  Libertas – Vienna, 49
  Normania – Tübingen, 115
  Olympia – Vienna, 49
  Silesia – Vienna, 49
  Teutonia – Halle, 14
  Vandalia – Jena, 14
Bursen, 2, 3

Cambridge, university of, 2, 27
cantons, 13, 38
Carlsbad Decrees, 16, 28
Cartellgesetz, 12
Cartellverband der katholischen deutschen Studentenverbindungen (CV), 84, 113
chivalric codes, 4
Clarenthal, Saar, 134
Coburg Convention (1868), 31
Codex Juris Canonici, 33
comment, 11–13, 29–32, 34, 36–8, 46, 66, 151
consilium abeundi, 28
Constantia, student order, 7–9, 11
conterranei, 2
corps, 12, 29 (*et passim*)
Corps
  Baruthia zu Erlangen, 24
  Bavaria zu München, 23, 128
  Bavaria zu Würzburg, 23–4, 160–1
  Borussia zu Bonn, 22

  Borussia zu Halle, 118
  Cisaria zu München, 159
  Franconia zu München, 65–75
  Franconia zu Tübingen, 160–1
  Guestphalia zu Greifswald, 92
  Guestphalia zu Halle, 11–12, 30
  Guestphalia zu Jena, 159–60
  Hannovera zu Göttingen, 22, 155–6
  Hercynia zu München, 128
  Hubertia zu München, 68, 71–2
  Isaria zu München, 70, 72–3
  Lusatia zu Leipzig, 118–9, 125, 158
  Misnia zu Leipzig, 159–61, 168
  Moenania zu Würzburg, 48, 106
  Onoldia zu Erlangen, 11–12
  Paliomarchia zu Halle, 105, 129–30, 133, 136–7, 160
  Rhenania zu Bonn, 23, 156, 160–1
  Rhenania zu Erlangen, 23
  Rhenania zu Heidelberg, 23
  Rhenania zu Würzburg, 23
  Rhenania Strasburg zu Marburg, 118
  Rheno-Guestphalia zu Münster, 157
  Saxonia zu Leipzig, 159
  Saxo-Borussia zu Heidelberg, 128–9, 132–3, 168
  Suevia zu Freiburg, 157
  Suevia zu München, 75, 117–8
  Teutonia zu Berlin, 80
  Vandalia zu Heidelberg, 19, 118

Danzig, 115
depositio beanii, 2
Derichsweiler, A. (NSD STB), 119, 122–3, 127, 131–3, 140, 142–3, 147–8, 153
Deutsche Baurenschaft, 116
Deutsche Hochschullehrer, 89
Deutsche Hochschulring, 46
Deutsche Landsmannschaft, 78, 111
Deutsche Sänngerschaft (DS), 123, 167
Deutsche Studentenschaft (DSt), 45, 58, 63, 70, 78–80, 83–8, 94, 107, 109–14, 119–22, 131, 149
Deutsche Wehrschaft (DW), 42, 48,

54, 56, 59, 76–7, 82, 86, 91, 111, 113, 123–4, 167 (*et passim*)
Deutscher Offiziersbund, 45, 65–8, 75
see also Officers' associations
Dimission, 30
Doenitz, Admiral Karl, 163
Druckery, H., 109–10, 112–3, 115
duel, 33–9, 58
see also fencing

Elbe, River, 37
Erfurt Agreement, 47–8, 60–3, 71–2, 76–83, 86, 89–90, 149
Erlangen Agreement, 59, 62, 88
Erlangen, university of, 11, 152
Etzdorf, Hasso von, 166, 169
Exeter College, Oxford, 2

fagging, 4
Feickert, A., 120–5
fencing, 33–9 (*see also* duel)
 glacé stance, 37, 39
 goggles, 37
 Losgehen, 8
 pro patria, 21
 Rencontres, 36, 38
 Revokation, 20
 Schiedsgericht, 19, 89, 91–2
 Schläger, Glockenschläger, 37
 Schläger, Korbschläger, 37, 163
 seconds, 39
 side-arms, scholars carrying of, 4
 Stossdegen, 37
 trial by combat, 35 (*see also* Gottesurteil)
 umpires and judges, 39
 Waffen belegen, 53, 65, 75, 106 (*see also glossary*)
Fichte Hochschulring, 42
Finkenschaft, 41
see also Free Students
Frankfurt Assembly, 20
Frankfurt/Main, 98
Frankfurt/Oder, university of, 10–2
see also Viadrina
Frederick the Great, 7
Free Corps,
see also Lützow, 14

Free Students, 13
Freemasons, 6, 7, 104–5, 113, 116, 127, 139, 142
Freiburg, university of, 12, 152, 154, 157
French Revolution, 6, 8, 9
Frick, W., 99, 101
Friessen, F., 14
Führer principle, 87, 94, 99–100, 153, 159
Füholzer, D., 73

German Protestant Princes, Union of, 9
Gemeinschaft Studentischer Verbände (GStV), 125–39
Gerloff, H., 80
Gerstein, Kurt, 166, 169
Gestapo, charges against Corps Misnia, 161
Gierlichs, H. (CV) (DSt), 83, 85
Giessen, university of, 15
Glauning, H. (DB) (NSDStB), 56, 127, 134, 140
Gleichschaltung, 86, 95, 97, 101, 106, 109, 159, 162
Göring, Hermann, 98, 111
Goslar Conference (ADW), 79, 81–6, 89, 91
Gottesurteil, 35
see also Trial by combat
Göttingen, university of, 30, 37, 152, 155, 158
Graz, DSt conference 1931, 63, 78, 86

Hagen, Albrecht von, 166, 169
Halle, university of, 5, 11, 17, 30
Harmonia, student order, 7, 8
Hassell, Ulrich von, 166, 169
Hederick, K. H. (DB), 97–8, 100
Heidelberg, university of, 8, 12, 132, 152
 Dozentenbund, 129
 Rector, 129
Heinricht, J., 80
Heringhaus (KSCV), 101, 139, 145
Hess, Rudolf, 73, 116, 143, 146–7
Hilgenstock, F. (DSt), 80, 83–4
Hindenburg, Paul von, 85, 101

Hitler, Adolf, 48, 70, 72,, 74, 93,
100–1, 103, 114, 124–9, 131,
133, 135, 137–8, 157, 168
Hochschulring deutscher Art, 42
Hoffman, Erik, 130
Holy Roman Emperor, 9
Holy Roman Empire, 9
Holzschuher, Leutnant Freiherr von,
65–75
Honour, 31–3, 114
affair of, 45, 59
code of, 8, 34, 44, 46, 57, 59, 60,
75–7, 95, 119, 149
point of, 12, 150
honourable student, 29, 31, 59
Hühnlein, Major, 72

Illuminati, 9
Immisch, Dr, of Heidelberg, 37
incarceration of students, 10
Ingolstadt, university of, 9

Jahn, Turnvater, F.L., 13, 14
Jena, Battle of, 13
Jena, university of, 7, 17
Jesus College, Oxford, 2
Jewish students, 48–55, 93, 96, 98–9,
104–5, 113, 123, 127, 129–30,
135, 138–9
see also Versipptenfrage

Kameradschaft
Axel Scheffold, 160
Carl Almenröder, 160
Freiherr vom Stein, 155–7
Friedrich Harkort, 157
Graf Spee, 159
Gustav Nachtigal, 160
Markgraf von Meissen, 155, 158
Number 10, Würzburg, 160
Schwabenland, 157, 160
Theodor Körner, 160
Yorck von Wartenburg, 156, 160
Kameradschaft waffenstudentischer
Verbände (KWV), 112
Kartell Convent: der Verbindungen
deutscher Studenten jüdischen
Glaubens, (KC), 51–2
Badenia – Heidelberg, 51

Viadrina – Breslau, 51
Salia – Würzburg, 52
Kartell Jüdischer Verbindungen, 51
Keppler, W., Secretary of State, 100
Kiel, 106–8, 155
Klinggräff, Friedrich von, 19
Kloss, Prof. Dr., 84
Königsberg, 86–7
university of, 106, 108
Körner, Secretary of State, 100
Körner, Theodor, 14
Köstritz, 17
Kotzebue, August von, 16
Kraak, W. (WB) (DSt), 83, 85
Kraaz, G. (KSCV), 87, 97, 101, 103,
136–7
Kränzchen, 10–3, 28–9, 34, 36, 167
Krüger, Gerhard, 79–81, 83–5, 87,
94, 97–8, 100
KSCV (Kösener Senioren-Conventen
Verband) 18–25, 31, 117 (et
passim)
Akademische Monatshefte, 32–3
Allgemeine Senioren-Convent-
Kartell, 17–18, 23
Bad Kösen, 17, 20, 88–9, 102, 160
Deutsche Corpszeitung, 102, 110,
146
foreign corps, 134
Grenz-und Auslandsdeutschtum,
Ausschuss für, 48
Kartellcorps, 24, 158
Kreispolitik, 24
KSCV – WSC Agreement, 42
reconstitution, 159–65
Rudelsburg, 20, 88, 160–1
tolerance principle, 49
Verband Alter Corpsstudenten, 22,
45, 92, 137, 145
Zehnerausschuss, 47
Kyffhäuser Verband (VDSt), 42, 51

Lammers, Hans, 100, 102, 111–14,,
117, 120, 122, 124, 126–38
Michaelson, sucessor to Lammers
(GStV), 138
Nordmann, assistant to Lammers,
133–4
Landfried, F., 99

Landsknecht, 3
Landsmannschaften, 3-10, 17, 29, 31, 40, 93, 154, 166
Landwehr Casino Berlin, 99, 117
Langemarck Fund, 80-1, 83-4
Langemarckstudenten, 156
Langhoff, F. (ADW), 116, 120, 123
Latvia, 51
Leipzig, university of, 1, 17, 158
Rector, 118
Leubsdorf, Thuringia, 108-9
Lienau, Walter, 60, 63, 70-1, 73, 76-81, 83, 87, 132, 167-8
Lippe, elections, 93
Louvain, university of, 1
Luther, Martin, 15
Lutze, SA Chief, 139-40, 168
Lützow, Major Ludwig von, Free Corps, 14-15

Mainz, Elector of, 9
Marburg Agreement, 40-4, 46, 89-90, 92, 126
Mecklenburg-Schwerin, 87
Mensur (Bestimmungsmensur), 21, 44, 46-7, 51, 53, 57-8, 93, 149, 154, 156-8, 161-5, 168
merchants and students, 13, 27
Miltenburger Ring (MR), 78, 109, 111, 114
Mohr, Karl Friedrich (KSCV), 92, 97-101, 103-4, 110
Müller, SS Sturmführer, Frankfurt, 114
Mumm von Schwarzenstein, Herbert, 166, 169
Münchhausen, Friedrich Freiherr von, 166, 169
Münster, university of, 156-7
Mussolini, Benito, 82
mutual assistance and support, 4, 12

Napoleon, 13, 167
Nationalsozialistische Gemeinschaft corpstudentische Verbände, 109-16
Nationalverband deutscher Offiziere, 45, 65
see also Officers' associations

nations at universities, 1
Naumburg, 99
Naumburger Senioren-Convent (NSC), 78, 90, 109, 116, 165
Naval Medicine, Institute of, 155
Nazi Students' Association (NSDStB), 20, 55-63, 66-7, 69-73, 76-9, 80-1, 83-9, 90, 94, 96, 99, 100, 108-12, 119, 121-2, 127-8, 131, 133, 137, 140-63 (*et passim*)
NSDStB code of honour, 57, 71-2, 76-8, 150-4
Kameradschaften, 107-8, 112, 120-3, 127, 140, 142-62, 165
Kameradschaften, organisation of, 147, 153, 156
Plauen Agreement with DB, 140, 144
Stammhochschulerlass, 150
Studentenkampfhilfe, 147-8, 151-2
Neue Gesellschaft, 10
see also New Society
New Society, 10, 13
Nobles, German Society of, 45
numerus clausus, 56, 94
Nuremberg Laws, 138

Officers' associations, 45, 59, 65
Olympic Games (1936), 139
Order of St John, 45
Osterhild, K., 159
Otto, H., 100-2
Oxford, university of, 2, 27

Padua, university of, 1
Pagels, NSDStB Freiburg/Br, 154
Paris, university of, 1
penal code, 29, 58, 66, 149, 163
pennalismus, 4, 167
Pennaljahr, 5
pietism, 5
Pfundtner, H., 99, 137
Philistines, Philisterium, 21, 32
praeceptor morum, 4
Prague, university of, 1
Prussia, King of, 11
Prussia, Wilhelm II of, 22

Prussian Emancipation Act (1812), 48–9
Prussian Law, 27
Prussian Student Ordinance, 93

Rainer, NSDAP fraternities office, 100
Ramsey, Chevalier Andrew, 7
regens bursae, 2
Reich citizenship, 138
Reichel, K. A., 73
Reichsdeutsche, 46
Reichsführer, (NSDStB), 59, 69
Reichsgericht, 46
Reichsjustizminister, 82
Reichsleitung, NSDStB, 60, 71–6, 86, 101–3, 108, 114, 126, 135
Reichspräsident, 85
Reichsrat, 58
Reichsstudentenführung, NSDStB, 112–3, 120, 149, 153
Reichstag, 32, 58
Retlaw, L., 79
 see also Leinau, W.
Ritterakademien, 5
Röhm, Oberstleutnant Ernst, 72
Roman Catholic students, 84, 113
Roman Civil Law, 2
Rosenberg, Alfred, 122
Rössler, K., 158–9
Rost, A., 154
Rostock, university of, 1
Rothenburger Verband (RVSV): Apollo, 74
Rudolstädter Senioren-Convent, 23, 43–4, 52–4, 78, 90, 109, 120, 165
Rühle, G. (NSDStB), 93
Rust, B., 93, 103, 122, 135

SA, 100, 105–8, 110, 114, 121, 139, 147, 151, 167
Sand, Karl, 16
Sandberger, SS-Hauptsturmführer, 150
satisfaction (sastisfaktionsfähig), 33, 41, 44, 52–3, 58–9, 62, 65, 67–9, 72, 75, 115, 135, 149, 151
Saurman, Dr (ADW), 105–6
Saxon universities, 17

Scanzoni, Oberleutnant von, 65–75
Scheel, G. A. (NSD StB) (DSt), 149, 153–4
Schirach, Baldur von, 45, 57, 59–61, 63–78, 81, 85, 87, 132, 167
Schlange, Dr E. (VAC), 145–6
Schmidtkampf, (DW), 112, 126
Schönerer, Georg von, 49
Schwab, O. (DB), 112–13, 115–16, 120, 123–4
Schulenberg, Fritz Graf von der, 166, 169
Schulz, H. H. (KSCV) (DSt), 80–1, 83–4, 87
Schwarzburgbund (SB), 18, 123
Senior, 4, 11, 105, 109, 153, 159 (*et passim*)
Senioren Convent – council of seniors, 4, 11–2, 29–32, 37–9, 49, 52–3, 60, 109, 151, 159, 164 (*et passim*)
Senioren Convent (SC)
 of Berlin, 43, 58
 of Dresden, 43
 of Erlangen, 23
 of Frankfurt/Main, 114
 of Frankfurt/Oder, 11
 of Hamburg, 145
 of Hannover, 22
 of Heidelberg, 93
 of Karlsruhe, 2
 of Leipzig, 155, 161
 of Marburg, 35, 105–6
 of Munich, 43, 45, 57, 66, 68, 70–7, 82, 85, 117, 119, 128, 159
 of Stuttgart, 22
 of Tübingen, 35
 of Würzburg, 23, 106
 of Zurich, 22
Seven Years' War, 9
Sikorski, H. (VDSt), 80
Silesian Wars, 7
societates, 3
Sonderhäuser Verband (SV), 78, 123
SS, 100, 108, 114, 121, 147, 151, 154
Stäbel, O., 80, 93, 98, 100, 106, 108, 112–14, 120
Stahlhelm, 87, 96, 100, 107–8, 130, 147

student-knight, ideal of, 3–7
student orders, 5–10 (*et passim*)
Studentenschaft, 94–5, 107–8, 118, 129
 Bündische Kammer, 94, 106, 118
Sturmfahne, Die, 79
Swoboda, (RVSV), 74–5

Tempel, W. (NSDStB), 57
Tenured Civil Servants, Restoration Act, 93, 98, 104, 116, 129, 135
Thomasius, Christian, 5
Tridentine Council, 33
Trott zu Solz, Adam von, 166, 169
Tübingen, university of, 12, 149, 154, 156
Turnerschaft Ghibellinia, 72
Turnerschaften, 31, 40–1, 85, 123

un-German spirit, 52
Unitas (UV), 18
Unitas, student order, 7, 13
USCHLA (Nazi Party court), 64, 103–4

Verein Deutscher Studenten (VDSt)
 see also Kyffhäuser-Verband, 51–2
Verruf, 30, 61, 66, 71, 73
 Waffenverruf, 68–9
 see also ban
Versipptenfrage, 98, 116
 see also Jewish students
Vertrauensleute, 86
Viadrina, university of, 10, 12–3
völkische, doctrine and activities, 42, 49, 55, 76, 96, 115, 124, 168
Völkische Waffenring, 123–6
Völkischer Beobachter, 70–1, 75–6, 99, 104, 125
Volksdeutsche, 46

Waffenring, 41, 71–2, 76–7 (*et passim*)
Waffenschutz, 62, 68 (*et passim*)
 see also glossary
Waffenstudententum, 40 (*et passim*)
Wagner, Dr A. (DB), 66, 75, 126, 130–1, 135, 137, 144, 148
Waidhofen principle, 50–1, 61, 76, 82, 124
War Graves, German National Association for the Care of, 83–4
Wartburg-Kartell akademische-evangelischer Verbindungen (WK), 115
Weimar, Duke Karl August von, 9
Weimar Republic, 42, 56–7
Weimar Constitution, 56
Weinheim/Bergstrasse, 22
Weinheimer Senioren-Covent, 22, 42–4, 78, 90, 109, 120, 123, 142, 159, 166 (*et passim*)
 reconstitution of, 165
Weishaupt, Adam, 9
Weizsaecker, K. (WSC), 165
Welte, K. (CV) (DSt), 83–4
Wetzel, U., 102
Windhoek Namibia (South West Africa), 48, 134
Wingolf (WB), 18
Wirth, Prof, 154
Wormser Rosengarten, 34–5
Würzburg, 149, 152

Yorck von Wartenburg, Peter Graf von, 166, 169

Zaeringer, H., (DSt), 118
Zander, L. (KSCV), 21–2

GPSR Compliance

The European Union's (EU) General Product Safety Regulation (GPSR) is a set of rules that requires consumer products to be safe and our obligations to ensure this.

If you have any concerns about our products, you can contact us on

ProductSafety@springernature.com

In case Publisher is established outside the EU, the EU authorized representative is:

Springer Nature Customer Service Center GmbH
Europaplatz 3
69115 Heidelberg, Germany

www.ingramcontent.com/pod-product-compliance
Lightning Source LLC
Chambersburg PA
CBHW031520100426
42873CB00013B/148